Creating
the Work
You Love

Creating

COURAGE

the Work

COMMITMENT

You Love

AND CAREER

Rick Jarow

BOOKS

Destiny Books
Rochester, Vermont

Destiny Books
One Park Street
Rochester, Vermont 05767
www.InnerTraditions.com

Destiny Books is a division of Inner Traditions International

LIBRARY OF CONGRESS CATALOGING-IN-PUBLICATION DATA
Jarow, Rick.
    Creating the work you love : courage, commitment, and career / Rick Jarow.
        p.   cm.
    Includes bibliographical references.
    ISBN 0-89281-542-6
    1. Vocation.   2. Self-realization—Religion aspects.   3. Success.   4. Chakras.   I. Title.
BL629.J37   1995
158.6—dc20   95-39793
                                                                                         CIP

Printed and bound in the United States

10   9

Medicine wheel mandala illustration by Cat Rocco
Text design and layout by Kristin Camp

This book was typeset in Minion
with Attorino, Micro Extended, and LucidaSans as display faces

This book is for Oshan—
may he walk in his own shoes.

Contents

Acknowledgments

There are many people I would like to acknowledge, not only for helping with this book but also for teaching me to live in such a way as to make this book possible. The following are but a few who come to mind, representative of the many.

Thank you to: My mother, who introduced me to the aspirations of the mind. My father, who passed on as I began writing this book. His deep love sustains me. Hilda Charlton and Orestes Valdes, whose lives on earth left a legacy of "hands-on" love. Swami Jnanananda, who still sits in the Himalayas in meditative inaction, representing the other polarity of the anti-career.

The New York Open Center, Wainwright House, Interface, and Kirkridge, sites of many anti-career workshops, were the ground upon which this work evolved. David Crismond and Rick Allen read through early manuscript drafts and made valuable suggestions. Andre DeZanger and Judy Morgan helped develop this material through numerous sessions, gently reminding me not to work too hard. Elizabeth Frost Knappman gave valuable suggestions for the improvement of the manuscript and graciously released it at the right time. Barbara Theiss introduced me to the staff at Inner Traditions. Robin Dutcher-Bayer saw the value in this work and helped bring it into form. Susan Davidson's unfailing editorial skills have greatly supported this project. Phil Marden walked down many anti-career roads with me. Ron Young has been part of my life for as long as I can remember; his work has inspired many of the concepts in this book. Celine Sigmen has been with me, in every sense of the word, through the evolution of this project. She has given me the future.

Introduction

The anti-career work with which I have been involved over the last several years grew out of the observation that so many people who had worked diligently to develop their inner lives can find no place for themselves in the world. It is now as it was over a century ago in New England, when Thoreau lamented that "The society which I was made for is not here."[1]

The "alienated worker" syndrome can be traced back to the rise of capitalism, and even before that when we consider that slavery was the norm of the ancient world. But it is only the postindustrial democracies that have dared to assume that any human being could, and indeed *should,* lift his or her face out of the muddied grind for survival and aspire to something higher. Indeed, my own baby-boom generation was raised on idealism mixed with Wheaties, and we recoiled in horror at the prospect of "Twenty years of schoolin' and they put you on the day shift," as Bob Dylan graphically described it.

It is no wonder that I am sensitized to these issues, for I am one of those who worked hard to develop my inner life and then had to come back and confront the fact that the society I was made for was not here. The first heroic career decision I made was to drop out of Harvard University. Early in life I learned to be the kind of game-player that a public school kid from Brooklyn needs to be to get into Harvard, and leaving that situation was a major assertion of my self-esteem, a declaration that what I felt inside was more important than what was rewarded on the outside. Like many of my generation, I was attracted to the East. I spent a number of years in India playing the role of the wanderer and practicing different forms of yoga and meditation. India was almost like summer camp to me, and being there was my path of least resistance. More than once I contemplated following the course of a few of my friends by throwing my passport into the Ganges, declaring myself dead to the world, and taking on a new identity.

Then a curious thing happened. In a middle-sized town in north India I happened across a volume of Carl Jung's writing in which he discussed the need to attend to the development of one's psyche through one's own cultural mythology. This idea struck a deep chord in me, and within a year I was enrolled in a Western university. This time, however, I was operating from my passion. In fact, I was impassioned by feelings of anger and indignation. I wanted to learn Sanskrit because I suspected that the gurus with whom I had studied in both India and America were presenting shallow and watered-down versions of a much deeper spiritual tradition. The only way for me to enter into the full power that I sensed existed in this tradition would be to learn to read the texts myself. Along the way I realized that I knew the Bhagavadgita but did not know Homer or Shakespeare, and this did not sit well with me. I desperately wanted to learn. I wanted to understand the roots of my personal search for meaning within the contexts of my own culture *and* the great civilizations of the past. With this as my focus I embarked upon a twelve-year course of East/West studies, a journey that culminated in a doctorate from Columbia University. While engaged in this study I also received a different sort of education, an education that I could never have planned but one that ultimately provided much of the background and basis for this book.

I will not go into all the details of this alternative education, but I will share some vignettes here that will be elaborated upon later. For a number of years while I was at Columbia I studied with a woman named Hilda Charlton who lived in a modest apartment on the Upper West Side of New York City. Hilda was a powerful and charismatic healer and teacher of meditation, but most interesting to me were her powers of manifestation. One day when a few of her students were in the midst of building a center in upstate New York, she off-handedly remarked, "We need windows." The next day eighty-some-odd windows, complete with frames, were left out on the street, abandoned by a construction company. Another time a number of us purchased "discount tickets" to India, paid for with cash. Unfortunately the man who sold them to us died of a heart attack a few days later, and we never received the tickets. When the officials went through the estate of the deceased salesman, they found that he was in debt to many people, owing on hundreds of tickets, and our own orders were nowhere to be found. The situation certainly did not look good, and after about two months I gave up hope of ever being reimbursed for my ticket. But Hilda refused to accept this finality; every Thursday night at the end of our meeting she would ask a group of a few hundred people to "Om for the tickets." She would then ask us to visualize the tickets being returned to us. After six months or so, I refused to participate in this ritual, thinking it obsessive and ridiculous. A year and a half later, however, when each of us received a full refund for the tickets, I had to admit that there were powers of manifestation that I had no clue about. Hilda would often say to me, "Don't worry about money, kid," as if such worry was a sign of ignorance and immaturity. I decided that I had something to learn from this woman. I stayed around for a while.

During this same period of my life I heard about an obscure shaman living in Little Cuba, New Jersey, who was able to lift spirits off of people. When I finally had the opportunity to meet him, I was a bit deflated to find that he looked more like a muscular delivery man than like my image of an exotic medicine man. But when he told me that I had a blind man in my aura I was more than intrigued, for I had been experiencing recurring eye problems. And when he told me that he was going to get rid of the blind man, I gave him my go-ahead. It took me six years to decide if what transpired from that point was imaginary theater or a legitimate psychic operation, but it seemed to work. For the next six years I studied with this shaman, Orestes, and learned about the powers of the imagination—not the imagination of fantasy but the image-making power of the human psyche.

Through my training with Hilda and Orestes, along with studies in cross-cultural symbolism at Columbia, I eventually started my own counseling practice. Due to my long association with both of these teachers, I had an open pipeline to the New Age community, and people came flocking to my door. I never advertised or claimed to have extraordinary gifts. But I did feel a deep calling to work with people, and I followed my heart.

I spent a number of years working as a "guru exorcist," helping people out of the trauma of gurudom—something I knew well—and felt very good about what I was doing. Eventually, however, I became aware of a different set of issues present in the lives of many of my clients. People would tell me about their remarkable past lives as pharaohs and queens, but these same people were still working behind the counter at Macy's. What was wrong? Why was it that spiritual people seemed to be chronically nonfunctional? Why was it that not long after having some ecstatic vision or transcendent experience, I would find the same person bogged down in the same morass that they had been in before their revelation? Clearly, there was a problem.

A major question that I began hearing over and again from my clients was, "What should I do? What is my particular place in the world?" And those who asked such questions generally did not have a clue as to the answer. It became increasingly apparent to me that the incongruities between peoples' inner worlds and outer possibilities were becoming magnified. As my practice expanded, I began to work with people on the other side, individuals in socially prestigious professions who were extremely frustrated with their inability to lead an authentic life in the straitjackets of their jobs. I also began working with students just getting ready to enter the job market who legitimately wondered if they could dare to pursue their dreams and still participate in what seemed to be a callous and irrational economic order.

After a number of years on this track, I put together a "manifestation laboratory." Ten of us met every week for nearly a year and worked together to understand—not only theoretically but practically—how to align our inner and outer worlds. We worked with rituals, meditative techniques, the power of suggestion, different forms of goal-setting, and the amplification of intention through collective effort. The most important breakthrough of our work together was the development of the chakra model as an aid to manifestation. The more we worked with it, the clearer it became to us that this model was an ideal tool for developing a strong interface between the inner and outer worlds. There was no dearth of information on the chakras themselves, and a number of people had done quite a bit of work on the application of the chakra model to health and psychological issues. When we began applying the chakra model to career questions, we found a perfect match: By clarifying the issues related to particular energy centers in the body, we could map the pathway from the inner to the outer world. This enabled us to begin conceiving of and creating strategies for creativity and career development that were actually centered in the body, as opposed to trying to fit the body into the workaday world.

Soon I realized that I had a genuine contribution to make to the study of manifestation. It felt right to "go public," and I began presenting various workshops on the relationship between one's inner being and one's place in the world. For five more years I developed this work, which was refined by the participation of hundreds of people from all age groups, social orientations, and walks of life. Eventually a series of tried and effective methods crystallized into the anti-career workshop, and into the material presented in this book.

The vocation issue is an extremely serious one, and it deserves genuine reflection as opposed to glib response. Is it, in fact, necessary to separate the truth of our being from our being in the world? For the spiritual ideal has, more often than not, been placed in opposition to the material world. Thus spiritually aware people are often seen (and view themselves) as nonfunctional, powerless to translate their inner visions into working realities. When we want to get things done we don't call the minister, we call the bank. Likewise, functional people are often considered to be nonspiritual, completely absorbed in a clock-run, workday reality—at least until they suffer their first heart attack.

Does one indeed have to lose the world to gain one's soul? Are we still, despite ourselves, operating through an outmoded paradigm that separates the inner from the outer world, the spirit from its concrete manifestation? If we are indeed the same beings in the working world as in the more shrouded realms of inward experience, then why shouldn't our inner and outer worlds support one another? I contend that until we move in this direction, none of our good intentions will change the nature of employment in this society, and unless we change the way in which we approach the act and art of making a living, it will become increasingly difficult to cultivate any sort of inner life at all.

Our reality around work will change when we re-envision work from the inside out, when we place economy within the greater frame of the evolutionary interdependence of each and all. From Karl Marx to Hazel Henderson, persuasive voices argue that the transformation of the workplace is a necessary prerequisite for human freedom. I hold that this transformation is also an essential step in the resacralization of our culture. More than any skill or product, the way in which we align our work with our deepest intuitions about life will be the genuine contribution we make to the emerging world community. To create this alignment—to make our lives into works of art— is an ambitious goal, but it is not unattainable. Prospering in boardrooms, in offices, in studios, and in fields that are described nowhere in vocational guidance manuals are inspiring people who have created inner/outer integration in their lives. Moreover, their prosperity—rather than robbing them of virtue, centeredness, and awareness—has actually resulted from this balanced inner state. In our hearts we know that we would all be better off doing what we love. The popularity of Marcia Sinetar's *Do What You Love, the Money Will Follow* and other books on right livelihood that have recently appeared reveal a groundswell of aspiration toward purposeful work. However, it is not so easy to convert our ideals into form, and often when we do try we find that there are variables in operation that we have totally neglected. What is needed then are tangible methods as well as visions of a new society. *Creating the Work You Love* offers a step-by-step process for creating self-sustaining conditions that resonate with our deepest levels of integrity, passion, and purpose. So let us take heart: As we move into a new millennium, what was possible for one may now be possible for many—for anyone, in fact, who is willing to challenge the life-negating suppositions of the current workplace and dare to become a force in the transformation of our world.

1
The Art of Work, the Work of Art

Your life is a work of art
A craft to be most carefully mastered
For patience has replaced time
And you are your own destination.

The separation between life and work, between our daily struggles and our dreams, plagues us as a people. The great majority take dissatisfaction with work for granted, thoughtlessly supporting a burgeoning entertainment and consumer culture as the only way to connect with the realm of the imagination. Others among us, despite a nagging feeling of having "sold out," accept working as a necessary sacrifice. Very few of us look forward to Monday morning. To make art forms out of the stuff of our lives, to create vital forms of living and working, may be our most current challenge.

Is it possible to be who we are in our work, rather than veiling our authenticity in order to survive in the job market? Can we create forms of work that will allow us to offer the fullness of ourselves to the world? Why have work and career become such areas of pressure that the struggle to simply maintain oneself increasingly crowds out the time and energy to live? These questions need to be addressed fully if there is any hope of stepping off the treadmill that we have created. Thoreau worked six weeks out of the year; aboriginal peoples can spend nine hours a day absorbed in mythology. In contrast, we have created portable offices in the form of laptop computers and cellular phones to accompany us on our vacations. And through the voice of the media we can hear an ever more compelling message that suggests we can get along on bread alone—provided that it is well-packaged. But without a basic, personal integrity and heartfelt energy associated with our work, nothing we produce or own will ever be enough, and we will continue to appease our deeper longings with one partial preoccupation after another.

A WORK OF ART

To affirm one's life as a work of art is more than a middle-class pastime. It is, in fact, a direct challenge to a class-ridden European inheritance epitomized by William Butler Yeats' contention that a man must choose between perfecting either the life or the work.[1] Such a split—between art and life, between those who work and those who create—is no longer viable, for we have arrived at a point in our social evolution where being the artist of our own lives, creating lives that are authentic instead of accepting or assuming ready-made models, is requisite for entry into the coming century.

Every age has its tyrants, and in this postmodern era tyranny is expressed through the interlocking webs of institutions that control our lives. The health, insurance, and banking industries, fixated on notions of "security" and "future," lead us to believe that it is impossible to fundamentally transform one's career, to live for something other than a salary. How can life be a "craft to be most carefully mastered" when the institutions around us favor the quick-fix and mass produced copy?

If patience replaces time, we may be able to reconnect with the natural rhythms of our nature. Instead of looking for a new job "out there," we can turn to the real source—ourselves—and allow our authenticity to recreate our lifestyles and our work, for the two go hand in hand.

To have patience may be the singular act of courage in today's world. Such patience appears when it is understood that "you are your own destination," that there is nothing and no one better to be than yourself. This is a genuine affirmation of the value of your own essence, a leap beyond the endless regression of doubt, and it will enable you to develop work situations that nourish your soul. The art of work thus emerges as a path. It takes courage to enter upon it, and commitment to stay on it, but as your determination to "work true" fosters inner growth, it becomes a "way."

VOCATION AND SELF-RELIANCE

To take away people's work is to take away their dignity, their sense of being able to make a genuine contribution to the life around them. Unfortunately, this is exactly what is occurring. The welfare-state model supports neither the self-worth nor the creative possibility of a person, but capitulates to a life model of chronic and never-ending need. The public, with little sense of rootedness, self-sufficiency, or community support, dreads scarcity and panics at the thought of losing jobs to immigration or foreign competition. A nation goes to war because its way of life—equated with the importation of fossil fuel—is threatened.

The welfare state exists, however, not only for the poor and disenfranchised but for all of us who are herded into vocational slots to fuel the needs of commercial productivity. When a company spends millions of dollars to advertise beer at a football game, we know that we have swallowed absurdity. After all, how many of us would name "beer-selling" as our choice for what we wanted to do with our lives? But we are seduced by the promise of future prosperity and controlled by the fear of scarcity. *We* are on welfare. *We* have given up the hope that we can re-create our destinies. In order to pay the electric company, the phone company, the insurance company, and the cable television company, we will go out and create advertising campaigns for beer, push pencils, and sit in front of computer monitors. We will farm out our children to daycare providers, relinquish a strong relationship with the land or community where we live, and force our internal rhythms to contort themselves to a nine-to-five nightmare. Why? Because we have bought into a vision that offers survival and distraction in exchange for our soul.

The plain fact is that our habitual way of working does not work. But the seeming absolute power of large, impersonal institutions induces a sense of helplessness and passivity. The alternative is to move through complacency and the many subtle forms of consumer-coated despair to re-create the spiritual basis of action. As this is done individually, we simultaneously address the social issues of overproduction and overconsumption, as well as apathy and the cutting-corners, cheating mentality that erodes the very integrity of our living together as a human community.

The central import of vocation is not foreign to our culture. As Westerners, our particular heritage is one of action. The traditions that we have been born into value human effort, and we carry within us the need to outwardly express our awareness, to manifest the right use of will. Thus, it is through the transformation of our work and our working environment that we may transform ourselves.

The transformative application of effort involves more than Emerson's exhortation to the individual to build his or her own world,[2] for the work of manifestation is both an individual and collective endeavor. It is individual because a person must have the courage to live from the heart, to risk loss of security and protective mediocrity in order to actualize his or her aspirations. It is collective in that we cannot actualize our dreams without one another.

To build our lives with each other's support, and with the earth's support as well, is the goal of what I call the *anti-career*. I use this term to distinguish it from what has been going on under the current guise of "career"—namely misery, pressure, and the struggle for status. With this in mind let us look at some traditional models of vocation, the collective fantasies around work that have become the unspoken structures informing our vocational possibilities. By examining their textures, qualities, and feelings, we may become more aware of the cultural visions that have crystallized into prevailing attitudes and beliefs around work, and begin to evolve into the new.

WORK AS A CURSE: "BY THE SWEAT OF YOUR BROW..."

The myth of Eden in the Book of Genesis depicts the unfallen condition as one of idyllic play, whereas the fallen human condition is one of hard work. "By the sweat of your brow you will draw bread from the earth."[3] Here God curses man to much work and little play, and this is seen as the necessary result of sin. Work is part of our daily prison sentence, and its purpose is bread, i.e., survival. The only reason that you have to work is because you are exiled from your original state, and the harder you work—the more rotten a deal you accept for yourself—the more you can expunge your inherent sinfulness. Such guilt-ridden thinking has supported oppressive structures for centuries. The priesthoods understood this well: condition a class of people with enough self-hate, and they will believe that it is their lot in life to suffer, to work until they drop. We may think that we are far from the serfdom of the Middle Ages or the slavery of the plantation, but we are the people who cannot leave the manor because we will lose our health insurance.

The issue here is not one of theology—whether man is a sinful creature or not—but is rather an issue of equating our very real condition of incompleteness and limitation with a negative sense of who we are, so that the work we do continually reinforces our lack of self-esteem. Our self-esteem, in fact, need not be determined by the work we do in the world. But if we feel that we need to do a certain type of work to prove our worth, we will remain on the job for the wrong reason. One woman, who had taken a leave of absence from work to raise her young child, told me of the rising fear she felt at a cocktail party when she was asked "What do you do?", as if she had to be a professional in order to be worthy.

If we remain imprisoned in the guilt-ridden associations of the past, our work will never approach exaltation. The more we struggle against ourselves, the more we will feel estranged. We need only slightly change the perspective, however, in order to see the myth of Eden in a much more constructive way. Yes, we humans are cast out of our innocent state; eating the apple, we have perhaps tried to become something we are not. But the expulsion from Eden is also the first step in our transformation, in our return. We are here to transform the earth and redeem ourselves through our work. Therefore, our work has a purpose. We are collectively rebuilding the road toward the holy city, the realm of our true nature. If our work does not have this sense of transformation, of working in congruence with an inner ideal, then it will be experienced as a curse. We will shirk difficult conditions and take the path of least resistance because we will not believe in what we are doing, and we will have no larger sense of why we are doing it. On the other hand, if we feel that our task is worthy, the smallest charge can be accomplished with enthusiasm.

What does it mean to draw from the earth through the sweat of one's brow? Must it be seen as a deep ancestral curse, or could it mirror an attitude that we have brought upon ourselves? Must one adopt a fallen demeanor to survive in this world? Must labor be equated with the denial of pleasure? The world *is* temporary and our knowledge *is* limited. Our position as humans is a precarious and vulnerable one. But is fear and cowering an adequate response? There are real alternatives, and a first step in reversing the idea of work as a curse is to move toward caring about one's work as much as about one's life. An office can become a shrine when we passionately care about what we do and respect the people and circumstances we engage. The alternative posture to the fallen demeanor is *presence*, being fully alive in our work. This creates mindfulness—the ability to live deliberately as opposed to partially. And this points us back toward Eden. But if we maintain an end separate from the means, we stay out of the garden and in the world of labor as drudgery. The curse of Eden is our own, and the necessary act of redemption is a work of renewal as opposed to toil, a work that holds a vision of fullness and whose performance is its own reward.

THE PROTESTANT ETHIC: *"WHAT DO YOU WANT TO BE WHEN YOU GROW UP?"* (SAVED!)

On the one hand we have been conditioned to believe that work is a curse. The Protestant ethic built upon this idea, developing an historically evolving obsession with vocation as part of the ideology of damnation and election. According to Calvin, there was no assurance of salvation since "by the decree of God," some were predestined to everlasting life and others to everlasting death.[4] Such an anxiety-producing condition would create a deep need to have some measure of one's election, and it was found in the ideal of "vocation." Performing work in the world for the "glory of God" may not insure one's salvation, but according to Max Weber, it was a good sign of it. If you had a vocation, then you may have been "elected." This fear-based vision of vocation ultimately translates into that most dreaded question, "What do you want to be when you grow up?" If it is a professional, then you may be among the elect, especially if your profession is valued socially. If you don't have a vision of what you want to be when you grow up, then you are markedly inferior.

Even the lofty sense of having a life mission may unsuspectingly participate in the dark side of the ethic of election. Have you ever noticed, for example, how humorless most missionaries are? Joyfulness, passion, and pleasure are sacrificed on the altar of hard work as a sacrament, and one concentrates on one's "calling" at the expense of everything and everyone.[5]

When I taught a colloquium on Asian humanities at Columbia University, Gandhi's autobiography was one of the cornerstones of our course. His life and work were presented to students as an ideal for our collective future. In my third year of teaching the course, a student raised her hand and said: "I do not quite understand why this work is presented to us as such an exemplary one. As a woman, I am quite sensitive to how people treat their intimates. This is, in fact, my most important criterion for judging a person. And Gandhi—at least in this work—treats both his wife and children miserably. Am I supposed to believe that one's role in the world, then, is the foremost value, and that as long as this is done well, the rest is inessential?"

I had no answer at the time, and that question forced me to rethink not only the text, but the whole ethos of "mission" and the heroic projections we place upon it. In retrospect, it stands to reason that the Western university promotes Gandhi as a missionary of morality—just as Hollywood voted the biographical film about him the best picture of 1986—for it reinforces our belief in election. The mission is more important than the person, the work more important than the life.

Being elected thus translates back into being safe and the resultant obsessive questioning about whether I have the "right" career. Once again we sell our birthright, this time for approval. As Alice Miller discusses in her book *The Drama of the Gifted Child,* from early childhood on we are encouraged to sell our enthusiasm for validation and approval. This training is reinforced in school systems that stifle spontaneity. Except for a rare few people, play increasingly disappears with age—even the *ability* to play withers. We become a nation of fans watching a few people play games for money while we keep track of the score.

THE RISE OF CORPORATE CAPITALISM: FROM CHESS TO MONOPOLY

The modern paradigm of productivity was spearheaded by emerging market economies that eventually broke through the medieval notion of a set hierarchy. In the hierarchical world, everyone knew their social and vocational role. Life was a chess game and you were a piece on the board. If you kept to your place you were assured salvation. Reward for innovation had to be balanced against any threat to an entrenched social order, insuring a deep sense of communal and personal security.

As the medieval construct gradually gave way to the market value as the determining factor in what you could and could not do in the world, expanded productivity and trade fueled unprecedented global expansion, along with its darker side of colonial and class exploitation. Expansion and technological development, however, still fit in with a mythological underpinning of progress leading toward the kingdom of God. Undesirable by-products, be they the exploitation of entire classes of people, the dictatorship of the proletariat, or radioactive waste, would disappear with time. Every human would have a wealth of goods and services, and heaven would arrive on earth. Both the capitalist and socialist world fully bought into this paradigm of productivity. I was unnerved on a recent trip to Warsaw, for example, by a Scylla/Charybdis-like vision of the main thoroughfare: on one side of the street was an old Communist-party building decorated with Stalinized sculptures of muscular factory workers forging out new goods. On the other side of the street were gaudy, larger-than-life posters of Marlboro cowboys flanked by bubbling glasses of Pepsi Cola. Each side promised heaven on earth. While seeking to free human beings from the

manacles of birth and fatalism, these systems contributed to a disorienta-
tion in the mytho-social order. Two world wars later, bloodlines are replaced by bank lines, and those not in line become dharma bums.

Since the second world war, and since Marx, Durkheim, and Sartre,
Western culture has been anything but secure in itself or its place in the
nature of things. And yet the monolithic market economies have gone on
making more and more products—as if objects are the panacea needed to
transform our basic anxiety.

More may have been better when the world was young, but productivity
has outlived its usefulness. If one employed a medical model, the current
measure of economic health, the GDP (formerly the gross national product), would be akin to cancer, the unrestricted, unintelligent, and chaotic
growth of cells. This is not a call for a return to some pristine past, it is
merely a recognition that more is *not* better and that the concept of "value"
needs to be understood in a different way. Do we really need new brands of
soft drink, toothpaste, and the rest? Do we really even need more jobs? Or
do we need depth, a life that can be lived as a work of art, with that much
dedication, care, and attention to detail? Productivity itself is not wrong or
negative, but when it is misplaced, when we try to fill the soul with *things*,
we reap the consequences.

The consequences of remaining in the hierarchical state were rigidity and
lack of creative possibility. The consequences of remaining fixated in the
productivity paradigm may be even more serious. For the productivity
model, with volume as its goal, reflects the male myth of potency, a myth in
which longer and larger is better. Such potency needs to prove itself and has
thus reinvented war in the economic sphere.

The often-stated goal of today's politicians is to create more jobs, as if
having a job will be enough. Ants have jobs, beavers have jobs, and asses
have jobs. To be able to offer jobs to everyone in society is no achievement
if they are not also accompanied by meaning. When industrial economies
were developing, productivity may have offered a certain heroic energy. But
the graduation out of the adolescent heroic role may be necessary for our
survival as a species.

FROM PRODUCTIVITY TO CREATIVITY: THE CROWN OF CREATION

To move out of the productive/consumptive syndrome, out of being a
nation of debt-ridden television addicts, there has to be a recognition of

core values, an expressed and understood need to live for more than objects, a belief in the possibility offered by life to become an integrated person, and a commitment to live out one's beliefs.

The serious issue of finding one's vocation will not therefore be solved by aptitude tests that help gear one to become a well-adjusted producer/consumer. What is needed is an anti-career—a throwing off of the shackles of obligation, approval, and mindless activity in order to enter deeply into the dynamics of co-creation. To make your work sacred is to believe in what you do, to do a good job as its own reward, and to feel proud of your work not by comparing it to the work of others but by feeling good inside, filled with integrity, neither fatigued nor drained of energy. It is work that does not destroy life, that honors pleasure, that promotes full presence and involvement and reflects your deepest sense of being. This is the challenge and the possibility offered by this book: to create a life work that will reflect your own nature, and to develop the courage and wisdom to bring it into form.

2

Creativity and Victimization: Two Modes of Manifestation

Manifestation has conventionally been viewed through the polarities of East and West. The Eastern way has generally been associated with the abdication of the will and dedication to experiencing an inner reality, while the Western way has been associated with the development of the will and its imposition upon an external reality. The West has been compared to a blind man and the East to a lame man. One can walk, the other can see, but they need one another to truly be whole. East and West may also be envisioned as existing inside our own experience. We are both East and West, and the task of finding our right work is about reconciling these two aspects of our being.

It may be helpful to consider a number of common career glitches as we lay the groundwork for creating work we love: there are those who have pursued the ladder of corporate success only to find that the top, as Steven Covey so aptly puts it, is leaning against the wrong building.[1] Then there are the burned-out health-care professionals, those who have exhausted themselves trying to help others. Another prototype is the person who has pursued a very particular interest through academic paths, and now finds no marketable place for him- or herself in the world. And then there are those who never took the job market seriously until the birth of their first child.

Is it necessary, then, for all of these people to adjust themselves to the marketplace, to put on a mask and compromise their deepest passions in order to fit into the work force and survive? These are serious questions. One may sincerely say, "Just do what you love and the money will follow," but what if the money does not follow in pace with your real needs? And what if you have no idea what it is that you love? What is crucial to addressing these issues is understanding the dynamics of co-creation. There are deeper laws behind the economic and social systems that appear to dominate our lives. The task at hand is to learn how to integrate those laws into our lives so that they support the fullest expression of ourselves through our work.

There are many ways of introducing the dynamics of co-creation, but for purposes of clarity I will lay out two career paths. The first is that of the victim—the victim of layoffs, of the economy, of society, of family, of lack of education—the list can go on indefinitely. The second is the way of the creative—the one who lives in such a manner that the world begins to evolve around his or her vision, creating an environment in which that vision can develop and flourish.[2]

To follow the second path is no easy task. It requires courage to live from one's authenticity and commitment to stay the course, but the effort to do so reveals subtle laws that are as real as the rates of currency exchange. Only this currency—from the word *current*, meaning "power transmission"—is of another nature. And it is this other nature, this intrinsic current, that we can tap into and work with in terms of manifesting an outer reality that corresponds to the inner laws of our beings. By doing so we can begin to resolve the tension between economics and spirituality, for it is the vision of them as distinct that has created such chaos on so many levels. This is what the Buddha called *right livelihood*. The questions we need to ask are: What is right? That is, what is needed to live? What is my *dharma*, the law of my own being? The answers to these questions can best be understood through process. They are revealed neither in a flash event nor through a flowchart, but are uncovered through painstaking determination to come down to the bare bones of oneself and one's life.

The anti-career, then, entails more than having a vision. We may romantically speak about our vision, but visions often change with the changing of our emotions, or they are captured and funneled through an unconscious participation mystique in which a group's vision is mistaken for one's own. The process of identifying a personal vision can be a confusing task because visioning is not an exclusively individual phenomenon. You cannot have a vision without a collective language and form, both of which provide external support for actualizing that vision. As we consider our personal visions, then, we must also consider the entire phenomenon of relationship—how, where, and why we fit in with those around us. A successful vision needs to be cultivated: like a garden, it requires planning, nurturing, and weeding so that it may grow in its own natural way.

How can one enter onto the creative path? The first step is to clearly distinguish between victim consciousness and "creative" consciousness. Once this distinction is clear, you can open the gates of visionary experience and inspiration from a place of strength and functionality. The creative being is not overrun by visions or other forms of inner experience, but learns to work with them. A creative person need not experience life through the screen of a particular discipline, but rather does so through the integrity of his or her own self and trusts in his or her inner authority.

CREATIVE ACCESSING OF THE INNER WORLD

A creative being does not allow him- or herself to be disempowered by "experts" who claim access to one's inner reality, be they gurus, career counselors, or Fortune Five-Hundred managers. To work with the inner world and receive the richness of its guidance is our heritage. It is our right, but we have to go through the door with key in hand and unlock it. Unfortunately for many of us that key was taken away in childhood when we were told that our imaginary playmates were not real. Subsequently we were conditioned to believe that imagination is lesser than conceptualization. Nothing could be further from the truth. For what has actually occurred is mass conditioning by collective imagery that masquerades as fact. We hear about the recession and the shrinking dollar, we tremble at the thought of paying higher taxes or the possibilities of a new health-care system and how it might adversely effect us. A creative response to the news of the shrinking dollar, for example, would first show as an understanding that, even during the Great Depression, some people made millions of dollars, and that by law of nature the converse movement of adversity is opportunity. The creative being, therefore, frees his or her imagination from the cloud of conditioned public belief and explores the very real and fertile terrain of his or her own being.

The inhibiting of one's image-making power is essential to enculteration of the paradigm of productivity. For reverie—taking long, slow dream walks and the like—wastes valuable, "productive" time. Instead of being trained in the possibilities and uses of the imagination, we are encouraged to have it siphoned off by television. The visionary dimension of the human experience is essential, but when it becomes devalued, it leaks out sideways and we become, in the words of T. S. Eliot, "distracted from distraction by distraction."[3]

In fact, both imagination *and* conceptual thinking have their proper functions. Both faculties enable the mind to negotiate and engage reality, and they can be used to complement instead of cancel one another out. In this book we will explore the imaginal, inner world and the ways in which it can be creatively accessed to conceptualize, plan, and take action. The prerequisite to this exploration is a willingness to let go of habitual concepts and judgments while allowing yourself to explore and receive information in the way of creative response. We can frame this process with the anagram TALL. One must stand tall in the inner world, one must be able to Trust, Ask, Listen, and Live.

Trust: The First Movement into Power

To trust is the basic energy of anti-career work. At its deepest level, an active trust indicates a confidence in the life process, a willingness to let things be as they are. Many of us who have received mixed messages from our parents, from the government, and from advertising campaigns have grown cynical and have consequently closed down our trusting faculties. We have become intimidated and thus hesitate to articulate the first flash that comes into our minds. We don't allow certain realms of experience, such as dreams, fantasy, or feeling, to nourish us, and playful spontaneity only manifests after we have had a few beers. But we can work to re-awaken these areas. Instead of condemning those who have proved to be untrustworthy, we can begin to restore trust by opening to the woundedness of our betrayal, by learning to forgive, and by contacting the fundamental and ever-renewing rhythms of the life process. This trust will not succeed if it remains on the conceptual level alone. It must enter into the very core of our behavioral and psychic configurations until we feel the flow of life stirring inside us. Such trust is essential in working with the inner world. Without it we will be tempted to manipulate inner phenomena, to make our visions and dreams appear to be more or less than what they are, and when the real thing comes we will wonder if it is true. As far as the inner world is concerned, the rule of thumb is to trust whatever comes up—this especially holds true for meditation—and to be honest and clear with it. If everyone in a group meditation is seeing angels, for example, but your image is of meat loaf, as incongruous as it may seem (and this actually happened to someone I know), this is the image you need to work with. This is what your consciousness has presented to you, and the more you are willing to work with *what is,* the more the unconscious receives the reinforcement that it is okay to reveal truth and that you are ready to engage core material.

Eric Erikson spoke of trust versus mistrust as the fundamental challenge of earliest childhood.[4] Many of us, as we work toward authentic career manifestation, will discover the need to recover this trust in ourselves and others. Therapeutic work can be very helpful for this and may be necessary if we are to move to a state of greater functionality. In terms of meditative experience, our level of trust is readily revealed through our breathing patterns. To what degree are you willing to allow the breath of life to flow through you, to heal and shape you? Do you constrict your breathing, try to control it, stop it from sinking down into lower levels of your body? Every day you can move deeper into universal trust by allowing the breath to move down to your edge, to that place where you hold on tight. Meet that rigidity, and then just let go a bit. Every day you can practice breathing a little easier, letting go a little more.

Asking: The Power of Articulation

The second letter of our anagram is A for asking. A seemingly simple directive, yet quite extensive in its application. To "ask" is to take up the way of inquiry as opposed to the way of complacency. The victim learns not to ask too much, for it may upset the powers that be. As one question after another is buried within, the child/adult is bent into the mold of acquiescence until true inquiry becomes next to impossible. Underneath the facade of the complacent, respectable victim there is always despair.

To ask is to maintain a state of alert energy—not questioning as a rhetorical ploy, but asking in a way that allows us to develop through our inconsistencies. We work with our doubts and questions, and we grow through our resistances. This is how creative careers are built—not by smooth sailing, but by the willingness to negotiate troubled waters.

To ask means that whenever and wherever we feel a disjunctive energy—be it within ourselves, in interacting with another, or in external processes of the world—we inquire into its quality, its texture, and its message. Media news conferences and public interviews do not usually engage in inquiry. The questions are framed by predetermined agendas or limited by the need to sell products. If you are going somewhere too fast, you do not have the time or energy to inquire. Furthermore, true inquiry is dangerous to those whose dogmas are already in place. Persistent questioning, more often than not, upsets the applecart of our preconceived notion of things. We have to start all over again, and we fear that we do not have the energy for that. Children engage in natural inquiry and are more often than not told to be quiet, or to stop asking "Why?". To ask is to open the floodgates of blocked energies, to move into communication, sincerity, and connectedness with others and with ourselves.

Asking, then, is not necessarily about questions and answers. In fact, one of the models we want to avoid is the problem solution model. The victim thinks, "My life or my career is a problem and I have to find the solution." Such thinking reinforces the hamster-in-the-cage mentality that keeps us seeing life as an unsolved problem.

There are many different ways to ask, and they are all valid. You can ask the universe. Go to a sacred place, a place that has meaning for you and ask the clouds, the trees, or God for whatever is truly urgent in your life. Ask from your heart, from your gut, not as a supplicant but as a being burning with inquiry, with a passion to know deeply. Ask, and energy is set into motion. But know that the answer you receive to your asking may not be the expected one, for this kind of asking opens possibilities for new pathways and nonsolutions.

Sharing our energy of inquiry with another is a powerful practice that pride or unworthiness often prevents us from doing. The entire field of counseling is based upon the fact that when we have another person who will listen to us, we are able to open up to new things within ourselves. To ask another is not to put oneself at the mercy of that person's judgment—such is the way of the victim. Rather, it is a willingness to share the life journey in good faith—not hanging onto another's energy, but asking as an opening to powerful interaction. Often we wait for answers to drop down from heaven when really the gift is being offered to us through the presence of another.

The final person we can always ask is ourselves. "How am I really feeling about this project? Do I really want to go to work this morning? Why am I resisting this particular situation?" Inquiry, then, does not have to be verbal. It is rather an attitude of constant attention to oneself and to one's environment.

Listening: The Willingness to Change

Listening is the companion to inquiry. Meditation is, in fact, nothing more than listening deeply. To listen is to acknowledge the possibility of a new way. When we are in victim mode, we do not listen, for we already anticipate habitual responses to our inquiries and tacitly refuse to break the molds of our expectations. The creative response, on the other hand, is deeply attentive, for the next message, the next opportunity, may come from the most unlikely source.

Asking is the active polarity that opens up energies; listening is the receptive polarity that allows these new energies to find their space. Listening is a mode of sensitivity, an awareness of all the messages we are receiving: the messages we receive from the body, from the earth, from our moods and reactions to others, and from our dreams. To listen is to establish a dialogue with everything and everyone that comes into our path. On the outer plane, our senses—sight, sound, taste, smell, and touch—are separate entities. The deeper we penetrate into listening, however, the more we may become aware of a realm where the senses converge—a realm in which seeing is hearing, for example.

To truly listen is to go beyond outer discriminations of what or who is important. In the 1950s the Indian poet Sharad Chandra once went on a pilgrimage to meet Nirala, "the Strange One," considered by many at the time to be India's greatest living poet but also something of a madman. Nirala lived alone and rarely acknowledged anyone. Willing to use any means necessary, Sharad Chandra finally accosted Nirala on the road as the poet was leaving his house. "What do you want?" Nirala angrily barked? "I just wanted your audience," Sharad replied. "If you want to see me," Nirala said, "you have to see everything and everyone."

To listen is to keep one's attention supple and sensitive, to allow a voice to speak through the natural as well as the human world. When tracking an animal, you bend your ear to the ground and pick up a vibration from afar. Listening, then, is an act of humility in the original sense of the word *humus*—not having one's head in the clouds, but being close to the earth and her signs, bending down low to hear the rumblings in the ground.

④ *To Live: The Power of Action*

Our anagram is completed with the letter L, standing for the courage to live. No matter what our experiences are in the inner world, if we are not able to cross over the corpus callosum into action, they will remain just that— inner experiences. The creative person does not revel in past experiences; the creative one moves into action. Action completes the circuit and inspires the unconscious to divulge new information, for it sees that the information is being heeded and put to good use. To truly live is to ground our intuitions and establish circuits of mutual interaction between our outer and inner worlds. There are thousands of armchair metaphysicians out there, but they remain in their armchairs because they have not embodied their teachings. The only teaching that has any effect, and hence the only one that can generate a career, is the one that has become embodied. The Jungian analyst and writer Robert Johnson speaks of this principle in dreamwork when he states that whenever he has a significant dream and has gone through the process of understanding its meaning, he will enact something in the physical world to commemorate that dream.[5] This is an example of the grounding that is necessary to manifest inner vision. In order to move from dream to reality, you have to put the dream to the test, and the only way that happens is by risking it in the crucible of action. It is through trial and error that information feeds back into the dream process and the inner world and outer world begin to work together.

To trust, to ask, to listen, and to live, then, are the activities by which we interface with the inner world to mold life into a work of art.

HARMONIZING OUR WORK WITH OUR LIFE PROCESS

Semiotics, the study of systems of meaning, teaches us that meaning exists not through independent units but through seeing an entire process. To see work as separate from life process and purpose is part of the fragmented worldview that we are growing out of. Patriarchal ideologies, even those spawned in the New Age, tend to devalue life by exalting the job. The efforts to replace rootedness, fellowship, and vision with work and loyalty to the firm (or even to a spiritual collective), mirror efforts to artificially create ourselves through one self-improvement ideal or another. Success in the workplace may be part of the spiritual journey, but it cannot replace it.

It is such thinking that leads to the illusion of economies sustained only by human laws, as if our good can be conceived of separately from that of the mineral, plant, and animal kingdoms. Our cultural bias toward career and self versus home and roots is dramatically visible in popular astrology. If you read ten random books on natal horoscope delineation you will find emphasis on the midheaven as a point of great importance. The tenth house (the midheaven)—career and status in the community—is given premium value, whereas the fourth house (the nadir)—home, roots, and the inner being—is given passing mention. We remain fixated with career as the

indicator of our well-being and quality of life when nothing in our empiri-
cal experience justifies this. But this is our predicament. We keep trying to
build that stairway to the sky without ever asking where we are going and
why.

If we really asked why, or better yet, if we really observed *how we live*—
seeing the hurry and the haste, the devaluation of entire classes of people,
the lack of connectedness with the very world that surrounds us—we would
have to face the terrible void that we try to cover with business, productivity,
and politics. If we want to integrate our work we have to challenge the
status-quo consensus—we have to take the responsibility to become truly
healthy. To be healthy is to be right with the world—its people, creatures,
and rhythms. No one else will make it right for us, for our essential nature
is unique to each of us. To return to essence is to return to inner balance,
and such balance is the only basis from which a true career can be created.

3

The First Chakra: Abundance as the Root of Power

One of the main cultural mechanisms of denial is to assert that one is or has "the best": think of such claims as "the master race," "the white man's burden," "the highest standard of living," and so forth. That facts do not bear these ideas out is irrelevant. They are pounded into the cultural mind until only the slogans remain. The political leaders we hire and the hero-icons who appear on our dolls and cereal boxes grimace in poses of certainty and confidence—all because, when we dig deeply enough, we find a pervasive feeling that something is missing. No matter what one has, it is never quite enough. In truth, with regard to our working lives, we are in the same position as the alcoholic, enmeshed in mechanisms and strategies of denial. Somewhere we will have to move off this downward spiral, or else the laws of economics will do it for us. As in the first and single most important step in Alcoholics Anonymous, the denial must cease and the admission must be made: Our working lives have become unmanageable. Whether on the janitor's stool or in the executive's chair, there is a feeling that forces out of our control are creating uncertainty, dispirited fatigue, and a muffled frustration that makes it seem normal to dread Monday mornings.

One poignant example of this comes from an interview with the late comic Sam Kinison. When asked why he felt his brand of off-color humor that rants at the Japanese, Iranians, homosexuals, and others was so popular, he explained that by now his audience realized they weren't going to get the dream—the American Dream, that is. His brand of humor resonated with this frustration by projecting it outward onto others who could be viewed as already "out of the dream." By mocking these people, the pain felt by those in his audience was mirrored in a less obtrusive (although not in a transformative) way. But herein lies a key to creating authentic work: it is the ability to break the fever of wanting to be someone else or somewhere else, the ability to take off the mask that claims "all is well" or that "they are ruining us" and to squarely face one's situation.

The feverish pace that we call "normal" and the self-righteous denial of three trillion dollars of debt are signs of an inward poverty. This poverty is not always visible to economists but it is all too familiar to families who live in frustrated inertia, to friendships that change with the marketplace, and to professional associations where infighting supplies the major drama of life. Underneath the facade we present to the world, many of us, indeed the great majority of us, actually feel poor. That is, we feel that we lack something. Either "my nose is too big," or "I didn't get enough education," or "I married the wrong man (or woman.)" Why is our cultural self-esteem so low that we must live in the denial of the confident but secretly impotent cowboy, for example, or in the constant feeling that we have not succeeded in our lives? What is it that we have missed?

A colleague of mine who travels abroad for six to nine months of every year once remarked that, upon returning to the United States, he is always impressed by the frenetic speed and the facade of motion, as if incessant movement will enable us to capture some elusive state of satisfaction. Underneath all this activity, do we doubt that we are actually alright? Do we doubt our goodness? Do we doubt our very metaphysical moorings, and keep the charade going to avoid admitting to this doubt?

ACCEPTANCE: THE ROOT OF POWER

What is being described here is the energetic source or the "root" of our being. It is here where we come in contact with the earth, and it is here where we must take our stand if we hope to establish authentic and powerful careers. In the body, the root is known as the first chakra. The word *chakra* simply means "wheel"; the chakras are visualized as seven wheel-like energy centers within the spinal column. Conceived of as subtle energy centers, the chakras act as nodal points, uniting the psycho-energetic and physical aspects of our being. An effective map for helping bridge the realities of the inner and outer worlds, the chakra system has garnered quite a bit of attention recently as various healing traditions employ it to identify blockages and psychological issues that tend to constellate around particular disease conditions. The origins of chakra symbolism are commonly traced back to Indian schools of tantric yoga, but Joseph Campbell found the same system present in ancient Egypt, and Edgar Cayce suggests that the seven churches in the Book of Revelations is a code indicating the seven centers in the body that may open one by one.[1]

I was a bit reticent about introducing esoteric symbology into a discussion on vocation, for my purpose is not to mystify the process. On the other hand, it feels more than appropriate to actively locate career issues in the pyscho-physical body, and the chakra system is the most compact, direct, and cross-cultural energy-body map that I know of. As we go through vocational issues and recognize their correspondence with the chakras, we should not confuse the map for the territory. The *issue* of authentic career choice is what is important; the model can give you a handle, a new and effective means of working with the issue.

The first chakra is traditionally visualized as red and is connected to the element of earth. It is located at the very tip of the coccyx (the tailbone), the lowermost bone of the spine. The first chakra is the place where we connect with the base energies of our being, where we can find the power as well as the spirit to actually accomplish something. This relates to the issue of abundance versus scarcity, the base matter that must be resolved if we are to move into working from passion. The teaching of the first chakra is to live from a place of acceptance rather than the debilitating unworthiness that is nourished by mass conditioning.

The antidote to this conditioning is a deep self-acceptance. Ralph Waldo Emerson speaks of this in his essay entitled "Self Reliance."

> There is a time in every man's education when he arrives at the conviction that envy is ignorance; that imitation is suicide; that he must take himself for better, or worse, as his portion; that though the universe is full of good, no kernel of nourishing corn can come to him but through his toil bestowed on that plot of ground which is given to him to till.[2]

The message here is to accept ourselves on every level (not simply at the level of an idealized spiritual self), to accept our backgrounds, histories, perceived weaknesses, and disappointments as well as our hopes, dreams, and desires. The building must arise from the foundation, the very bottom of our being, with no pretense. Ideas such as "I need more education," "I need to move to a different place," "I need to learn another language," and so forth, are secondary and often mask the scarcity mentality that keeps us bound to a frustration of our own making.

The term *abundance* has been thrown around the "prosperity arena" for some time, and is just as often a synonym for denial as it is for reality. Anyone who has spent time in the Third World, or in the South Bronx for that matter, may cynically question the concept of abundance, and this should be so. To consider the concept that abundance is real and all else is illusion we need to begin with ourselves, not with judging the world. We need to understand abundance as genuine self-acceptance and recognize its fundamental relationship to the quality of trust.

The millionaire afraid to spend two dollars on an ice cream sundae is not living in abundance; neither is a prosperous nation that turns back refugees, afraid that it will lose its coveted and limited number of jobs. Abundance is not a question of how much one has but of what one's attitude is toward what one has.

To truly accept what you have—your gifts, your experiences, and your chronic shortcomings—is no simple matter. But this is where your riches lie, for no one can duplicate your experiences; no one is born under the exact same set of circumstances, and therefore no one else can make the same contribution to the world that you can. From life's point of view, each one of us is special. If you have not been told this enough, you must uncover it for yourself. And we have to uncover it for each other. No one is born in the same place and time. No one can do what you can do. No one can take your place in the universe. If an idea or a way of doing something is truly your own, no one else will steal it. It is yours, and it will amplify your power.

To be abundant is to accept the validity of your destiny, no matter how seemingly small or insignificant. Such an embrace of your uniqueness generates a presence that flows out over your heredity and environment and creates unforeseen opportunity. This is as true for one's so-called weaknesses as it is for one's apparent strengths. Behind the chronic weakness or seeming disability is a message that needs to be received and a healing force that needs to find its place. The percentage of healers who have themselves experienced traumatic illness is extraordinary. Whoever we may be, there is material to work with, material that will yield its form in proportion to our attentiveness and care.

Abundance is, above all, the belief—and even more importantly, the feeling—that one is loved. When we feel loved by life itself, we begin to feel that there will always be a place for us in the world. The terrible fear of abandonment needs to be met and seen for what it is—a valley that must be walked through in order to move into a place of trust. How do we get the strength to walk through this valley? I remember Martin Buber saying that even in one's moment of greatest despair, when one retreats from the world, one will peek out and eventually see that life goes on anyway. Even in our moment of greatest disillusionment, the river flows, the birds fly, and the clouds blow through the sky. There is a great paradox at work here: True abundance arises from emptiness, from letting go of the idols that support our partiality. To drop into life, to let go of the hope that this person, this idea, or this institution is your salvation, is an entryway into abundance. To test life, to allow life itself to lead you and to care for you, is not a parlor game. In order to move into your way, you may have to put everything on the line. You may be asked to give up the rewards you have coveted for so long. But life will respond because you have asked it to; you have looked into life itself. And the results grow slowly, but they develop into a deep self-worth and trust in life. One can then accept the various aspects of one's existence—the heavens and hells, the places of awkwardness and of skillfulness—and exalt in one's self as the poet Walt Whitman exalted in "Song of Myself":

> I celebrate myself, and sing myself,
> And what I assume, you shall assume,
> For every atom belonging to me as good belongs to you.[3]

Affirming abundance is not holding mindless cosmic optimism. Perhaps it would be better to rename abundance *regenerative trust.* The resources of the earth are abundant. Mineral deposits, for example, reappear long after they have been believed to be used up. However, when one engages in unconscious appropriation there is neither trust nor regenerative cooperation. Greed, often socially sanctioned, is a gross manifestation of the scarcity principle. The trusting person on the other hand senses that what is needed is available. There is no need to hoard or to take more than one's share at a particular time. Cosmic optimists and success cults that do not respect the cycles of nature and the so-called downsides of human experience harden into ideologues. They find themselves frozen in smiles of denial. Such people are often forced to become esoteric used-car salesmen—always on the make, always preaching. One basic principle regarding abundance is this: If there is obsession, if there is a hidden agenda, if you feel the pull of need—whether it is the need to be heard, to convince, or to sell— then somewhere within there is a sense of lack that demands investigation.

This is not to say that great careers cannot arise out of need. More often than not, they have. And need is nothing to be ashamed of. But if need is all we know, we will remain caught in the paradigm of work arising from necessity as opposed to work as an expression of one's innate creativity. And this is the juncture at which we stand.

When there is trust and self-acceptance, mutuality can come into being. In the scarcity situation we either crave others to fulfill our own needs or are afraid of being controlled—we either suck others in or push them away. Abundance makes room for the other. The corollary of abundance is the ability to function in mutuality, be that with family, friends, coworkers, or whomever. When we work in mutuality, we no longer need to convince clients or patients that they are missing something and that the savior, expert, or product has the answer. As a culture, we have become victimized by the loveless pose of the expert; with each ounce of power given away, we lose trust in ourselves, in our fundamental goodness, and in our ability to cooperate with others for mutual growth and benefit. Just as the sign of abundance is mutuality, the signs of scarcity are dominance and dependency.

INTEGRITY AS THE ROOT OF POWER

On this base level of the root chakra, we also touch an evolutionary polarity. It is here that we become aware of the human as suspended between the predator and the giver. Ingrained in some part of the reptilian brain are millions of years of evolutionary coding to eat or be eaten. From the natural world of predatorship comes the predominate mode of basic root energy— survival. The will to live, struggle, and survive is genuine and should not be minimized. The struggle for survival—the emergence of autonomous power—is a primary initiating energy in the human experience, and this needs to be recognized. If we do not learn to stand up on our own two feet, we will wither away. If the chicken does not peck its way out of the egg, it does not survive. And yet we do not want to stop at this point and go no further, for the purpose of initiation is to bring us to a new platform of experience.

Above and beyond the need for struggle and survival that lies at the base of one's being, there is another dimension. Integrity appears when our principles become so established that they supplant survival as the motivating human mechanism. From this place, principle may be worth more than life itself. This is the basis of the power of alignment.

A powerful model of integrity may be seen in the life of a Gandhi, not Mohandas but his wife, Kasturbai. When violently ill and possibly near death, Mrs. Gandhi refused to take the beef tea prescribed by the attending physician, for it violated her basic principles. She preferred death to abandoning her integrity. Kasturbai Gandhi's particular concept of integrity may be different than yours or mine, but the point is that when an ideal becomes so much a part of oneself that it is more powerful than the will to live, it brings in tremendous power and energy of accomplishment.

Such integrity may be evident in the commonest of situations. On one of my first visits to Mandolin Brothers music store, a great success story in creating the work one loves, a customer was bargaining for a guitar at a lower price and offered to pay cash so that the sales tax need not be charged. The salesperson answered simply, without any trace of self-righteousness, "I'm sorry, we're straight arrow here." There was something about the way he said it—so definitive and yet not challenging. It was a statement declaring that here our business is selling musical instruments, the best musical instruments. There is no need to cut corners or to be dishonest on any level. Mandolin Brothers is a store owned and operated by lovers of musical instruments, and you get that feeling the minute you walk in the store. Unlike most stores that sell vintage guitars, no one discourages you from playing the instruments on the floor, and no one hits you with a hard sell. And business keeps increasing, for the integrity of the business has created a worldwide reputation.

THE LIFE CURRENT

Genuine self-acceptance translates into self-respect, which then becomes self-reliance. Self-acceptance is really life acceptance—accepting the current, finding and tuning into the energy of life itself and all its subsequent potential. The experience of abundance cannot be found at the discursive or even at the emotional level. It must be experienced within the body. This is a cardinal anti-career principle: The career starts in the body. Isadora Duncan discovered her vocation by imitating the movements of the ocean waves in front of her mother's home and connecting to the visceral experience of energy. "I realized early in my life," she said, "that there was this kind of energy, some animating spark."[4]

This spark is what sustains us. To contact the spark of your abundance,

To contact the spark of your abundance

you might ask yourself, "What sustains me? What nourishes me?" Then list all the things that come to mind, everything from food to friendship to manifestations of more subtle energies. As you consciously recognize these things and begin to own them, you familiarize yourself with your prime territory, the place where your abundance is found. This is where lies the strengths that you have to share with the world.

One successful process that has been developed in the course of exploring the art of work is the abundance meditation. This meditation is not accomplished in one sitting. It must be practiced with regularity until you can literally feel the current of life connect with and penetrate your system. You may want to tape the following meditation (as well as the others in this book) and work with them in that way, as they were created in alignment with the spoken word.[5] The most important factor in working with the first chakra is to learn to begin every day from a place of fulfillment and a sense of being supported by the forces of existence, to feel in your very core that you are riding the energetic crest of life as opposed to constantly paddling upstream.

The Abundance Meditation

Sit in a comfortable position. Be aware of your feet or your buttocks touching the ground. Feel the strength and suppleness of your spinal column and begin to gently breathe in and breathe out. Allow your breath to flow freely, smoothing out and relaxing your entire being. If you feel any tension or resistance, breathe into that place and gently invite release. You may voice a long "aah" on the exhalation, to assist with the release.

As you release the breath, remain aware of all the places in your body where you are holding on, trying to maintain control out of scarcity. Gently release your energy into the ever-present current of life. You are plugging in to a circulating electric current that fills you and enlivens you. With every breath, feel yourself more deeply in the current. You can now feel yourself being supported by the earth, as if your entire being is rooted and is receiving nourishment. As the breath drops you down deeper and deeper into the earth, allow your body to be breathed by the rhythm of the inhale and exhale. Every breath now synchronizes with the rhythm of life itself. Your breath connects you with the flow of the tides and the seas and the movement of the stars. Your rhythm is the rhythm of life—the changing seasons, the progression from dawn to dark to dawn again. The current is ever present and it fills you, energizes you, permeates your entire being. You feel the flow of the unlimited life force, the energy that is ever available as you let go and align yourself with its beauty, its power, its presence. Feel your being harmonized in this moment. Allow the fullness of existence to enter you and work through you. Feel free, open, and easy in this flow of ever-abundant energy. From this state affirm to yourself: "This abundance, this flow, is the natural energy of being itself, and I am ever supported by this flow of energy."

Breathing in and out, lightly and easily letting yourself expand to receive the fullness of the life force, allow an image of abundance to arise from deep within and enter your consciousness. Do not force it. Just ask and it will form within—an image, literal or abstract—a gift from your inner wisdom that shows you a form of abundance. The image need not be understood. Just allow it to form and then hold it in mind, feeling it energizing you.

And as you breathe in and out, slowly return and integrate within your physical form, keeping the image alive, knowing that you can return to it at any time to remember the reality of the life force. The image of abundance affirms regenerative trust from deep within.

THE IMAGE OF ABUNDANCE

The image of abundance permits us to overturn limiting and conditioned structures. The image and its attendant feeling, the current of life, is the first step in forming a true and new structure that will support our work in the world. One person was gifted with an image of a woman in a rocking chair nursing a child. Upon closer inspection, she found the child to be herself and the woman to be the mother of all. Another person found herself to be a smooth stone. The stone was saying, "To look at me, you may think that I am plain, but when the water covers me I glisten in the sun like a diamond! Here in the water I can change position. I can work with others to provide refuge. And I have learned that with patience I can shape-change, if I submit to the power of the water."

The image of abundance need not fit into any conventional category. Its power is not in its literal form. Rather, its power is in its ability to activate the psyche to begin to move toward its inherent possibility. Many people see images from childhood during this meditation, indicating that there are untapped riches from the past that are seeking their way into life at this time. Others see fields of green, an image of fertility. The color may be significant. Sometimes by simply accepting a new color into our field— wearing it, eating it, or noticing it in our environment—we can bring in needed energy that will effect the external levels of life.

The purpose of the abundance meditation is to establish this current on an everyday basis. The current works as tangibly experienced energy. It is our own energy opening to receive the energy of life itself, to receive and be renewed on a constant basis. Psychologically, this corresponds to Erik Erikson's first developmental stage of childhood, that of trust versus mistrust. With this meditation we are rewiring our lives. By establishing a daily pattern of trust, we are, in fact, reparenting ourselves and learning to receive the support of the Earth Mother, not as a metaphysical idea but by coming into touch with the actual current of life. When we connect with this current, feeling it supporting and nurturing us, we can allow ourselves more space—space to experiment, to make mistakes, to learn, and to accept our present situation, being fully responsive to it. We need no longer paralyze ourselves with explanations. At the very foundation of being we begin to operate from a kinesthetic mode—touching, feeling, plugging in, and allowing ourselves to be carried by life.

As soon as this current is met the various scarcity issues such as unpaid bills, shortage of time, fatigue, and so forth can be brought into a new focus. We are not attacking these issues, but are placing them within a wider perspective—this is crucial to understand. The authentic career must proceed from this wider perspective, from the place of our fullness.

At this point you may want to stop and identify your "power shortages." Notice where there is frustration and resistance in your daily life. Do you feel frustration around time constraints? money? relationships? Know that these are never the underlying issues; these are the symptoms. Instead of bending ourselves out of shape in order to fit into the world, the anti-career path uses the strategy of recognizing that the basis of our work is to accept, receive, and expand into our maximum energy, which is our birthright. By connecting on a kinesthetic level with the life current, it becomes more difficult to do things that block the natural expression of our energetic capabilities. We begin to look for creative involvement with the life force. This involvement will affect our physical posture, food choices, time scheduling, and language. This relationship deeply affects our life rhythm. And the great joy is that, as we move into our full, unqualified life rhythm, nature itself begins to support us, financially as well as emotionally. Where we once thought there was no time we now find there is more time. Where we once thought there was no one, we now find people are with us—all because we have accepted our abundance, our trust in the life we have been given.

Success may not come at once because we are habituated to living in a contracted state. But we must begin somewhere expanding into the energy of life. Start with an hour. Move to a day. Go for a lifetime.

4

The Second Chakra: Tracing the Thread of Passion

Such, such were the joys
When we all, girls and boys
In our youthtime were seen
On the Ecchoing Green.
                    William Blake

To get what you want, the success books tell you, you have to be able to see your goal, to visualize the object in detail, to affirm its reality daily, to hold it in your mind. Then your dream will come true. The problem with this strategy is that what we want on a conscious level is often at odds with what we crave on the unconscious level. We are adept at finding countless ways to sabotage ourselves, and we blame it on circumstances such as the boss or the economy. Or else we actually do get what we want—like Midas, who was granted the boon that whatever he touched would turn to gold—and are destroyed by it. Certainly we would find it attractive to have the power to turn all that we touch into gold. And there are people who have powers like this. My own mentor, Hilda Charlton, was able to manifest money for people. Satya Sai Baba, the Indian holy man, has the ability to materialize objects. I and countless others have seen him do this, and it has been documented on film. In such cases as these, there seems to be so little interference between thought and its actualization that manifestation oc-- curs instantaneously. If the man and woman on the street had this power, however, they would probably end up, like Midas, making a royal mess out of things. This is because most of us have so much unprocessed debris floating in our emotional and subconscious realms that what we actually want and what we *think* we want are often quite disjointed.

Rosalyn Bruyere of the Healing Light Center in Los Angeles speaks of an acquaintance who decided to practice creative visualization in order to acquire a new automobile. And she did not want any ordinary vehicle—she wanted a Rolls Royce—so she continually visualized a red Rolls Royce in her garage. She practiced the visualization and affirmed it day and night for months. Sure enough, one night a red Rolls Royce crashed into her garage! This woman had never bothered to clean out her garage first; that is, to make psychic space for the thing she wanted to bring into her life. Similarly, Mary and Byron Gentry, teachers of healing in the human energy field, speak of a woman who visualized the man she wanted to be with. She visualized the car he would drive and the places they would go, all in exquisite detail. She eventually met this man. He drove the Lincoln Continental she visualized and took her dancing, just as she had seen it. What she had not seen, however, was that he was involved with organized crime and treated her terribly. She visualized the externals but they were not aligned with her source. Such an alignment is essential if visualization is to be ethical and beneficial.

If our wanting is to be positive and productive, not only for ourselves but for others, we must develop the clarity that comes from cleaning out and understanding our psychic space. This means that we must first become aware of the various and largely unconscious comedies, tragedies, and farces whose scripts inhabit our inner beings. In the root-energy area of the first chakra, we give ourselves permission to want things, and this permission is crucial. Desire is the creative energy of life. It does not have be envisioned as an enemy to be ferreted out, an activity of the old-world, life-denying model. As human beings, we are intrinsically worth something. We belong here and are here to create *with* the world, not to find a way *out* of the world. Therefore, we can be ourselves. Moreover, we do not have to spend years seeking out our "true" selves for, more often than not, such a search runs on a problem/solution model that suggests we not take action until we perfect ourselves. Rather than seeking perfection or improvment, let us begin by trusting ourselves, by trusting the promptings of our inner being, and by increasing that trust through action.

The question to ask, then, is greater than "What do I want to do?" Such a lukewarm question will not generate breakthrough passion. If choosing a career was simply a matter of choosing what you want or what you like, you could sit in the career counselor's office filling out forms that try to match your personality profile with the job market. The anti-career needs to come from a deeper level, from the soul level. So a more appropriate question to ask might be this: "How can I fully express the desire energy of life that nourishes and runs through me in a way that will enhance life itself?"

In order to answer such a question and set viable goals and priorities, the emotional labyrinth of our past needs to be processed; our motivations, insecurities, fantasies around achievement, employment, money, and much more need to be listened to. Otherwise we become either high achievers to please someone else or victims to past sufferings, or we manifest other undesirable outcomes, all of which reflect our unconscious patterning.

THE SCRIPT IS IN THE INTESTINES

The emotional patterning of our unconscious is represented by the second chakra and is symbolically visualized in the lower intestinal area. This is where we can either assimilate the nutrients we need (information) or leave them to lie dormant, held-in, blocked, and putrified to the point that they start to poison the rest of the system. The element of this area is water, representing the emotional realm of our being. Its symbolic color is orange, a color that is rarely seen in the clothing worn by Westerners—the warmth and expressive quality of orange is not something that our culture is very comfortable with. The second chakra is located in front of the spine, at the level of the reproductive organs.

The method of visualizing our vocational concerns through particular chakras gives us a means by which to recognize core issues that ultimately determine the quality of our careers. The anti-career process is, above all, an organic one. Our present work situation accurately reflects particular aspects of our psyche. If we go out knocking on doors or sending off resumes, we risk repeating the same self-defeating patterns that got us knocking at the wrong doors to begin with.

Myths provide us with stories so deeply resonant with our own that they open up new possibilities for our lives and work. When we see that our predicament has been shared by many others we can stop feeling sorry for ourselves and begin to explore our unique potentials and capacities through our own stories. Instead of trying to solve our problems, we allow our situations to find their own unique solutions.

One myth that strongly mirrors the second chakra situation is that of the Minotaur, the human-eating monster to whom the residents of Crete were obliged to sacrifice their children. The Minotaur reflects the destructive energy within that devours our talents and creative possibilities.[1] The birth of the Minotaur resulted from a king's desire to hold on to something that was not his own. King Minos of Crete was made ruler of this sea region by Poseidon; in exchange, the king was to offer his beautiful white bull as a sacrifice to the god. In the ancient world, the principle of sacrifice had to do with acknowledging the interdependence of all living beings, an important first law of economics. In an anti-career, wealth is created through sharing, and one's prosperity serves the prosperity of others.

King Minos, however, had other ideas. He hid the bull in his herd and offered a lesser animal in its place. In retribution, Poseidon had Aphrodite afflict Minos' wife Pasiphae with a passionate desire for the white bull. The queen persuaded Daedalus, the chief artisan of the realm, to build her a wooden cow, which she entered. The bull then entered her and satisfied her desire.[2] The Minotaur, a beast with a man's body and a bull's head, was born from this union. The Minotaur fed on human flesh and was insatiable. In shame and fear, the king hid the creature in the depths of a great stone labyrinth. Every year, in order to appease the monster, two of the most beautiful youths of Crete would be sacrificed to it. They were driven by force into the labyrinth, from which no one returned.

In this way, we, in the second-chakra labyrinth of our hoarded secrets, sacrifice our beauty and possibility to our hidden shame and to unconscious permutations of family secrets and horrors. Every day we sacrifice parts of ourselves because we do not deal with the dark, disowned energy in the twisted folds of our past. We may be driven, but we do not really know who or what is driving us. Or we may be apathetic, but we dare not uncover the reasons for our fatigue and inertia.

The way out of this situation is suggested in the myth. Minos' daughter, Ariadne, aids the hero Theseus, son of Poseidon, by giving him a magic thread that will enable him to find his way out of the labyrinth once the Minotaur is slain. Ariadne's thread represents the recovery of our psychic history. It is not the male hero alone, but the union of intuitive feeling with active intelligence that allows one to negotiate this realm. For this domain is the emotional wetland of our shame, the womb of our being where there resides either creativity or the swamplike festering of crippling complexes, real or imagined. The hero too often remains wedded to his fraudulent ideal of himself, the ego ideal, and goes off to conquer another world (i.e., begin another project) without facing the issues underlying the discomfort and restlessness that accompany him on his journey. As the daughter of Minos, who is the culprit in a sense, Ariadne's action shows us that the solution is in the same family as the problem. We are not obliged, then, to go outside of ourselves to find our "calling"; instead, our authentic work will grow out of the very symptoms that currently block the way. The resources we need are present if we are willing to "stay at home" and deal with our situations. "The way out is the way in"—the labyrinth must be entered if we want to uncover our passions and convictions.

One way of entering the labyrinth is to pay attention to our feelings and our unwanted symptoms. Symptoms represent the feeling energies that are seeking to communicate themselves to us. They are the messengers of the gods who can lead us into the core of our genuine concerns and hence to our work in the world. Why? Because feeling is the correlate energy of the second chakra, and symptoms are manifestations of deep feelings. A career can develop from any feeling, joyful or painful, but not through numbness. If I am aware that I do not like my job, I am still working on the surface. What is it that I do not like? Who is hiding down in my labyrinth? Is it the boredom I despise? Is it the mindless authority and hierarchy of a company? Is it living at breakneck speed when I always wanted to waltz through life? Being frustrated with work is not unusual, but only when we can recognize the frustrations and enter the labyrinth can we begin to evolve plans of action.

Joyce Critendon worked at Northwestern Mutual Life in data processing; her husband Paul had a position in marketing. Good soldiers in the corporate realm, both developed much technical proficiency and had risen up the corporate ladder. Both of them, however, were people-lovers who liked to entertain and be outdoors. They had been mildly frustrated with their jobs for years. Every so often they discussed the possibility of buying an inn or opening up a clothing or liquor store, any situation where they could spend more time connecting with people. Nothing ever came of it, however, for they were haunted by the perennial fear of self-employment: who would pay the health insurance? After all, their jobs were secure, the pay was good, and so were the benefits. This is the position that many of us find ourselves in. Work is okay, but it doesn't make our hearts sing. At some point in midlife we begin to wonder if we will ever sing again. We know that we are not being joyful or spontaneous, but our world has become such a juggling act that we would rather remain precariously afloat than risk opening the floodgates that would carry us into the labyrinth.

In Paul and Joyce's case, he kept dreaming and she kept resisting, even though it was becoming increasingly difficult for her to go to work every day. The heaviness, she realized, was not that the job was not good. It came from the fact that she did not want to face the sadness at having forfeited her dream about working with people. I hear this question constantly in my counseling work: "My job is okay, but is this all I want to do with my life?"

When we settle for "okay," we have to pad the second chakra, dulling the anguish over not receiving and acting on our passion. One prevalent way to do this is through food, and it may very well be that this orality is a necessary anaesthetic. We are filling ourselves up, with work as well as food, in order to relieve the pain of our inauthenticity.

One Friday Paul came home and told Joyce that he had just been offered a "lateral promotion." There was a good chance that relocation might be involved, and he realized he did not want to uproot himself from his community and life for a soft drink. After years of mild annoyance, this incident crystallized their frustration. They went away for the weekend and spent their time reflecting on and ultimately listing what made them happy. Making these lists was their entry into the labyrinth, for it brought up emotions and desires that had been muffled for years. Both made their lists independently, and when they compared them they found one thing in common: nothing they did at work was anywhere on their lists! Joyce had "being with her family" at the top of her list. How could she be with her family when Paul was gone all day long? She had to work, and their young son was at a day-care center. High up on both of their lists were entertaining and outdoor sports, not easy things to do when you are in an office from nine to five every weekday.

Further soul searching told Joyce and Paul that the element in life really worth living for was people. They wanted to use their skills in a way that would make them feel connected with others. Joyce had held an ongoing fantasy about starting a bed and breakfast in the Door Country region in Wisconsin. During one of their vacations they had driven down through the county noticing inns that were for sale. This time, they acted. They both took Monday off and drove down to Door County, staying at a friend's house along the way. As they told their story that evening, their friends told them of a spot that might be just what they were looking for. This illustrates another anti-career principle—hidden alliances work to move you into your authentic vocation as soon as you begin to commit to it.

The Critendons eventually took a chance and bought a small property on the lake that they converted into a bed and breakfast. The inn idea was appealing as a vocation because it was a people business and allowed them to do so many things they enjoyed—cooking, baking, decorating, and entertaining. And they plunged right into it, painting, advertising, and working to create a warm and welcoming place. They knew it would be difficult in the beginning, but the enthusiasm of finally doing what they loved overrode the fear of losing their corporate benefits.

The banks in Milwaukee wanted nothing to do with the project, of course. When asked about their applicable experience, all Joyce and Paul could say was, "We entertain a lot." But they were determined to find a way, and again an ally appeared. A friend of Paul's father agreed to loan them the needed start-up money, and within two years they had turned the Griffen Inn into a booming business. Paul and Joyce have never looked back.

Opening to and tracking feelings of restlessness and frustration instead of trying to mask them is the second stage in developing an anti-career. You need a considerable store of self-worth to do this, in order to work through past disillusionments and disappointments without turning them against yourself. There is a big difference between not succeeding and thinking you are a failure. You need to be able to honestly open to your personal and social history so that you can feel your genuine passions and convictions. Such openness needs to be tempered by the discipline of inquiry and by the willingness to deal with whatever one may uncover. Joyce describes how, before they bought the inn, she and Paul had to face all their fears of failure as well as the idea that they were both completely crazy. In fact, one of the vice presidents at their company actually told them he thought they had gone mad. This was not an easy time, but it was an important one. Once they worked through their major resistances they were able to reason that the worst that could happen was that they would return to the city and get jobs and health insurance. And once decided, they received unexpected encouragement. Another of the vice presidents told them how much he had always wanted to do something like this.

WE BEGIN AT THE BEGINNING

If one is intent on establishing a career that nourishes one's soul as well as one's body, there is serious excavation work to do, and this work almost always involves coming to terms with one's parents, the deepest embodiments of our conditioning. It is said that, if one wants to understand one's own destiny, one need look no further than the life path of one's parents, as much for the roads they have not taken as for the ones they have. Stan Jay, the owner of Mandolin Brothers Music Store, had a father who was in retail and who, in fact, dissuaded him from following in his footsteps. It was too hard, he said, and the rewards were slim. So Stan became an English teacher. But the universe kept giving him a different message. One summer he was traveling in California and wanted to rent a car. He had purchased a guitar a while earlier and found that he was able to barter the guitar for a car for the entire summer. "If I could do this all the time, why should I work?" he thought. But before he could create a business that corresponded to his nature, he had to get clear on his nature, including his past and his real vision of the future.

One of the most powerful exercises I have worked with in this regard is writing a parental biography. This work is very potent in a group setting; however you can do it on your own and derive significant results.

The Parental Biography

Sit in a quiet place and begin to meditate upon the life journey of one of your parents or your significant childhood caregiver. Allow the echoes of the past to reappear, the bits and pieces of your mother's or father's life that you have seen and heard over the years. When you feel ready, begin to write that person's story. Once you begin, you will feel the energy start to flow. This is neither a report requiring factual accuracy nor a work of art, and it is being written for no one else's attention or approval. Take as long as you need to write all you can. The piece can be a page long, or ten, or thirty. Some people will find it excruciatingly difficult to begin. For others the words will just flow out onto the page. Allow your feelings and imagination to guide you. Let the writing take any form it wants: a narrative, a drama, an epic poem, a dialogue, or even a letter from that person to yourself. As it takes form, you may begin to feel your parent's life journey in a new way and be surprised at the manner in which their struggles and hopes relate to your own.

When the biography is finished, read it aloud. Even if you are alone, reading the work out loud will enable you to hear and react to what is genuine and deeply resonant. Once you have done the reading, you can continue to work with it internally. It may stay with you for some time. There is no fixed format or set of questions for working with the parental biography. Writing and reading it through is enough to reveal how many of the themes of your parents' life are your own, and how you are often called upon to deal with similar circumstances. The purpose of this exercise is not comparison but feeling and amplification—to be able to appreciate that your work in life is not an isolated phenomenon, merely a product of the current job market or of your particular interests or aptitudes, but rather that you are in a process of re-enacting and reworking patterns that span generations in families and are often shared by entire cultures as well.

Sometimes I am asked how I got into this line of work, and I have to look no further than my own father. My father was trained to be a dentist, but due to illness he had to give up his practice before he ever really started. I have vivid memories of him coming home from work, irritated and defeated, slumping into his chair in front of the television set, and saying nothing. He sold pharmaceutical products for fifteen years and was pretty good at it, but the silence in the evening spoke of something else, of what it's like to be doing less than what you feel capable of and how that gives you the message that you are less than the unique being that you really are.

At a certain point in his life, my father went back to dentistry. And although it took me thirty-five years to ask him how he did it, I will never forget what he told me. "I was sitting in a diner having a cup of coffee one day," he said, "and suddenly I asked myself 'What the hell am I doing this for?'" In my language I would say that his feelings went deep and touched his true sense of self-worth.

"*What the hell am I doing this for?*" Sometimes when a person asks me how he or she might possibly ever change, I answer, "When you get angry enough, you will make the move." When Paul Critendon was asked by his company to move to a different city, he had the same reaction, "What the hell am I doing this for? If I am going to relocate, why not relocate for something that has meaning?" If we are dissatisfied with our work, that is a beginning. Then we have to believe that we were born for something better than what we are doing.

In my father's case, he called an old friend from dental school who had a clinic in upper Manhattan. For two years he went to the clinic after work and retrained himself, and for the last twenty years of his working life he ran a dental clinic in New York City. I witnessed how the change in work went hand in hand with a change in his life and in our family relationships. The imprint of that experience will remain with me always, for I have seen at intimate range what it is like to work at something that does not make you feel good about yourself, and I have also seen the other side, the self-esteem that comes into your life when you feel that you are making a contribution to the world.

By opening to our life history, then, we see that our work in the world brings into play the entirety of our past and its power. That power is there, whether we acknowledge it or not. It will either nurture us or thwart us. There are no "how to's" here. This is not a simple matter of listing five qualities that you have taken from your family and wish to continue to develop, or identifying a family pattern that you want to change. When the world of our feelings truly opens, we connect with the power of our lineage—not just our familial bloodlines, but our professional and spiritual lineages as well. We thus allow ourselves to open to possibilities of employment that include the conscious engagement of the deepest feelings and issues in our lives. We seek neither to idealize nor to damn our past, but to relate to it in an empowered way.

The demons that we have stuffed into our labyrinth—lust-fed by media images, spite-ridden by anger at the success of others, consumed by greed for wealth or position—will yield their insights, teachings, and positive conduits of expression if we are willing to listen to their messages. As in the aphorism "The stone that was rejected becomes the cornerstone," the dissipating effects of lust and misaligned eroticism, when rerouted toward our discovered passion, fuel the fires of growth and achievement. One person I know started a successful business manufacturing and selling essential oils. On the day while I was interviewing him he swung his chair around, kicked his heels up on his desk, threw out his arms, and exclaimed, "This is even more fun than dealing dope!" Gandhi's career was precipitated by his coming to terms with the humiliation of getting thrown off the train in South Africa for being the wrong color. Florence Nightingale's drive to reform the medical profession in Britain arose from her anger and indignation at the way patients were being treated.

There are times when it is extremely difficult and painful to come to terms with our past in an empowering way. But the greater the difficulty, the greater the reward. In one of my workshops, a woman spoke of her struggle to deal with being raped at the age of eighteen. After long and hard work, a powerful image of a spade in the earth came to her. This image spoke of the very real fact that a wound had been inflicted, but from that wound had come her insight and power, her ability to seed her future with an experience planted deeply in the soil of her life. Her present work as a crisis counselor reflects this recognition. As for this woman, so it is for survivors of child abuse, those uprooted by war or illness, or anyone affected by countless other traumas. Within the wound is the foundation for great power, if we are willing first to grieve and then to allow the healing processes to occur. To grieve means to let it bleed, to allow the flood of hurt, vulnerability, disappointment, and heartache to flow on its own course. We might fear what could happen if we remove our finger from the dike, but we have to ask ourselves if it is worth the energy expended trying to continually patch the make-shift wall we have constructed to meet the world, the padding around the second chakra. The "blood" of the wound may flow and flow, but if we can allow ourselves to be nonjudgmental about what is happening, this grieving process will eventually take us to an entirely new place.

Even privilege can be problematic from an anti-career standpoint. Children whose parents are powerful public figures often have difficulty coming out of their parents' shadows and defining their own authenticity. Many people who have inherited wealth are known to make unwise investments, feeling inwardly unworthy of their situation. In the workshops I have given over the years, I have also encountered a number of people dealing with shame and guilt about inheriting money. The process for them is no different than anyone else's—if we ignore our labyrinth, we will wind up sacrificing the most cherished parts of ourselves. To meet the Minotaur is to meet and welcome whatever has happened to us so far in life, no matter the source. To meet and welcome this history is to acknowledge it and have enough self-worth that we can open up and let it in without fearing that it will destroy us. Whether it be abundance or shortage, the expectations of being a child prodigy or the inherited lethargy of middle-class boredom—whatever the history, we must come to terms with it and be energized rather than debilitated by it.

The roads to follow in exploring this history are the empty spaces, the anxieties that reveal incompletions in our emotional make-up. Just as there is a choice between the way of fulfillment and the way of shortage at the root of our being, the emotional center asks us to choose between the way of inner work and the way of reaction. Our emotional reactions to people and situations can be used as keys to enter into our past, to seek and find the complexities within our own being that trigger certain reactions, and to use those keys to release the energy by consciously experiencing the triggering process and thus allowing the energy to pass through.

The emotive energy in our labyrinth will either fuel or paralyze us. If the bull remains locked in the labyrinth, we will sacrifice our goals and objectives to it. The inner folds of our beings—the important influences of home, nurturing, and family—must be acknowledged for the *positive* roles they have played in our lives. Without this recognition we displace our emotional energy, using work to either forget or compensate for inner imbalances. The connection with the world through our work should be an outgrowth of our connectedness to the people and the land where we live, not a substitute for it. The contacts made in a thousand seminars will not replace the sharing of warmth and the gut-level interactions through which our lives are nourished. Without these we are building houses of cards, and all of our work-related activities will be riddled with repetitions of our family patterns.

Psychotherapy or other forms of therapeutic support may be helpful in bringing our wounded self forward and getting him or her involved in our career. This process is not about regressing and indulging in our woundedness; rather, it is a process of taking the time and energy to explore and release the imbalances of the past. This will allow us to bring new elements into our work. *Work* is reserved for grown-ups because it is not fun; it is about the serious business of survival or status-seeking. But when we have converted our basic energy into integrity, dismissing survival as the foremost imperative, we feel the bliss of our being, and status-seeking is seen for what it is—a poor substitute for loving and being loved. When we have made this shift we can then align our feelings and all the lost wonder of childhood into our work.

OWNING FEELING

When we allow genuine feelings to operate within and through us, we become capable of doing what we want to do. Then our careers can move beyond a grasping need for love and approval. Feelings are one of the most potent energies available to us as human beings. The exaltation of reason over feeling leads to a society of reasonable duds. There is no fire, no life, no excitement in a society where feeling has been devalued or siphoned off into mindless distraction. When feeling is not aligned it becomes chaotic, connecting to thought patterns that have no solid grounding. The power of feelings are in owning them, not in being owned by them. To own feeling means to experience the depths of possibility of one's life-force—to care deeply, to act enthusiastically, and to feel an inherent value in what you are doing.

Joy is the essence of being oneself. When we do what we feel good doing, joy flows and is infectious. Such joy does not imply an easy path of nonresistance. Athletes, artists, and dancers labor strenuously, but it is joyful labor, the kind of excitement that flows when one's feeling is aligned with one's rootedness in self-worth. Joy should not be confused with superficial happiness or pleasure. Pain and anger are also "joyful" if they come from the base. The feeling energy must flow from the root power center. This enables one's passion to progress in the direction of authentic action.

William James, the eminent American psychologist (who himself agonized over his career direction for a long time), ranked the "sick soul" above the "healthy soul" in terms of profoundness and insight. The idea is to liberate feeling, not to simply ignore pain. Tragedy, nostalgia, and depression can all move one toward a more authentic working situation. Isadora Duncan experienced a "conversion" when her two children were killed in an automobile accident. All the children of the world became hers and fueled her art. We do not seek to court tragedy or other such intense experiences for the sake of inspiration—that would be a return to scarcity. I know of an artist who, after being hit by a car, exclaimed, "Thank God something has *finally* happened to me." Instead, we trust the ground beneath our feet. For that, it is said, is where the medicine lies.

All genuine feeling fuels our fire. The power to create an authentic career grows out of feeling unencumbered by shame or rationalization. The word *passion* originally referred to pain, but it is a pain that serves the organism. The word *joy* is part of the word *enjoy*. We have a need and a creative drive to enjoy life. The fact that most people do not enjoy their work tells of a painful imbalance in our allocation of time and energy. This pain, if owned, will begin to align feeling with power and create the space for joy to enter. When it does we will begin greeting one another not with the question "What do you do?", but with an engaged "Hi. What's your passion?" From this deep feeling our life work will be born.

TAKING INVENTORY OF OUR SKILLS

The questions to ask, then, are "What is my passion?" or "What are my base convictions? What do I care about more than anything else?" This is where you can make your contribution, and this is the place where you can begin to take inventory of your talents and abilities. There are a great many methods that will help you do this; if you feel the need for guidance I suggest using Richard Bolles's *What Color is Your Parachute,* a book about creating meaningful work that is still uniquely helpful a quarter-century after its initial publication. A good many of Bolles's and other career counselor's exercises have to do with processing one's life history by looking back at what you did well, or at the times you felt best about what you were doing.

This is exactly what we do in the anti-career process. We focus on the feeling, on the passion, on what has truly motivated our lives and will continue to do so. A mere inventory of skills, however, will not achieve this. After deciding that he did not want to teach school, Thoreau followed in the footsteps of his father, a man who manufactured lead pencils. He applied himself diligently to this pencil-making craft, constantly experimenting to make a better instrument than any other in current use. He exhibited his finished work to chemists and artists in Boston, who certified that his pencil was as good as the best one manufactured in London at the time. His friends applauded him, thinking that his future was set and his fortune made. But Thoreau decided that he would never make another lead pencil again. "Why should I? I would not do again what I have done once," he said.[3] "He resumed," says Emerson, "his endless walks and miscellaneous studies, making everyday some new acquaintance with nature."[4] Thoreau had a particular skill, but that skill was not aligned with his passion, which was for nature. In *Walden* he refers to himself as "the self-appointed inspector of snowstorms." And he eventually evolved a lifestyle that allowed him to deeply experience the natural world and its wisdom.

Wherever your passion is, that is where your life will gravitate to, regardless of whether you are consciously focused on it or not. If your labyrinth is not relatively worked through, however, you will repeat your family history in the office (or wherever). To move into your labyrinth, you must move your feelings into focus by investigating what is most important to you, where you want to spend your time and energy, and what skills you have developed that fit your concern.

PASSION COMPROMISED FOR APPROVAL

When you begin to explore this arena you often find that there have been many times and places in life when you compromised your feelings. What were the circumstances around that experience? One person's earliest memory in this regard was when she was asked in kindergarten what she wanted to be as a grown-up. When she answered "A hairdresser," both the teacher and the headmistress of the school laughed at her, shaming her deeply. From that point on she retreated from her dream. For the message she received was not "Do what you love," but "Do what is sanctioned."

When feeling energy does not function strongly, it is often due to continually receiving mixed messages. "I love you, but . . . " as the saying goes. As Alice Miller documents, the child is thus coerced into speaking and acting for parental approval, which can be given or withdrawn with just a gesture.[5] From very early on, most of us learn to tone down our acts. In the guise of values such as courtesy, cooperation, and control, we are given the message that social approval is the quintessential value in this culture. So on the one hand, a young person is encouraged to develop his or her talents and abilities. Yet on the other hand, if one's particular ability happens to cut against the grain of approval, it is given little credence. It is good to be passionately attached to the fortunes of a baseball team, but not to the beauty of passing clouds. No wonder it is so difficult to find, and then do, what we love. To develop an authentic mode of work, we must get down to the feeling level, to a place where the life current that we contacted energetically expands into a feeling, into a desire to act, to do something that is meaningful. Meaning in this context can only come out of one's genuine spirit. It is not a question of existential choice. Choice is only effective when it is aligned with feeling and life current. Otherwise we pit the mind *against* life, which is what we have generally been taught to do.

Even a great search for truth can become a smoke screen for not coming to terms with our feelings. The ego is swept away by a movement or ideal, but its actual moorings are flimsy, so the movement or the ideal substitutes for the missing power of feeling. When the war is over, however, or the movement turns into an institution, the heroic stance cannot be maintained, and the ego searches for another cause. This is not to say that causes may not be just and powerful channels for life energy. But if they are substitutes, if they provide us with a reason to live and move rather than being natural expressions of our passion, then our true feeling energy is still on hold.

Perhaps even more insidious than the "great search" ideal is the attitude of cynical relativism that, out of its own despair, conspires to undercut attempts at authenticity. Here, as Alan Bloom poignantly notes in *The Closing of the American Mind*, we lose the ability to believe in anything, to feel or act passionately at all.[6] All this may be covered over by talk or by filling our days with activities such as shopping and the like, but the unspoken complicity in this strategy is to avoid coming to terms with our ultimate feelings. For many, the career issue is compounded by this resultant lack of passion, a despair in the face of so much possibility with "so little compelling reason to choose."[7] This is why it is so important to begin with the physical-energetic core. An authentic career *must* originate in the body and its relationship to the life current. If you do not know what to do, go into the woods for a while and feel the flow of your own body. Go into life and its rhythms, which constantly display the capacity for rebirth.

The liberation of our powers to feel has to do with casting off the bonds of both cynicism and idealism by accepting the truth of our feelings. When we accept ourselves for what we are, we can accept what we feel as well, and such energy will create both the appropriate words and actions that will take us into authentic lives and livelihoods. Here we can move through mixed messages around money, power, security, and success. We can be unabashed about what we want, and live and work in the world from a place of genuine conviction.

Second Chakra Meditation: The Feeling Flow

Find a comfortable seated position in which you are aware of your body touching the ground. Feel your spinal column extending upward from your pelvis. Feel its strength and suppleness. Begin to breathe gently in and out. Allow your breath to flow freely and deeply, relaxing your entire being. Feel it flowing through your arms and legs, through your spinal column, and through the wide bowl of the pelvis. If any part of you feels tension or resistance, breathe into that place and gently release it. You may voice a long "Aah" on the exhalation.

As the breath drops you down deeper and deeper into your inner world, allow your body to begin to be breathed by the rhythm of the in breath and the out breath. Notice all the places where you are holding, trying to maintain control, and gently release your energy with deep trust into the ever-present current of life. With every breath feel yourself more deeply in the current, connected to the earth and its subtle power and great patience.

Begin now to focus on your second chakra in front of the sacrum. Let the breath rise and fall on the ebb and flow of the great inner waters. Breathing merges with the flow of the tides, the flow of blood rivulets and lymphatic systems, of the liquid life forces within the body: water, the great ocean, dancing coin waves and deep-cold depths, the faces of the Great Mother, unfathomable depths within. The past, the womblike folds of memory are protected inside. Allow yourself to enter into this great inner space through memories of your own life.

Imagine yourself walking backward now through an underwater cave. On the walls of the cave find pictures of your own life, of the roads taken and not taken, of times of hurt and times of joy. Move gently. If you feel stuck, ask for a guide to come and take you by the hand as you go back, back, all the way back in time, into the labyrinth of the past. Notice the roads you could have taken but did not. Notice the places along the way that are blurred and murky, the places where energy has been obstructed.

Now let your guide take you by the hand to the first moment in your life when you felt the swell of feeling, when the wonder of the world burst into your being and you suddenly realized that there was so much more to life than you had been led to believe. It may have been a moment of great joy or sorrow, a vision of the beauty of nature, the excitement of discovering how something works. You might be led to a different moment each time you do this meditation. Trust in the wisdom of your inner being and move deeply into that moment, into its form, texture, sound, taste, and smell. How did you feel? What was it like to be alive at that moment? Hold this moment for as long as it remains powerful and then slowly begin to let it go, leaving a door open, knowing that you can return to it at any time to be nurtured and empowered by its energy.

And as you breathe in and out and slowly return and reintegrate within your physical form, keep the imprint of the vision with you and, for a moment, juxtapose it with the life you are currently living. How does your current life reflect your deep inner experience? Have you let the experience of joy, of wonder, of passion, of conviction into your day-to-day life, or have you kept it boarded up somewhere? Now, in this moment, conceive of one thing you can do every day, be it the smallest thing, that will breathe life into your way in the world. What can you do, every day, that is an expression of your deepest joy? Be it singing, meditating, watering a plant, cultivating a garden, working out in the gym—whatever it is, let it become a practice that will begin to link your inner joy with your outer life.

5

The Third Chakra: The Right Use of Will

It furthers one to install helpers and to set armies marching.
I-Ching

The question "What line of work do I want to go into?" does not suffice in the postmodern world, for most people will not only change jobs at least three times in the course of their working lives (and probably much more than that), but they will change their lines of work as well. The underlying and more important questions to ask ourselves are "How do I want to be? How do I want to live my life and have my work be a part of my life?" Answering these questions requires us to focus not only on our skills and interests but also on our passionate convictions. If our job choices are congruent with what we care about most, we will have the possibility of empowered choice and clarity.

At any given time our priorities may change, and so the criteria we use in choosing our work may differ. What is important is that we *know* what is most crucial to us at any given time, be it family, creative expression, or money, to name a few possibilities. Congruence between our work and our convictions does not necessarily mean that they are the same. Victor, for example, had been a peace activist in the New England area for over ten years and was well known in his circle. He had become a full-time organizer out of passionate idealism, and while that idealism was still present, there were new and very real concerns in his life. After working through his labyrinth he realized that his most important concern at that point in time was his relationship with his son, who was thirteen years old and who would soon be out of the house. Victor knew of a job opening as a social worker at an organization in his neighborhood, a job that would permit him to be both helpful to others and have the time to spend with his family. At first Victor thought it was a demotion to go from working as a high powered peace activist to being a "mere" social worker. Once he saw what was most important to him at this juncture in his life, however, he realized that social work was indeed congruent with his conviction, and he was able to make the choice for taking the job.

Creating the work you love subordinates itself to creating the life you love.

THE LOCALIZATION OF WILL

Our choices around work, no matter what the field, are unavoidably influenced by historical notions around choice itself. The possibility that we can actually choose our way or create our career is the result of long-fought battles for freedom contested on many fronts. To speak of the right use of will is to speak of something more than immediate choices facing a single individual, for in many cases true choice is about choosing what or whom to align ourselves with—be it social or political movements, green businesses, or new ways of exchanging goods and services. The alignment of will, which is the alignment that takes place in the third chakra, entails more than personal preferences as we seek to make choices that are aligned with spirit and its power. This is no simple affair, for it seems that choices that lead toward growth and individual freedom often do not possess much market value, and are therefore not encouraged. And there are all sorts of influences around us asking to be chosen. There are the voices that tell us, for example, that we have no choice, that all our career possibilities are determined by existing market conditions or by the government or by fate, and we should consider ourselves lucky to just get by. At the same time, other voices tell us that we have unlimited choice, that we can accomplish anything we want to if we just think in the right way. None of these voices, of course, are completely true, and it is therefore up to each of us to find our own voice, to choose from our own place of clarity and power.

In many traditional cultures choice was not such an issue. Authority was localized in the figure of an all-wise or powerful man or man/god. In the modern Western world, authority has been localized in the scripture and sanctioned religious and political institutions. In the last century we have also witnessed the mindlessly cruel results of following the wise men and their institutional power. We in the postmodern West would like to believe that we have overthrown the false-god authorities. At least this is the initial image we have of ourselves, although one can argue that the new god has become the market, and that popular pressure dictates the direction that people follow. To better understand our relationship to authority and our resultant possibilities around choice, I have chosen three figures from our collective culture who personify varied strategies of the will. These three figures still live within us, although I would argue that the best thing we could do in establishing an anti-career would be to exorcise each of them. The following history of choice-making is a visionary sketch, a case study of archetypes. Its purpose is to depict different applications of will. By becoming more aware of our cultural models, we may then be able to reformulate them and create stronger avenues of choice.

Oedipus: Like Father, like Son

In Oedipus' world, fate reigns supreme regardless of human will. Sophocles' drama, appropriated by Freud, (who kept statues of the Greek gods on his desk), is enacted around a fated situation and the efforts to avoid it. King Laius receives a prophecy that his son will kill him. In response, he has a spike driven through his son's foot and has him cast out on a mountain to die. The boy is found and saved by a shepherd and is adopted by the King of Corinth as Oedipus [the swollen-footed one]. Oedipus, now the prince of Corinth, likewise receives an oracle. He is fated to kill his father and marry his mother. In order to evade the prophecy, he flees Corinth but gets involved in an altercation at a crossroads. The altercation erupts into a fight and Oedipus kills the herald who opposed him and, unbeknownst to him, his father Laius, who is in the carriage.

After later solving the riddle of the Sphinx, and thus saving his city Thebes from danger, Oedipus is made king of the land. He unknowingly marries the widowed queen, Jocasta, his natural mother, and all seems to be well. It is not until a plague descends upon Thebes, a plague that can only be lifted when the murderer of Laius is found, that the truth is gradually discovered by Oedipus himself.

Fate, in this story, appears through prophecy as the voice of the oracle, and it touches all. Laius the king, Oedipus his son, and Jocasta the queen try, each in their own way, to circumvent fate. Laius has received the prophecy that his own son will kill him, so he casts his son off to die in the hills. Jocasta, fearing the worst, tries to persuade Oedipus to turn back from his efforts to discover the truth about his situation. And Oedipus, in his intense effort and determination to solve his own mystery, destroys himself and his house.

The initial problem in the play is a plague, a blight upon the kingdom (not unlike the blight upon our own present-day kingdom). This is a sign that, despite outward appearances of order, something is deeply wrong. And this is often the case with our work. The pay is good, the benefits are good, and the job is good, but inside we feel that we have let ourselves down, that we are not living for the reason we were deemed to.

The office of the king, symbolizing the cohesiveness of the collective, is intertwined with that of the father, for Laius is both father and king, and the ancient king is a father to his people. Authority is transmitted in an unbroken chain from the gods, to the father/king, to the populace, and this is the order that sustains the people, an order whose validity—like the job—is unquestioned until things begin to go wrong. Right action in this instance means being in right relation to the gods and their authority, no matter how capricious, as revealed through the elders of the community and their institutions.

When something goes wrong in life we may feel that somehow we have violated the order of things. We have sinned or cheated the government and are now getting our just due. And this is true to some extent. We are the king of our own kingdom. The blight upon our kingdom is that queasy inner feeling that tells us that something is not right. But if we see fate as irrevocable or react from fear of retribution as Laius does, we paint ourselves into a corner from which there is no way out. Likewise, when we believe the numbers game to be the sole arbiter of our working possibilities, we fall into the trap of fatalism. As Richard Bolles has convincingly shown us, unemployment figures do not tell us anything at all about actual job vacancies, about the million jobs openings per month that are never advertised in any newspaper.[1]

The chain of irrevocable fate in *Oedipus* begins with an act of fear. The voice of authority, of prophecy, is heard but not listened to. Its quality is not questioned. The ego simply tries to avoid its consequences and reacts: "If the prophecy says my son will kill me, I will kill him first." Thus the chain of karma is set into motion.

Oedipus calls witnesses, listens to accounts, and becomes infuriated when the prophet Teiresias declares that the king is ultimately responsible for his own misfortune. He scoffs at the prophet and angrily sends him away. Gradually the mystery unfolds, and Oedipus is horrified to discover the awful truth that he has so stridently sought after. He is the man!

This story illustrates, among other things, the tragedy of the obedient mind. Upon initial reading it may seem to be quite the contrary—trying to avoid the clutches of fate, Oedipus and his family are systematically thwarted—the message being that one should just play out one's allotted role in life and hope for the best. But the reactions of avoidance are *just as bound to the prophecy!* And so the obedient mind label is appropriate to the one who mindlessly reacts, as well as to the one who mindlessly follows. Perhaps it would be more apt, then, to see this play as the tragedy of the reactive mind. Postmodern people might no longer obey, but we do react. We hear on the news that the recession is coming and we immediately fold up our tents. We hear that "The Ph.D. is out and the MBA is in," and suddenly the concrete and steel of the Wharton Business School looks better than the ivy walls of Princeton and Yale.

On either side, obedience or rebellion, there is but a one-dimensional perspective. The patricide that Oedipus commits unawares fulfills the prophecy, in part because the prophetic voice is feared to begin with. If authority is externalized and obedience automatic, one has no other options. We can see how this leads back to the fundamental importance of genuine self-worth. How do I feel inside about the information I am receiving? What is my power of choice here?

If we externalize authority we are blind to ourselves and our own possibilities. If we react blindly against the system we still find ourselves caught in its webs. But there is another way to respond. When Laius heard the prophecy, perhaps he could have faced his fears about his son usurping his power. Perhaps he could have found another way of working with this energy.[2] The voice of the prophet rings in our ears—in *our* ears. How we respond to this voice depends upon our willingness to let go of the initial panic that we will be destroyed by the wrath of God, the recession, or the I.R.S., and to open to another way, a way based on our inherent worth and the true validity of our feelings. The first failed strategy with regard to authority, then, is obedience/reaction. A father calls gruffly to his five-year-old son to come in from playing outside. The son asks why. The father answers, "Because I said so." The child, somewhat bewildered, complies or throws an enraged tantrum. Once again, the ancient spiral is set into motion.

Hamlet: The Paralysis of Choice

The story of Hamlet, another long-standing cultural icon, illustrates the dilemma of the person who has lost the ability to contact a higher power and plummets into his own fractured thinking processes. As in Oedipus, there is a blight in the kingdom. The king of Denmark has died, apparently from natural causes, and his brother, Prince Hamlet's uncle, has been made king. Hamlet is disappointed with his uncle, the new king, and with the general state of affairs at court after his father's untimely death. More pointedly, however, he is shocked and bewildered by his mother, who hastily marries his uncle without so much as mourning the loss of her husband.

Unlike Laius, Hamlet cannot accept the words of prophecy that are his own father's words. Or are they? Hamlet's father appears as a ghost and declares that he has in fact been murdered by his brother, a most foul and unnatural murder. This Hamlet has already suspected. But is the ghost real, or is the apparition Hamlet's own projection? Hamlet cannot be absolutely certain; the first words of Shakespeare's play—"Who's there?"— underline this dilemma. Unlike *Oedipus*, in which the claim of authority is absolute, in *Hamlet* we witness a situation in which trust in the preceding generation is broken. The form of the father is insubstantial. It can only speak from the grave.

Hamlet, "sicklied o'er with the pale cast of thought," is so self-absorbed that he cannot choose. The possibility that the voice of authority is false haunts him.

> The spirit that I have seen may be a devil,
> and the devil has power
> T'assume a pleasing shape, yes, and perhaps
> Out of my weakness and my melancholy,
> As he is very potent with such spirits,
> Abuses me to damn me.
>
> (II.602-7)

Hamlet, then, must test the word of the ghostly father, something unthinkable to his premodern counterpart. He trusts no one, and this speaks to the modern condition. The mind, pried loose from its archetypal moorings, is unable to decide on its own what is the best course of action. Hamlet cannot act until circumstances compel him. And by this he foreshadows the predicament of the free-thinker—caught by his own mental parameters, in denial of the supernatural, and, as we shall see, in fear of the female.

Hamlet is unable to take anyone else into his confidence, especially women.[3] He feels betrayed by his mother and cannot trust his love, Ophelia. On an inward level the women Hamlet spurns may be representative of his own feminine side, his ability to intuit and feel. With no external certitude, and little inward trust, it is no wonder that Hamlet cannot decide what he wants to be when he grows up. If we do not recognize that certain choices are indeed beyond our deliberative powers, and refuse to allow ourselves to be guided by another light, we too will become victims of the dissonant chorus of conflict within the mind. After all, how do we know our inner promptings are valid? To whom should we listen? We are so easily suggestible—one day we are determined to leave the city and become farmers, the next day we want to go back to school to get MSWs.

There is no discursive solution here, and this may at first be disheartening. No aptitude test, no process work, no visualization technique will necessarily tell us what we are meant to do. But there is the ongoing process of trusting, inquiring, listening, and living. Hamlet refuses to trust and is thus unable to live. With all his ingenuity and integrity, he violates one of the cardinal laws of manifestation—he rejects human relationship and support and tries to walk through the labyrinth alone.

If *Oedipus* illustrates the problem of localizing the will in an infallible other (the ancient way), then *Hamlet* exemplifies the problem of lack of initiative due to loss of faith in the other and in oneself (the modern way).

The Tightrope Walker

Nietzsche's Zarathustra is a luminous being who comes down from the mountaintop to offer his wisdom to humanity. On his way down, he stops to preach in a marketplace and witnesses a rope dancer engaging in his tightrope-walking act. The rope dancer moves high above the crowd, but is then rattled by the appearance of a clownlike figure who emerges from the tower. The buffoon jumps up and down on the rope over the head of the rope dancer, who stumbles and falls to his death.

Jung saw this scene as a metaphor for Nietzsche himself, his inflated self trying to walk above the crowd and his disowned, unconscious self—his shadow—toppling him.[4] We live in a tightrope world. We swagger with weapons and tall buildings, banks and insurance companies that rise above the human community. We speak about making our own destiny and developing unlimited power (as if we would know what to do with it), while we still do not have the slightest idea of who we are, where we came from, or where we are going.

Zarathustra proclaims the death of God, and we follow in his footsteps. Clerics and prophets no longer intimidate us, oracles and visions no longer appear to us. Instead, we will to create our own reality. We will to build businesses that gobble up the earth, and when we have finished with that, we will to seek new markets in outer space. When human productivity replaces our humane-ness, we walk the tightrope, still not imagining that nature, being duly violated, will respond in kind. And then when the forests disappear, the floods strike, or diseases rage out of control, we simply cannot understand it.

The anti-career has to do with neither limited nor unlimited power, but with being in your own power. Nietzsche carried off a volume of Emerson on the way to the mental institution. For Emerson enjoined, "build therefore your own world."[5] But this is only half of the story, which if taken as the whole creates chaos. To be in one's own power is to also be in relationship with everything and everyone. Only then can the individual support and, in turn, be supported by the whole. This is where empowered choice comes from.

The separated ego thinks that affirmations or psychological systems can substitute for being in relationship with the living power of the world. The separated nation thinks that platitudes and gifts of foreign aid can cover up a basic posture of self-interest. What happens to the rope dancer in *Zarathustra* is exactly what happens when we say our affirmations, or do one hundred push-ups and pop protein pills, but neglect to align ourselves with Spirit and its power. The same will occur on an international level if we neglect right relationship with the "insignificant" nations of the world.

To make right choices is to align our will with the great forces of life, not to separate decision-making from our feelings, energies, heart, or soul. If we see our fate as sealed, as in *Oedipus,* we remain locked in a tragic hero mode or in dissipating apathy. If we see our fate as only our own and not enmeshed in everyone else's, we are filled with disturbing ambivalence and lack of trust. We constantly wonder, "What should I do? Is this right?" Like Hamlet, we become paralyzed. If we think of ourselves as Superman, we may indeed act and even create marvelous monuments and machineries, but we will destroy the world. What is needed is neither a new authority or system, nor a subjective turning inward, but rather a renewed relationship to the life process that allows trust and its resultant experience to re-create the language of choice, the forms that choice may take, and the path that results from such forms. This is the path of the authentic career.

To follow this path is to accept a power of will that is neither chosen by self nor by another. It is to live a law that is neither written nor unwritten. It is to follow neither through obedience nor denial, to be neither paralyzed within one's mind nor driven out of one's mind. Let this living law be confirmed through meeting the other in relationship. Let it be the groundwork for our actualization in the world of form. An anti-career requires the development of a strong ego, but an integrated one as well. A strong ego is one that is able to choose—to choose from a place of alignment—and this is no small matter. Never before have there been so many choices, with the resultant possibility of diffused energy and interest bespeaking a lack of genuine or committed direction. How then does one get beyond temporary infatuation and unconsciously coerced commitment to begin living a life of awakened choice?

Sartre claimed that man has to invent himself. But can we choose independently of everything and everyone without going headlong into despair? Do we really know what we want, or if what we want is good for ourselves and for others? If we knew all the variables involved, perhaps we could make logical decisions about what career to take up and what not to. But the fact is that we do not have the slightest concept of the full range of factors that underlie our choices. Not only is there heredity, environment, opportunity, and the prevailing market conditions, but there is also a plethora of unconscious needs, patterns, and desires, as well as collective realities: recessions, famines, earthquakes, totalitarian governments. These myriad crisscrossing currents influence any one person's destiny.

HASTEN SLOWLY

We cannot invent ourselves with only the known parts of ourselves, but we can allow ourselves to be invented by the vastness of life. To invent oneself is to take on the burden of knowledge and ever repeat the fall from Eden, to try and *be* the father and know, or to *be* one of Sophocles's characters and try to re-create fate to our own design.

To be invented is to simply be aligned, to live in trust, and to follow the law of concern. Where our concern is, that is where we are, and that is where our pleasure is. When we are aligned with our self-worth, when we live our bliss, we can feel the creative spirit of life leading us in a particular direction. Then we can take initiative, for true initiative is aligned action. By being connected with our feelings and their energies, we can begin to cultivate intention and its power. I use the word *cultivate* deliberately here. It is not sufficient to engage in goal setting, for our original choices are often as much a product of our denial as of our alignment. We must be willing to nurture our goals, to see if they are indeed being nourished by our feelings, our dreams, and our life force. Nevertheless, we must choose on some level so that we can move into active participation with our possibilities. If you don't choose your fate you'll lose it, you'll risk becoming another passive "being of light" who is so light that you are again and again crushed by the world.

DEVELOPING WORKING PRIORITIES

The most important question you can ask yourself at this juncture is, "What am I concerned about, and how much is this concern worth to me?" We are talking about values, and the question is so important because our values are often unconscious. If you believe this is not so, record an honest time log for one week. See if your hour-by-hour and minute-by-minute deeds match your image of yourself. If they do, put this book down or give it to a friend. You are an anti-career person.

If your time log, on the other hand, shows that you are scattering energy, wasting time, filling pages with to-do lists and not crossing them off, or, more importantly, if your day does not make you feel that your are nourishing the soul—both your soul and the soul of the world—then it is time to act. It is time to become aware of the core beliefs that are actually dictating your daily life.

What is really important in terms of how you spend your days and nights? What has empowered the basic movement of your life so far? What are the passions that rule you? Who are the gods and goddesses at whose altar you sacrifice your time and energy? Until you have done substantial investigation here, do not enter into the activities of decision making and prioritizing. First you must see where your attention has been focused, and why.

THE FIRE IN THE BELLY

The capacities of will and discrimination are traditionally associated with the third chakra, which is located in and around the region of the solar plexus. The congruent element of the third chakra is fire, and its color is yellow. The fire element heats, burns, and transforms. It can also be powerfully focused to a pinpoint, like a laser beam. It is this inner fire that has to be activated in order to choose from a place of power, commitment, and completeness. This fire is also the fire of digestion. It assimilates not only food but also information such as past experiences, other people's points of view, and the constant flow of data that enters our energetic field. This fire needs to be ignited and focused to strengthen and sharpen the intellect, so that we can make and stand by our choices. Once a choice is deeply rooted and clear, tremendous power is generated, and obstacles that once seemed insurmountable become capable of being handled. Instead of sitting in a daze waiting for the millennium to arrive, we act from our place of strength. It is through action that guidance is received.

We do not need to find one absolute burning mission, one point of focus that excludes all else; we need instead to develop some sort of inner consensus between the various aspects of self. If our work does not reflect this unity it will not express our sense of the sacred, and it will not withstand the strong tides of contradictory energies that are ever present in our world.

Third Chakra Meditation: The Inner Fire

Breathe in deeply and relax completely. Allow your body to be centered and supported by the earth upon which it resides. As you breathe in and breathe out, open yourself to deeply connect your own being with the ever-present abundance of beingness that is everywhere at all times. As you breathe in and breathe out, let go of the distractions of the superficial level of the mind. Feel the power at the root of your being, the power of abundance, the earth-based power that becomes the vessel that can support the great waters of feeling and form. As you breathe, feel your passion and your convictions. Feel what it is that you really care about, the things you want to do before you die.

Relax your shoulders, the back of your neck, and your spinal column all the way down to the tailbone as you begin to feel the alignment between your first and second chakras, the root and the sacrum, the energy centers of abundance and feeling. As you do so, bring your attention upward to the solar plexus, allowing the energies from the first and second chakras to begin to move upward as you direct your breath energy to the solar plexus.

Now bring to mind, the last year of your life—the roads you have taken and the roads you have not taken, the paths you have walked on and the paths you have neglected, your comings and goings, relationships, working situations, health, financial situation—all the deep energies that have moved you. At this point gently ask yourself, "Who are the gods who have been calling me this year? What are the energies that have been calling me?"

What do you feel in your depths is the most important thing for you to accomplish in the next six months of your life? As you contemplate this question, you may begin to feel a certain focusing energy that you can breathe into the solar plexus. Feeling this focus, allow yourself to come into contact with the energy of fire. The fire of digestion transforms food into fuel for nourishment. The fire of the laser beam pinpoints areas of concentration. The fire of conviction lends determination to your endeavors. Feel the flames of these three fires; feel the incendiary energy of fire itself. Begin to burn away the nonessentials. Begin to burn whatever you are carrying that is not necessary for your growth at this time. Allow yourself to visualize unnecessary materials, places, and activities literally burning away, giving you more time and freedom to focus on what is truly important to you.

Breathe in and breathe out. Let this fire get even hotter. Notice how you are able to bare the heat without getting burned. This is the power of the third chakra—to glow like a coal and still be able to hold that burning energy because it has begun to move into focus. As you offer to the fire and burn away more and more of that which is not necessary to you, you will be able to focus more strongly on what is important. You will be able to concentrate your attention on that place from which you really need to be for the growth of your soul, the place where you can make a difference and impact the world around you.

Allow your mind to receive a message about whatever your emerging priority is at this moment in your life. Just begin to feel it inside of you. You are not creating it consciously: you are not deciding it but are instead allowing it to emerge from your abundance and your passion, and from there allowing it to move into your power. Where is it most important for you to focus your energy, to spend your time, to give your attention in this next period of your life? Who are the gods who are calling to you? What are you being called to accomplish in the coming period of your life? As you breathe in and breathe out, allow a response to come into focus—a priority, a point of attention. Without forcing it, see how clear that focus can become.

Every day as you do the third chakra meditation and get rid of things that are not necessary for you, you can feel the moving power of fire in the belly, the power to take action, the power to move through blockages, the power to say "No," the power to mobilize your energy and set achievable

goals. Every day see this priority coming into clearer focus. When it becomes totally clear, know that this is your working priority, and that you are
ready to engage this priority in a way that will support the giving of your gift
to the world.

6

Moving Ideas into Action: The Wheel of Manifestation

Until one is committed there is hesitancy, the chance to draw back, always ineffective-ness. Concerning all acts of initiative (and creation), there is one elementary truth, the ignorance of which kills countless ideas and splendid plans: that the moment one definitely commits oneself, then Providence moves too. All sorts of things occur to help one that would never otherwise have occurred. A whole stream of events issues from the decision, raising in one's favour all manner of unforseen incidents and meetings and material assistance which no man could have dreamt would have come his way. I have learned a deep respect for one of Goethe's couplets: Whatever you can do, or dream you can, begin it. Boldness has genius, power, and magic in it.

W. H. Murray, Mount Everest Expedition, 1951[1]

As your inner consensus moves into focus—a word that is etymologically related to *fire* through the Latin *focus*, which means "a point where light rays meet"—it is possible to create a set of six-month priorities. Six months is not an arbitrary number. It is one full course of our earth's travel around the sun, from solstice to solstice or equinox to equinox, reflecting the contrast and balancing of darkness and light. Moreover, it seems to work as a strong cycle within which to gestate an idea and move it into action. Depending upon your own rhythm, however, you may want to alter this time frame, and that is fine. What is important is to begin to frame your ideals and ideas into units of space and time. Writing them down begins the process of their incarnation.

It is important to realize that these priorities are temporal. We conceive of them in a way analogous to the Hindu concept of *sva-dharma*. While *sanatana-dharma* is the eternal occupation of the soul and does not change, sva-dharma refers to one's position in the world. Ideally, one's sva-dharma, one's place in the world, leads toward and supports one's sanatana-dharma. The development of a soul-based career is an organic, step-by-step process; it does not come in a sudden flash. The process asks us to be realistically idealistic, that is, to find a focus and then to patiently allow the path to unfold. Our priorities will change over time. This is only natural, and knowing this can fuel current projects. We understand that they are not forever, and so for now we can give them all we have got to give, for they are aligned with the ongoing process of our coming into wholeness. We are therefore neither identified with nor attached to our priorities. They have grown out of our lives and their energies will lead us, but we are not beholden unto them. Our doing flows in and out of our being. Our being need not subordinate itself to our doing.

You can set several priorities to work toward in this six-month time frame, but do not set seventeen. In other words, do not set yourself up for failure. Know where the bulk of your energy needs to be focused. Understand that this is neither a goal nor a fixed decision, but a beginning, a galvanizing of your energy that will permit you to define and focus your career. Ideally you should write your priorities on index cards and keep them in places where you will see them every day. Some people even color code these cards or write their priorities, not in words, but as symbols, and then leave them in strategic locations throughout the house. In this way, you are continually feeding the message to your unconscious, which actually does the work. This is crucial to understand: To the degree that your priorities are clear and aligned with your whole being, the job, the place, and the people will manifest like clockwork, because you have done the necessary inner work. No more effort is needed, and there is no effort more important than developing this clarity of vision.

Such clarity of vision is the province of the third chakra, the power center. This center, which allows us to focus and discipline ourselves to achieve a goal, is often the least developed among people who identify themselves as spiritual. Perhaps this has to do with the fact that so many of us have witnessed outrageous abuses of power in this century and have become extremely sensitized to the negative polarity of power. When one looks at the genocide that has been perpetrated over the last one hundred years on our planet, one cannot help but wonder if a more willing or skillful use of power by those being oppressed, or by those who would help those in danger, could have changed the outcome. We cannot remake the past, but we can understand that, by refusing to develop our power center, we remain ineffective and unable to participate in the world around us. And we can also be inspired by those who have broken through the gloom and inertia and have actually made a difference. The firm resolve of Nelson Mandela, for example, stands as a testimony to the power of aligned determination. From an anti-career perspective, one seeks neither to use nor abuse power, but to align power: to focus on a priority and feel it aligned with your energy, your life force. To feel it means that you are ready to cultivate it, to do the actual work of manifesting your inner vision.

THE WHEEL OF DESIRE IN ACTION

The following model is based on a Lakota medicine wheel, which was introduced to me by Native American teachers in my own area, and which was powerfully amplified by the teachings of Reverend Rosalyn L. Bruyere. Her teachings impacted me greatly and made me think about the medicine wheel in terms of career issues. I have been working with this model, with some modifications, for a number of years now. Some people feel that the medicine wheel should not have been shared with non-native cultures, but the act has already taken place, and it seems as though there must be a higher design to this cross-cultural seeding. My purpose in using the medicine wheel model is neither to divulge a sacred practice nor to vulgarize a traditional teaching. My intention is to effect positive and conscious manifestation, and the medicine wheel does just that by presenting a sophisticated and effective model that enables us to process desire—that is, to align our individual intentions with the fullness of our being and the world around us.

In the Theravada Buddhist and many other Eastern traditions, desire is conceived of as an enemy, the cause of worldly suffering. Since desire naturally leads to other desires, perpetual wanting is viewed as the human predicament. Such a paradigm may be helpful if we conceive of human action as being based solely on an illusory desire for personal fulfillment. But desire may also be viewed as the very energy that sustains us, spawning creativity and ecstasy, creating new possibilities, and proceeding from bounty as opposed to lack. In truth, if you never want anything, you will never have anything. Now, if you are honestly aligned with having nothing, that is fine. The musician John Cage made a career out of this, working consciously from a place of nonpurpose. But even this was a discipline. For most of us, however, having or being nothing is not in alignment with our passion. We need to learn new ways of dealing with our desires, ways that will lead to positive models of living and sharing.

This issue has plagued the Western world just as much as the Eastern. One of the great historical controversies around desire in action took place between the Catholic Church and the so-called Manachaeans in the twelfth century.[2] The core of the argument was over the value of the world. The Manachaean-Gnostic perspective declared the world to be fundamentally unreal and leading only toward death. Therefore the only value of the world was to renounce it and cultivate the spiritual essence that lies beyond the world. The Church countered by declaring that the world had value due to the incarnation of Christ, and therefore action performed in the spirit of Christ redeemed the world. Such action, unfortunately, was all too often seen in its most limited perspective—action that served the institution of the Church. But this idea can be amplified to help us open to possibilities of desire that align themselves with love, compassion, and human freedom as opposed to the devaluation of the world.

The devaluation of the material world is a principle common to various absolutist teachings, including Vedanta, Gnosticism, or monastic Christianity. While such teachings are often romanticized by those with no firsthand experience or acquaintance with the actual texts and social ramifications of these traditions, they actually offer few models of positive action in the world and thus offer little hope for the betterment of human society. Is it any wonder, then, that avowedly spiritual people seem to have such difficulty in the material world?

Some people have responded to this schism by leaving the mainstream society and establishing alternatives such as spiritual communities or sects. Such people usually manage to stay energized through the emotional ecstasy of group-induced experience. These alternative communities, however, all too often become ingrown, and the members find their social lives limited to the confines of the group of believers. They cannot easily extend their experiences into mutuality, into a wider community, or into creative cultural diversity. Once again, the possibilities of positive action become limited. The nihilist vision—be it adolescent-minded anarchism, linguistic deconstruction, or mindless hedonism—also sees the world as ultimately valueless, and while demonstrating time and again that the emperor has no clothes, still remains stranded in despair over prospects of affirmative living.

There are and have always been alternatives to the denial of the world, alternatives that seek to honor the beauty, mystery, and wonder of the world and to make our work a reflection of these qualities.[3] Working with the medicine wheel is one such alternative.

The wheel is a primordial, archetypal form that signifies states of ignorance as well as illumination. The circular uroboros, the serpent chasing its own tail in womblike unconsciousness, evokes the sleepy depths of unawakened energy—whole, yet static and unaware.[4] The archetypal wheel appears in two very different symbols in the tarot deck: as the Wheel of Fortune, indicating the fate-ridden wheel of blind circumstance; and again as the World, emblematic of the awakened state and essential integration in one's being. These two images may, in fact, be viewed as the beginning and end of the anti-career journey. Instead of avoiding the material world or becoming hopelessly enmeshed in it, we use our vocational situation as a vehicle for our own awakening. Thus, the Wheel of Fortune, as uncertain as it is, can become an ally. For the wheel is always turning—even monks who live in mountain caves depend upon lay workers for their sustenance. The wheel turns, and we turn with it—it is *how we turn* that is crucial.

The wheel also turns as the mandala of meditation, used to move toward inner freedom, and as the enclosing circle, drawn around oneself for protection and focus. The encompassing wholeness of the wheel represents desire in all its possibilities, and the issue of desire and how to work with it is what an anti-career is all about. The intent in working with the wheel is to neither escape nor indulge, but to align our desires.

A story told to me by a holy man in India is appropriate here.

Once, while on a bus in the Himalayan region, the holy man met a wandering Westerner, and they began talking. "What do you do?," the holy man asked him.

"I am an ex-guru," the man replied.

"Oh, that is very good," said the swami, "And what do you do now?"

"I follow my heart and follow my desires," said the Western traveler.

"Oh, very good, excellent," replied the swami. "Will you permit me to make one adjustment?"

"What is that?," asked the young man.

"Follow *the* heart and *the* desires."

Aligned desire offers the possibility of being part of the movement of creation itself, so that our actions inspire and are inspired by life around us. Vocation, then, becomes more than "my work," "my career," and "my life." We are not bound to the wheel of fortune, nor do we seek to escape the wheel and become saints. We accept who we are and what we want, but need not conceive of this as a problem. Rather, we integrate ourselves with what is by seeing how and where we can make a contribution.

There are eight areas or lodges on the Lakota wheel, and each one enables us to better understand and strengthen our priorities. To begin with, you must have an idea, a priority that you can commit to. The idea is the first lodge. I used to call this place the place of initial desire, but a number of workshop participants felt that concept was too narrow and could be misconstrued as mere ego motivation, and I have come to agree. The way I now conceive of this initial point, which corresponds to the cardinal direction of east, is as the place of contribution. Here we ask, "What contribution can I make to my community, to my world? How can my desire serve the whole?" The first lodge works with the element of fire, with the ability to assimilate and choose, the ability to direct energy. It is in this lodge that we say, "This is what I want to accomplish during the next six months. This is my goal." Goals need not be external. One can name "developing patience" as one's priority, or choose the goal of increasing one's income. What is important here is clarity and direction. The quality of focus is what we seek to develop in the third chakra, and this focus manifests as the ability to pinpoint your commitments in a given period of time. If the priority is thoroughly genuine, the energy will be there. To see how genuine it may be, we continue around the wheel.

The Lodge of Peace

Once our goal/priority is set we then ask, "Am I at peace with my goal? Does it ring true? Does it make me want to get up early in the morning and get right to it?" If our priorities are still couched in "shoulds" and "oughts," we do not really move with them. They are masks for other, more important issues that we have not yet uncovered. So the next activity on the wheel of manifestation is working to be truly at peace with what we want. One workshop participant said that her priority was losing weight, but all her diets and exercise regimens never developed any momentum. Things were not working. When she finally looked into the lodge of peace, she realized that she was not aligned with this priority. She was not at peace with it. What she really wanted to do was play, and her idea to lose weight was hardly playful at all. As she moved into her playfulness, taking time in her life to relax, walk in the park, be with friends, and just breathe, her anxiety dropped away and eventually so did her waistline.

The all-important message of the anti-career path is to come from your place of fullness, not incompleteness. This is true for any career you might

THE PLAINS INDIANS'
MEDICINE WHEEL MANDALA

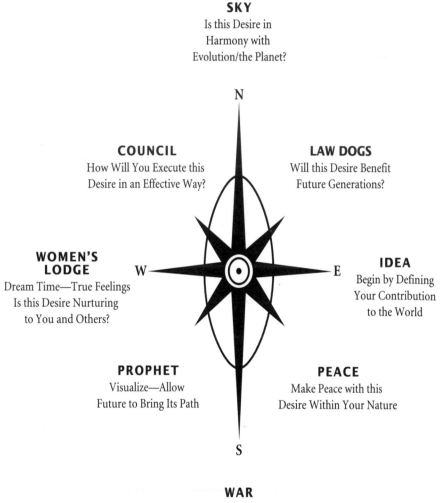

SKY
Is this Desire in
Harmony with
Evolution/the Planet?

COUNCIL
How Will You Execute this
Desire in an Effective Way?

LAW DOGS
Will this Desire Benefit
Future Generations?

**WOMEN'S
LODGE**
Dream Time—True Feelings
Is this Desire Nurturing
to You and Others?

IDEA
Begin by Defining
Your Contribution
to the World

PROPHET
Visualize—Allow
Future to Bring Its Path

PEACE
Make Peace with this
Desire Within Your Nature

WAR
Enthusiasm/Motivation
Mobilization of
Energy Allies

ENLIGHTENED ACTION
In Harmony With Everyone and Everything

choose or develop. Jack Schhwager, the director of Futures Research and Trading Strategy at Prudential Securities, insists that the most successful traders in the stock market believe that they have won the game before they begin. They are not trading out of a desperate need to "make it." Moreover, when asked why many of these traders continue to work long after amassing personal fortunes, he answers that it is not out of compulsiveness; rather, it is simply that they truly enjoy what they are doing.[5]

Are you morally at peace with your work? Does it feel right to be doing what you are doing? Is your conscience clear? If it is not, there is some part of you that will rebel or will sabotage your efforts. I have often thought about this in regard to Hitler. How is it that someone who created and organized the most efficient war machine of his time, who never even came close to losing a battle, suddenly started making the most irrational military decisions possible, such as the invasion of Russia? Could it be that somewhere deep in his inner recesses, Hitler felt that what he was doing was life negating and wrong, and, being unable to consciously acknowledge this, he had to sabotage his own endeavors?

This lodge of peace is really about getting honest with yourself, about feeling right about what you are doing down to the bone, which is quite different from wasting energy trying to convince yourself and others that what you are doing is good. In the manner of conferrring with others, if you are asking too many questions or seeking a lot of advice, you are not yet at peace. Take the time to process whatever needs to be processed. Allow the vision to crystallize. The feeling of being in the flow is well worth the wait.

The Lodge of War

Once you are at peace with yourself, then and only then are you ready to go to war. War, in this context, refers to the ability to mobilize energies, to discipline yourself, and to eliminate whatever is not carrying you toward your goal. The Vietnam war is a tragic example of what happens, on a national level, when one tries to mobilize energy without being at peace with oneself. With half the nation opposing the war, it could neither be won nor cleanly abandoned. In terms of personal manifestation, you must be clear before you can mobilize energy. And how does one mobilize energy? Through the power of the warrior. The warrior as an archetypal energy is discussed by Robert Moore in *King, Warrior, Magician, Lover* as the part of the human psyche that allows one to "sacrifice for the mission."[6]

The warrior energy, or energy of mobilization, can be activated through dual movement. To activate the warrior you must bring in energy, re-sources, and allies to accumulate power, and you must eliminate whatever is obstructing the primacy of the priority in order to streamline and focus on your goal.

Receiving support from others is a natural outcome of alignment. When we are clear about our intent, others whose intentions consciously or un-consciously resonate with our own will appear. We need not even call them in; it is enough to be open. However, we would do well to learn to receive support. One of the foibles of mobilization is the belief that we must do it all by ourselves. Every mobilization is a cooperative effort and need not be a Machiavellian enterprise. Clear purpose and goodness of heart will, by law of nature, draw support. As mentioned previously, when Joyce and Paul Critendon explored the possibility of opening up the Griffen Inn, they needed capital. Since the banks were not anxious to fund an unconventional project hundreds of miles away, they had to look for other resources. The resources appeared through friends and family. Joyce and Paul had real estate holdings in Milwaukee that could not be sold right away, but a friend of Paul's father was willing to put up the money for the property and receive his share whenever the property sold. Now one may call this luck or good circumstances, but such haphazard thinking will never convince others to open their wallets and pocketbooks for you. On the other hand, when you are fixed in your intention and at peace with yourself, alliances often appear mysteriously, for you are ready to receive them. We will explore this process in more detail in the next chapter.

In order to receive this kind of support, there has to be space for it. That is why one of the strongest means of mobilizing energy is to begin getting rid of what you no longer need. On the literal level, this means cleaning stuffed file cabinets and address books with dead people's names in them, throwing away your third-grade biology notes, getting rid of the clothes your mother bought you that you never wear and the tapes and CDs you no longer listen to, and so forth. See who may actually need these items—send for the Salvation Army if you must, or perform a ritual and ignite them in a bonfire—just get rid of the excess "stuff" in your life. We are too weighed down by grandmother's china, extra furniture, clothes, books, and the rest. One workshop participant, a corporate think-tank employee, reported get-ting rid of eight hundred books and suddenly feeling light, free, and ready to receive life in a way he had not felt since adolescence. The first time I consciously engaged in this exercise I decided to tackle my file cabinets, which had been overloaded for years. As I was throwing out one useless piece of paper after another, I came across a file that contained a bond my grandmother left me eight years before, at the time of her death. It had now matured and was worth five hundred dollars.

Streamline. Simplify. This is the way of the warrior. This is the way to invite more life to enter.

The ability to wage war is usually conceived of in terms of the masculine energetic of martial discipline, but this need not be the case. In Goddess-based lunar traditions, the energy of accumulating and streamlining corresponds to the phases of the moon. The new moon represents the beginning of an endeavor. As the moon waxes there is a natural impulse to accumulate and energize, which culminates in the full moon. As the moon wanes, there is impetus to eliminate and streamline. By following such lunar rhythms, you may feel connected to and empowered by the ebb and flow of nature, and may begin to feel the joy of doing the right thing at the right time.

When your talk and actions are pared down to essentials, you will immediately find yourself taken more seriously. For you transmit the energy of the warrior: the one who is single pointed and willing to sacrifice for the mission. Until your priority is aligned in this way, it will remain weak: the book will remain half-written, the song unsung, the house just an idea on paper.

The Lodge of Prophets and Visionaries

Once we streamline and empower ourselves, our visions take on meaning. We move from fantasy to creative vision, acting not from haphazard energy bursts but from naturally occurring dreams of the possible. When your purpose is clear and your energies are focused, the vision of what is possible will begin to manifest through you. You won't have to use manipulative visualization methods because your own natural enthusiasm will lead you into the visionary realm. You will begin to dream, imagine, and feel the future, allowing yourself to be led by the future instead of trying to plan it and thus losing all the magic in your life. To live in vision is to ever be created in the here and now, to defy the limitations that others put on you and, above all, to allow yourself to be led by the unknown.

The element of vision adds magic to the mobilization of energy. We do not know how our vocations will turn out, but we begin to intuit possibilities. A career that lacks this component becomes dry, brittle, and predictable. When our visionary energies are activated, on the other hand, they actually begin to create circumstances—ideas, markets, and organizational paradigms—that will move our priorities into manifestation.

Stan Jay was busy collecting vintage guitars and selling them, mostly through classified ads. He had one major competitor. One day his phone rang. It was his competitor, whom he had never before spoken to, calling him to let him know that there was a cache of vintage instruments available. The competitor was not particularly interested in this brand of instruments, but thought that Stan Jay might be. They wound up going down to look at the instruments together, and on that day a partnership was born that became known as the Mandolin Brothers. Stan Jay was an excellent collector and his new partner was an excellent promoter. The partnership worked, not through extensive planning or an act of will, not through a series of market evaluations, but because both men shared a vision that brought them together at the right time.

As we open to our own visionary wisdom, our sense of timing opens as well. Instead of being run by the clock, we begin to find ourselves in the right place at the right time, and as we do, we become cognizant of a different type of clock, one that runs not by strict economic or mechanical laws but that instead synchronizes with the rhythm of our beings as we begin to trust its accuracy.

The Women's Lodge

Once your priority has been extended, you must go back and ask "Does this really feel right?" You may have a vision of yourself as president of the United States, but how does that vision feel? Would you feel more authentic as a geologist? This is the place where we begin to connect with our inner feminine wisdom. Therefore, the women's lodge is also the place of the dream. Dreams, while connected to the visionary state, also indicate your true feelings about things. If you are about to embark on a project but keep getting contrary information in your dreams, or if in your dream you continually have images of being chased, judged, or examined, then there are feelings that have to be processed before you can manifest your vision. Just as a vision may take us up the mountain, the dream leads us into the valley, into the hidden corners and densely covered regions of our interior. As dreams are not consciously conceived, they may be even more insightful (and sometimes disconcerting) than visions. The richness of the dream, therefore, responds to our patience and attention. The intellectually based practice of decoding dream symbols may actually prevent us from developing familiarity with the inner terrain, and if the inner terrain—what Jung called the province of the anima/animus—is not consulted and included in our career planning, we find ourselves hampered by moods, by the mess in our rooms and offices, and by the seeming opposition of circumstances around us. This is the value of the wheel. The cluttered office or overscheduled datebook cannot be remedied by efficiency strategies—the mere "straightening out" of these areas—for they will just fill up again. Simply answering want ads or going to job interviews will not solve the problem either. Until feeling and will are aligned, until our unconscious and conscious places move into dialogue and cooperation, we will always be at cross purposes with ourselves and, no matter how hard we try to shore things up around us, our outer life will reflect our inner disharmony.

Dreams are the level that must nourish our work if our work is to nourish our inner development in return. And that, after all, is the true purpose of any work. To include dreams in our work of manifestation is to begin to bring our masculine and feminine sides into dialogue.

John Dempson saw the movie "Wall Street" at nineteen years old, and immediately knew that he wanted to work with the stock market. His intuitive sense of the marketplace, however, was that it had to do with more than money; to him, it was the international meeting place of values, and he wanted to understand its psychology. Following his innate feeling, he did not go to business school but began knocking on the doors of Wall Street firms, and in his early twenties was hired as a trader. At night he would have dreams about commodities, and his hunches were very often correct and financially rewarding. Eventually the older traders began asking him about his "system," and they did not quite believe it when he told them that he had none. What he had was a strong connection to his inner world that kept offering up new information. He knew he was doing what he wanted to be doing, and the dream that was leading him was one of understanding. He was not afraid to go "big time" as he honored the forces that were moving him. I have followed John's career for over seven years now. It has had its ups and downs, like anybody else's, but every new turn in the road adds a piece to the puzzle, and as a result, this young man in his late twenties knows more about markets and about people than professionals twice his age.

Our dreams need not, of course, yield literal indications about our career situations. More importantly, they may reveal our inner terrain. The dream of the abandoned parking lot we find ourselves stranded in, for example, may reflect a state of the soul, a place where we feel alone or alienated. And if life and work does not address this space, we will be moved to encounter it someplace else, which fragments our energies. We want to create a situation where our dreams are working on our work, and our work is working on our dreams. The parking lot tells me that I must connect with this feeling of urban desolation. Perhaps the office where I work is an urban desert, and I feel stranded there. If I can recognize this, I open to the possibility of change.

We may think that we are accomplishing something in the world, but if that accomplishment does not yield insight or penetrate into the inner levels of our being, it is wasted time. For our work is ideally preparing us for death, familiarizing us with the inner spaces, allowing us to make transitions in love, appreciation, and even glory. One's work in the world need not be a fight against entropy. When Dylan Thomas rages against the dying light—"Do not go gentle into that good night . . . rage, rage against the dying of the light"—he poignantly and powerfully epitomizes the male heroic ego, still not at peace, raging against its inability to ascend beyond itself. This is the model that is still largely glorified. There are many who would show us how to live; there are few who can show us how to die.

The women's lodge is the place where we listen to the wise woman within. It is here that we gestate our dreams and let them contribute, in their own ways, to our priorities and ultimately to our vocations. Here is where we consolidate and coordinate the various aspects of being one with another.

The Lodge of Administration

The next lodge is that of the administrative chiefs. This is where daily planning and strategies are taken into account. If we want to acknowledge our priorities, we must be willing to give them time. It usually takes a *minimum* of three hours a day to work a new idea or project into manifestation.

In the Aquarian age, wars will be fought through the weaponry of ideology and information. This lodge, then, is the place where we decide what information we need to receive and transmit. In the way that contemporary society is evolving, it is safe to say that if you do not devise a plan to manage your time and energy, you will spend the rest of your life reading junk mail. You will be the victim of Ed McMahon and Publisher's Clearing House sweepstakes, spending a good hour every day looking for the right stamps to stick on the right envelope! Let this be known—time management is the yoga of the nineties!

The strategy for managing your time and energy is to have your priority so rightly and deeply ingrained in you that you can naturally work your day around its power, as opposed to working around other people's agendas.[7] In this lodge, we make a craft out of life because we employ the discipline of the artist every day. This kind of discipline is one of the accepted definitions of yoga. The Bhagavadgita actually defines yoga as "skill in action." In the 1960s, many were eager to march but few were ready to do their kitchen yoga and clean up the mess of cups, paper, and other assorted trash left behind. But if we do not attend to our messes they will attend to us. The day-to-day sculpting of life is the essence of this lodge. Our ideals need to be supported by our form of daily living.

Are you scurrying around all day answering the phone? Are you playing therapist to all of your friends and receiving no compensation for it? Are you letting your husband or children set the entire agenda for your day? Minute-by-minute awareness of your daily activities is as important, if not more so, than any meditation. And it is your responsibility to manage your daily energy flow, to know what is important to you, to know where and how you want to spend your time and how you are going to administer your own day-to-day life. Many busy people know all of this on an intellectual level, and some may have taken professional time-management seminars. But the exhaustive repetition of things to do day after day, the seemingly overwhelming amount of information that a working individual needs to digest on a regular basis, and the apparent never-ending pressure to produce, make it very easy to forget, to lose focus again and again. As this happens, you must seriously question and commit to transform the models of productivity and efficiency that drive this insatiable movement toward exhaustion.

The anti-career application of time management does not focus on time in the sense of clocks, schedules, lists, day planners, and the like. Rather, we begin with the all-important concept of space. Space is one of the important elements most lacking in our modern lives. I am speaking of something more than the need for a cushion and time to allow room for reflection. I am speaking of the quality of space that allows for new people and possibilities to enter our lives, of creating enough room for the creative flow to come in and dance with us. Space is the fifth element, the complement to earth, air, fire, and water. Space is the container that allows creativity to unfold. Space gives birth to different dimensions and qualities of time. Space allows one to maintain an inward dimension, a sense of connectedness to the whole. If we do not develop a very real, palpable sense of space around ourselves, we get caught in the unreflective net of linear time. We run on the treadmill until our time runs out and we completely lose the moment of incarnation, the intersection of the timeless with time, which is the possibility that authentic work offers to us.

The prerequisite to sane time management is thus learning to inhabit space, to literally feel the space in and around your body. Again I will say that a true career begins in the body. You must first feel comfortable being what you are before you can be what you do. Movement, martial arts, walking, and breathing all help a person develop a sense of space, and hence a sense of time, that is inherently rhythmic and not contorted into a date book. When you have space around you, you can feel things coming before they actually arrive; you can sense others' thoughts, resistances, and support. This is not part of any esoteric mystery. This comes about because you are not filled to the brim with "to do's." Keeping the space clear around you is the same operative principle of health that tells you not to stuff yourself at every meal. It makes total sense to be available in this way if we want to cultivate the ability to respond to the world around us.

Do not "list" yourself out of existence. Time management need not make you an automaton, walking up and down hallways with appointment books held in hand. When you take the time to cultivate the quality of space around you, time management becomes an ongoing energy discipline, and it is in this way that it can be regarded as the yoga of the nineties. Just as the yogi has to manage body, breath, posture, and thought processes, the anti-career yogi has to manage all incoming and outgoing energy flows—phone, mail, fax, food, friends, television, and the like—for optimum awareness.

It might therefore be better to speak of visionary time awareness, for time management, as it is often practiced, has become synonymous with efficiency alone and thus participates in the archetype of man as machine. Visionary time awareness, on the other hand, sees efficiency as growing out of one's vision. For the visionary, one's understanding of time is not limited to linear time. Rather, linear time is integrated into cyclic time—the particular season one is in, both psychologically and temporally—and into a sense of the timeless as well. True management of time is that which reveals the timeless and thus imbues our daily activities with a sense of the higher laws and natural rhythms that can regulate our lives.

The Lodge of Guidance

The next place on the wheel is the North, the world of the gods. It is here that, after we have done everything we can—nurtured an idea, made peace with it, mobilized our energy, visualized, dreamed, felt, and planned—here we can do nothing more except give it up to the universe, to God, to our own sense of the Higher Power. Here is where our plan moves into alignment with the universal plan, and so we are very conscious that it is not just ours alone. Here we actively ask for help from the gods, and in so doing we begin to align our will with the greater will. This can only work if we have made all the preparations. You can fail a math test and say it was God's will, but if you didn't study for it, you rigged the deck and you will never know whose will was stronger in this situation.

Asking for guidance may be the key to feeling that our work is genuine. Here is where we experience the inspiration and the exhilaration that tells us we are not alone in our endeavor. Here is where we actively enlist the higher forces. Instead of believing in them, we begin to work with them. This is also the place where little miracles start to occur because here we move beyond the egotism of I, me, and mine. There is admittedly an element of risk here, but if we do not take this risk, we paint ourselves into our own little corner. To ask for guidance does not guarantee any particular result, but it does place our work in an entirely new context. We no longer carry the entire burden; rather, we begin to acknowledge that our life's work is, in fact, life working through us. This alone gives our work a meaning that no external label could, and this position, when taken in sincerity, lends true nobility to any type of working situation.

The Lodge of Earth Community

The final stop on the wheel fittingly belongs to the earth community. What will be the ramifications of our actions for those around us, for the Earth, and for her future generations? What legacy will our vocation leave behind? Will our children's children and their children be proud of what we have done? Will the Earth herself appreciate our endeavors? This concern for progeny and the Earth's future may seem sentimental at first, but it is actually becoming the determining factor in whether an enterprise will succeed in the coming millennium or not. For the industrial paradigm of productivity is no longer generative from the planet's point of view. Those careers and enterprises that are truly serving the needs of the Earth will be supported, the others will not. In this, the last lodge, we test our careers against what is truly needed, we make our work part of *the* work, and this automatically lends dignity to the seemingly smallest task.

We have all been hearing for quite some time now that the service-based economy is replacing the industrial-based economy. But the idea of service itself needs to be extended. It is service to the Earth, to the totality of eco-existence that will create the enduring jobs of the future, because our planet is interested in its own survival. Recently I heard that a small ecological think tank approached a major oil company in Oregon and demonstrated to them that instituting recycling in their plant would prove cost effective within five years. Ordinarily, businesses might not want to think in terms of half-decades until losses are recouped for environmental purposes, but seeing the larger picture has now become essential for economic survival. I was told that the company has agreed to implement the plan.

Our own vocations must likewise gear themselves toward *the* future, not simply our future. This means that we have to see how our work will support the future, not as a rationalization but as a commitment to the wheel of life itself. In doing so we will gain a most inestimable ally—the Earth herself.

As we begin to nurture our ideas and move into action, we will inevitably be presented with obstacles. At times we will be tempted to take them as signs that we are on the wrong path, but there is no wrong path with the anti-career. Every experience is a learning one, so there can be no failure! Whenever you did something that seems like a wrong move in retrospect, remember that you believed it to be the optimum thing to do at the time. Otherwise you would not have done it. The fact that you can now see it as a mistake indicates that you have grown, that you have learned something. There is no point to retroactive judgement. What we need to do is to act and adjust, to flow with circumstances and let them bend our actions, to constantly reprocess our intentions into greater alignment, and to use resulting feedback from the world to move into ever deeper levels of right will.

Once while performing an excavation in Egypt, archaeologists ran across a hieroglyph that read, "Eat this book." What did it mean: Eat this book? As with Oedipus, the search for a literal answer was futile. For the answer is in the power of assimilation, the third chakra's ability to process information, to adjust, and to refocus. Priorities are made to evolve. To absorb the power of the obstacle is the reward of encounter. Whether you assimilate it or it assimilates you, there will be synergy, and thus more energy, available for your next move. On the other hand, to separate, conquer, or flee from the obstacle is the road to withering away and dying.

Therefore it is incorrect to assume that, just because obstacles have arisen in your path, your path is flawed. If you are fluid and attentive, if you are willing to assimilate the experience and let it re-create your direction, you will become empowered even through seeming defeat. When New York City went bankrupt in the 1970s and laid off a number of teachers at the city universities, Stan Jay did not take it personally, feel rejected, or consider himself a failure. He used the situation as an opportunity to finally turn his sideline of collecting vintage musical instruments and selling them into a full-fledged business.

This is how we actually begin to move into our vocation: We open to ourselves and to our feelings, we know what our priorities are, and we process them so that our actions are aligned with our enthusiasm. The focusing mechanism is about fire—the enthusiasm to choose and remain committed to your choice, the fire to assimilate and digest, to come to a sense of purpose from which we can build. This is still the beginning. We have built the base triangle, the fusing of self-worth, feeling, and will. Once this triangle is strong, we can begin to engage the collective in a new way. No longer exclusively motivated by survival, scarcity, or the need to impede the other to uphold ourselves, we can move into the realm of the heart, into the beauty of sharing, where our visions blend and create new forms of love and work for all.

APPLYING THE MEDICINE WHEEL TO VOCATIONAL ISSUES

There are many different ways to work with the medicine wheel. I have worked with native teachers who have had us build them on the earth with stones, and then sit or stand in their different positions and connect the directions to particular attitudinal places within. The following exercises are very helpful when considering any particular undertaking, especially once you have put the wheel and its positions to memory. The prerequisite to this activity is that you have worked through the first three centers and have a particular priority at hand. Then you can put the priority onto the wheel, focusing on one particular lodge, and see what needs to be done to bring it to fruition. The following exercises will demonstrate how you can take a priority and work with it.

East: Focusing on an Idea

Bring your chosen priority into focus. See it, feel its texture, and gently allow it to constellate within. You are now entering the lodge of the East. See yourself walking into this lodge, carrying your priority with you. Is it clear? Is it focused? Is it defined? Does your project feel like something that has grown out of you, as opposed to something you are trying to graft on to yourself? Hold your priority in the lodge of the East until you experience its definition and focus. This will allow you to empower a new career direction.

Southeast: Having a Clear Conscience

Holding your project with you, enter into the lodge of peace and open to your inner knowing. Do you feel at peace with your idea? Is your conscience really clear about it? Can you work at your new career without any inner qualms and half-hearted efforts? Feel inside your body and notice any places that are not comfortable with your idea. Listen to them. If there is any place within where you do not feel at peace now, you will have to stay in this lodge, or return to it at the appropriate time and allow your project to bend and shape itself differently. If you find that there is resistance here, call upon the peace chiefs. Ask their advice. Ask "Why do I not feel peaceful with my desire?" Ask, and be willing to receive.

South: Mobilization

You are now entering the southern lodge, the Lodge of War. You are now at one with your endeavor and you are ready to mobilize yourself for action. As you breathe in, feel the fire strengthening itself in your solar plexus. As you breathe out, let go of anything that is impeding your realization of your objective. Perhaps you need to let go of so-called friends who are hanging on to you but not contributing to your direction at this time. Perhaps you need to let go of false security needs, or of a relationship that has been over for some time but keeps reappearing in your mind. Feel your Being aimed like an arrow; feel yourself lean, taut, and in training. Make a mental list of all excess baggage that you are ready to drop and see it all falling by the wayside. Feel the power of the warrior—the one who is dedicated to his mission, the one who is undaunted by difficulty, the one who is alert, ready, and determined to succeed.

Now begin to scan your field for allies and resources—people, places, information sources, training programs, and institutions that will help you advance toward your goal. Once the list has been presented, notice which names burn with a fiery glow and remember them, writing them if necessary. Now call on your inner power to receive any support that you have contracted with on another level or in a previous dimension. Open yourself to receive all support from all levels in your quest. Being at peace with yourself, you know that you deserve this support and there is no need to worry—there will be ample opportunity to return the favors later on. Visualize the life patterns around you consolidating, taking form, and working with you, magnetized by the power of your intention. If you feel resistance in this lodge, you know there is work to be done here, and you can return at any time to continue.

S o u t h w e s t : V i s i o n

You are now ready to enter into the Lodge of Singers and Visionaries. This is the place from which you can begin to transform your habitual patterns by conceiving of new ones, by imagining a greater reality for yourself and letting the currents of your imaging power rearrange your inner structure. Breathe in and breathe out, allowing the power of the breath to move you into flight. With utter ease your vision opens and you see the future possibility coming to take you by the hand and show you how your idea may take form. See, feel, sense, taste, touch, and smell your project in its complete power. How does it look? Where is it located? Who is around you? Do not try to create a preconceived future, but instead trust the inner power of creation to move you into this possibility. Perhaps what you see will surprise you. Perhaps what you experience is not literal at all. Instead you are taken into a world of shapes, colors, or sounds. Trust this inner process. Explore your visionary possibilities. If you see no future for your idea, ask the chiefs in this lodge to guide you, to point out where you can take this project to move it along. Be patient. Do not try to force the future into being. If things appear to be stuck, that is where they need to be at the present time. You can return to this lodge whenever necessary to renew and expand the visionary faculty.

You can also work in this lodge with others who are your allies or part of the project. You may sit down together and brainstorm, or take dream walks together in which you and your partners articulate your hopes for the future or give vent to your imaginations of what could be. The time spent at letting the creative imagination play is as important, if not more so, than any hard work you may do to bring a project to successful completion.

West: The Way of the Dream

You now enter the Women's Lodge. Here you examine your deep feelings and primal concerns and see if your vision is truly congruent with them. Feel your idea within your body and take a detailed inventory. How does it feel? What is your gut reaction to your vision? Do you feel nourished, whole, and at ease? If not, notice where the resistances appear and how they appear. Open your heart to them and listen. Go far back in your memory, back to your childhood. Does your idea flow with your childhood feelings? With your prenatal memories? Go back even further. Allow scenes to come in from the watery underworld, from your dreams, from what may even be past existences. Allow the inner landscape to appear and follow its winding contours, its hills and valleys. Where have you been spending your nights in your dreams? Have you been building an inner landscape that will support your project, or have you had different agendas vying for your night attention? What have you actually been working on in this deep inner world that rarely crosses over into the light of day? Do you have helpers? enemies? judges? teachers? Allow the wise women chiefs of this lodge to take you into your hazy zones of awareness; allow them to show you the concerns of this region. If they are not congruent with your conscious priority, you may need to hold an inner conference and reprioritize. Take as much time as you need here. The women's lodge often communicates through silence alone, and great patience is needed to cross over into this realm. But the rewards will be considerable. You will leave the lodge with a new integrity, a power that comes from no known or definable source. You will be more intuitive and more at ease with your work in the daylight world. For the beings who inhabit the deep recesses of the interior are content that you are finally ready to listen, and they will begin to serve you with information that emerges from within as long as you are true to this innermost place.

Northwest: Time-Space Strategies

You now move into the Lodge of the Administrative Chiefs. Your idea is clear and you are at peace with it. You have begun to mobilize your energy, have visions of your possibilities, and are linked up with your intuition. But how will you make this happen in the day-to-day world? What kind of space do you need, and what kind of schedule? How are you to manage the everyday operation of your endeavor? Even if your first priority is a personal one, such as developing patience, under what circumstances shall you develop this quality—with whom, when, and where?

See yourself functioning on a daily basis, accomplishing your endeavor. What are your surroundings like? How are you sustaining yourself and handling the inflow and outflow of information? See yourself fully at the task at hand and notice your set-up. Ask the chiefs of this region how you can support your priority by balancing your daily time and energy situation. Perhaps you fiddle away a lot of time because you neglect to give yourself real quality time and space for recreation and relaxation, or perhaps you lose time fulfilling all sorts of obligations to others, real or imagined.

One of the most important qualities necessary to achieving your goal is developing the ability to say "No." When you are working toward your goal and the phone rings, see yourself politely but firmly saying "No" to the invitation or request coming in. When Ed McMahon invades your home with the latest credit card sweepstakes scam, see yourself saying "No." When your recently converted friend tries to drag you to his latest miracle workshop, even though it has nothing to do with where you are at right now, see yourself saying "No." Say "No" to the energy chiselers and prana-suckers, to the mass marketers, to the latest tournament of champions, and say "Yes" to your soul, to your goal, and to the better world that your goal will inspire.

North: Making the Heavenly Connection

You now enter into the Lodge of the Gods. You have done all you can and you are ready to "lift your eyes on to the hills." You are ready to accept the verdict of the universe, whatever it may be. You are not here to bang down heaven's door, but to be open and to receive the light from above. And you do receive it, because you are ready to. In this lodge you drop your pretenses, your ambitions, your idea of how it all is. Here, along with Brother Klaus, the great Swiss holy man who is said to have kept the Nazis out of Switzerland during the war with the power of his intention, you ask: "Whatever I am doing that is bringing me closer to Thee, let it be so, and whatever I am doing that is taking me away from Thee, let it go."

Here, in your own way, you lay your burden down—the heavy, illusory burden that you are the controller of your life and work. Allow the Great Spirit to fill you, to permeate your body and soul. Ask for nothing but guidance, that you may be in the right place at the right time, that you may find and be found in those circumstances that are aligned with the will of heaven, that you may function as an instrument of universal grace and compassion, that your heart and your desires may be at one with the Great Heart and the Great Desire for world evolution, awakening, and compassion.

Northeast: The Legacy of Our Work

You finally come to the Lodge of the Northeast. Here the final arbiters ask you one simple question. Your project, your desire, your idea, your career: Will it serve our children's children's children? Will your work be remembered with love and appreciation by the future generations? The sweat and toil, the effort and training, the planning and execution, the meditations and prayers you have done: Will they leave a legacy of peace and harmony, of openness and caring, of growth and prosperity upon the earth?

This does not mean that your work has to be in direct service to a known goal. The artist who struggles with an inner vision provides possibilities for the future, the homemaker who loves his child creates a place where the child will grow free from fear, the mechanic who loves her tools and respects their power, who guides them to serve and not to harm, is helping to build the blueprint of a future technology that will be earth supporting and humanity sustaining. The gift you will give to the planet will be the love and care that went into your job—nothing more and nothing less. The earth knows this, the children know this, and you in your heart know this. To the extent that you stepped out of your fear and into the greater community of the world, to that extent will your legacy be remembered.

Here you offer your work, your talents, your dreams, and your aspirations to the generations to come, and see your work—no matter how large or seemingly small—as part of the great work that is beyond the human, but that is nourished and sustained by the human.

We have now come full circle on the medicine wheel. Each place on the wheel represents a place inside ourselves. In some sectors we will be naturally vibrant. In others we will be tentative; these are the places we need to develop. Start from where you are, accept where you are, and allow the various places on the wheel to integrate themselves within you. In this way your priority will begin to crystallize into its own unique form, and you will find yourself moving in a direction that is authentic and representative of who you are on the wheel of life and where you want to go.

7
The Fourth Chakra:
At Heart Thou Art

Look closely at his aims,
observe the means by which he pursues them,
discover what brings him content.

Confucius

We now arrive at the pivotal juncture in the process of establishing soul-centered work, the place of transition from ego-centered motivation into the radiance of conscious participation with the whole. The movement of any individual through this juncture will make a measurable difference in the potential of the collective. This kind of conscious participation should not be confused with "doing good." Heart-centered action, which is compassion, comes as a result of tempered strength and an understanding that deepens beyond perspectives of good and evil. Such activity is fully aware of the futility of separateness and fear as motivations for action, and it thus does not lend itself to instant gratification. Without the energetic of conscious participation in operation, our work efforts will, at best, continue to yield a legacy of imbalance.

THE SEAT OF PROSPERITY

The heart is the seat of prosperity. If one's prosperity is achieved without an open heart, one will still feel poor. No matter how much is accumulated on any level, something will be missing. The notion of the heart as the center of prosperity exposes the myth of "hard work" for what it is, as there are quite a few beings on this planet who are able to manifest materially without working. Millions of people have witnessed the Indian holy man, Satya Sai Baba, manifest materials from the universal field into his hand. Swami Jnanananda Giri, upon finding a sack of potatoes dumped in front of his cottage, would say something like, "Somebody must be coming for dinner," and indeed people would arrive later that evening.

This does not equate an anti-work ethic with any form of freeloading. Richard Dominguez, the one-time stockbroker who preaches financial independence through radical voluntary simplicity, notes that people who succeed in being supported without working for money are usually people who have an intense sense of mission.[1] They are inner directed and their directedness supports those around them. What needs to be fully appreciated for prosperity to manifest is the way of the heart in the world, the way of giving and receiving. This basic movement of the heart is mirrored by the in breath and out breath; the inhale receives from life and the exhale offers itself back to life. In truth, no one can say where one movement ends and the other begins, for the words giving and receiving are but human approximations of a much greater universal law. Nevertheless, when we speak we are bound to these terms. Receiving is mentioned first because it is conspicuously absent from our lives. Notice how most people react to compliments, for example. It is not unusual for any of us to shy away from them, saying—often with our body language—that we are unworthy of receiving such recognition. On the other hand we might be so starved for support that we are continually seeking new ways to market ourselves, thrusting ourselves on people whether they would benefit from our gifts or not.

Both sides of this polarity indicate an inability to receive. Receiving has to do with having a fundamental openness toward experience, a willingness to accept all that life has to offer—the good and the so-called bad. Often we do not allow ourselves to receive because we have not developed a strong, centered ground. We simply cannot hold the energy of bounty. We are bowled over by heightened spiritual experiences or by perceptions of "too much" money, authority, responsibility, and so forth. In order to receive we must begin at the root, establishing ourselves in our fullness and in our right and need to be exactly who and where we are. We align our feelings with this energy and can then choose reasonable priorities to focus on. But if we are not able to receive, our priority will not make contact with the greater community.

Receiving can operate on many levels. We can learn to receive praise or constructive criticism; we can allow ourselves to accept money, beauty, and affection, as well as quality friendships and quality items, not feeling unworthy or awkward at participating in all of life's treasures. Receiving also involves accepting rejection and pain without blocking it out and forming judgments that will not allow us to transform the energy. When it is our time to drink from the cup of poison, we can drink it completely. In this way we receive the impact, and hence the wisdom, of the experience. In the midst of our darkness we then find a jewel forming, a treasure that is ours to share because we have allowed it to form through our genuine openness. If we are unwilling to open to rejection, criticism, or illness, we waste much energy trying to push these things away and are therefore constantly in a defensive position. In order to receive such gifts, we must be convinced of our innate goodness and value. We must believe that we are inherently worthy. Finally, in order to receive we must give, for giving opens up our field and sets up the flowing circuit of prosperity. But in order to give, we must believe that we have something *to* give. No matter what kind of talents and abilities or seeming handicaps and shortcomings we might think we have, what we have to offer is essentially our own God-given essence, and no person or thing can minimize this or take it away.

The first thing we can do to retrain ourselves to receive, then, is to practice receiving the fullness of our breaths. By beginning each morning as a conscious receiver of the breath of life, you will feel so energized that you will *want to* give, you will *want to* get up and do something. Image yourself as an open vessel. Invite the breath of life to flow through all the organs of your body. One by one allow the lungs, heart, liver, stomach, spleen, pancreas, kidneys, bladder, and sex organs to become energized and filled. Every morning invite your limbs, muscles, bones, tendons, and skin to be filled with vital energy. Receive! The next time someone compliments you, do not cringe or belittle yourself but instead allow yourself to fully take in the compliment. Take the time to feel yourself filled consciously. Giving will then become a natural outcome of your condition.

Giving is not about doing good, nor is it about service to God, guru, or country. Such concepts can further the illusion of separation and are often based on some subtle form of self-hate. Most of us have lived our lives filled to the brim with injurious platitudes about how we should give and help the needy. Conseqently, many people harbor "healer's disease" and so sit in watchful wait for someone in need, swooping down upon them in order to justify the healer's existence. Thoreau once said, "If I knew for a certainty that a man was coming to my house with the conscious design of doing me good, I should run for my life."[2] And so would we, because we are being attacked by the grasping need behind the act. Much so-called giving is based on a sense of obligation and therefore prohibits the natural flow of receiving. The same is true of tithing and any similar type of saving, if it is calculated to bring a profit later on. All such methods have in common the desire to create a specific end, which means that they are coming from one form of attitudinal poverty or another. There is no spontaneity, no magic, and no meeting. This is why so many wealthy people need to continue accumulating money; they do not know how to do anything else. Even with all matter of comforts they are still not receiving, and thus they remain haunted by what they do not have.

In the Tibetan Buddhist tradition, this mentality is known to belong to the realm of the "hungry ghost." Hungry ghosts are visualized as disembodied spirits with enormous bodies and tiny mouths who are always trying to suck up more experience because they can never get enough. The Vietnamese Buddhist teacher Thich Nhat Hanh observes that America seems to have a hungry ghost syndrome. The feverish energy of consumption—intellectual and emotional as well as material—is never satisfied because there is little earth-centered groundedness or a regenerative cycle of giving and receiving.[3]

Giving, whether it is of an emotional or a material nature, is not a calculated act. Giving flows from fullness, and it is spontaneous. When we feel full, we are free to give and to receive. Every time you find yourself hoarding, ask yourself what you are actually trying to fill. (This includes the hoarding of knowledge.) Each time you find yourself giving out of compulsion, look to the root of the compulsion, for true giving is an expression of our value, and every time we give, in every way we give, we are making a statement. With every dollar we spend we are supporting something or someone. Do our expenditures reflect our values? Do we see spending as giving, or are we still trying to extract bread from the world? If we only spent money on what we believed in, every expenditure would be aligning us with our priorities and moving us toward our goals. Every time we paid a bill we would be actively supporting a new vision of the world. For example, many people now buy organic food whenever possible, not only for health reasons but also because it supports the natural foods industry, the small farmers, and self-sustaining agriculture rather than community-crippling agribusiness. These people are not simply buying food, they are giving. In a similar vein, new companies such as Working Assets and Seventh Generation have built the idea of giving into their corporate mission.

Every time you pay your telephone bill under Working Assets, for example, a percentage of that money is put toward environmental causes.

Another word for giving is support, and support is something that occurs on all levels. Joyce Critendon remarks that if the customers at her inn feel the heart energy coming from the staff—that is, if they feel true support—then even when there are defects in the service, the guests are likely to return. For they are receiving something that cannot be measured, and yet it is palpable.

The opposite of support is envy—the same envy that Emerson declared to be ignorance—and it is the crowning emblem of our scarcity. Wherever there is envy in our lives, there is a place where we believe that we do not have enough, or worse, are not ourselves enough. To work through the heart center is to come to terms with our envy.

Envy is the serpent's tongue. It bites us and holds on, poisoning every part it touches. For many, the whole career game is based on envy, and all the traditional metaphors for getting ahead are tied in with it. Artists and career spiritualists are not immune: How often do we hear the tinge of envy in our critique of another's work or another's teaching? As long as envy holds sway in our hearts, we cannot function in a free capacity, for envy is based on a sense of poverty and nonacceptance of ourselves. This does not mean that we arm ourselves with goodness and go out to vanquish the enemy of negative emotion. That only leaves us with a humble and frustrated ego. Like any other so-called negative emotion, envy begs for care and investigation. And as we trace it down to its roots, we see our hidden hopes as delicate flowers that have been stepped on and damaged. We find things that we always wanted to do but never did, and ways in which we always wanted to be but never allowed ourselves to be. Once we see what underlies our envy, we can stop projecting the emotion outward onto others. There is new material to guide us and help us open to the desires of the heart.

If you believe the nature of the world to be dog-eat-dog competition, it will be that for you, and every encounter will reinforce this dreadful pattern. The way of the heart is the win/win alternative, and it entails coming to terms with envy, mistrust, and our basic contraction from the life process, not as saints but as courageous investigators of our personal reality. When you mistrust or contract in face of a situation, you can explore it. What is the emotional quality of the situation? Can you fully articulate it? Mistrust and envy are not the enemies but are instead powerful keys to exploring our scarcity-ridden mentalities, of deeply looking into the parts of ourselves that are not fulfilled, and thus giving us opportunities to reclaim them.

Many people recommend exercises in self-forgiveness for overcoming contraction, but one needs to be very careful in their application. Anger, envy, and so forth are genuine feelings aching to be explored. If forgiveness becomes a "should," then we will constantly torture ourselves trying to be better people. Perhaps a better word for working with heart-based emotions is *acceptance*, living inside a heartfelt acceptance that allows us to open to a situation *as it is.* The openness is achieved not by denying, but by admitting whatever emotion is present and exploring it from the heart center, that is, exploring it without motive, vengeance, or judgment. The places where we cringe are our personal edges.[4] They are the doors we have never been quite able to walk through, although we have always known they are there waiting for us. The edge is the place where we get tied up in knots in the presence of another person, where we panic at the prospect of turning on the light even when the darkness feels overwhelming. In order to establish life work that will support our fullness, we need to challenge this place, to walk through this door and other doors like it, even if we start by just sticking our big toes in the water.

One edge that appears time and again in career counseling is, "How am I going to get paid for it?" Many people in the public service and helping professions feel guilty about receiving payment. Uncomfortable with taking money from an individual, they instead milk the insurance companies for all they can. This scenario points to a misunderstanding of giving and receiving. When we are willing to receive from another (notice I did not use the word *take*), others will want to give to us because their true *need* is to give, rather than to "be taken." When you ask a doctor what his fee is these days, he more often than not feigns ignorance and passes you on to his receptionist. The receptionist can quote you the doctor's exorbitant fee without wincing, since she knows that the insurance company will pay for it. Bureaucracies such as the insurance industry remove all sense of giving and receiving. We have given away this power because most of us are ashamed of the way we give and receive.

In order to get right with money, we must get right with ourselves; we must establish our sense of self-worth and enter fully into the wheel of giving and receiving. We need not be afraid to receive because we have given, and we are certainly more inspired to give when we feel we are not being taken. A Himalayan dwelling holy man, Swami Jnanananda Giri, used to tell me that money is round to keep it rolling. To "keep it rolling" means to enter into the practice of giving and receiving. When we start doing this consciously we actually begin getting paid for our work because we value it, and others receive that which is of value. Our work itself becomes our way of giving back to life. It is an expression of our fullness rather than a need to extract bread from the earth. This is the dance that we negotiate as we work through the heart center.

One woman's life dream was to go to Israel and become an active peace-maker. She had very strong organizational and interpersonal communication skills but no other plan of action. Yet her ideal was more than a fly-by-night fantasy. She had been holding it in her heart for many years, and it had been incubating. Her children were now in college and she felt more ready than ever to set out and see what life would bring. Just as she began to conceive of this as a concrete possibility and actually plan a trip to test the waters, the company she worked for offered her a hefty raise. Her brain went into immediate action. She began thinking: "I could work for five more years, save enough money to secure my future, and then I'll pursue my dream."

This is the position most of us find ourselves in. Our heads and hearts are entangled, and we are forever trying to come up with some mutually satisfying compromise. There is no formula here, no way to say if, when, or how one should forego the security of salary, an established position, or credentials.

Following one's heart does not necessarily mean leaving the established world behind. Some do so in a flourish of heroism and are even lauded by the world. But a teacher of mine who worked with Albert Schweitzer in the jungles of Africa told me that the good doctor's organ music often sounded a bit out of place there. Many who leave the established world in a flourish return with a dejected thud. It is not emotion, then, that will carry us. The heart's energy should not be confused with emotion. What carries us is the incubation, the simmering, the constant reappearance of the dream, the inner call that strengthens with time and demands to be heard.

The distinguished Islamic theologian al-Ghazali (1058–1111), a teacher at the University of Baghdad, was held in the highest respect by his peers, though he secretly felt that his work was not fulfilling some greater part of himself. Something else was calling him. He would listen, consider making a change, and then lose courage, until one day his throat dried up and he could no longer speak. The doctors told al-Ghazali that there was nothing physically wrong with him, but that he was suffering a malady of the soul! Al-Ghazali left Baghdad and studied in seclusion with Sufi mystics for many years. He ultimately returned to teaching with a deepened sense of his calling, and did much to heal the rift between mystical and juridical Islam.[5]

Our calling, then, may often be revealed through our symptoms, illnesses, and discomforts. The heart need not judge. The very energy that may be crippling us may eventually lead us to our vocations. To listen to this calling, in whatever form, is the stuff of courage. It will lead to appropriate action, and you will know that it is appropriate because your being will feel clear, enlivened, and at peace.

To summarize: The basic principle of working with the heart chakra is to create a palpable circuit of giving and receiving. The heart center, the fourth chakra, is itself the fulcrum and can transmute our energies on its own. We need not manipulate, scheme, or even plan. It is enough to open the heart to the edge of risk, to allow the pain, the envy, or whatever other emotions might be present to surface. Letting go of a preconceived outcome, our destiny appears. In this way seemingly negative situations become meetings with destiny; illness and bankruptcy become doors that we walk through to move into a greater reality. As the spasms of nonalignment subside and the intellect settles in its rightful place, we can move more easily with our heart's desire. Rebirth into an anti-career means living the life of the heart.

SUPPORT FLOWS FROM THE OPEN HEART

The heart chakra is the juncture between the upper and lower worlds. Its element is air, the element of communication. The heart chakra is the place in the subtle body where our efforts are transformed through giving and receiving, the place where life is no longer envisioned as a battle, the place where our ideal takes on flesh by bringing it into contact with others.

Whatever we intend to do can never be accomplished in a vacuum. It can only be accomplished through the lawful mechanism of giving and receiving. This is the beauty of the heart chakra. As one moves beyond the bondage of chronic contraction, a vast pool of resources and support opens up. You no longer have to claw your way into corporate doorways or send out a barrage of resumes in the hope that one will land on fertile ground. Rather, by connecting to your core and nourishing that connection, your conviction begins to touch a resonant core within the community. Tom Chapin, Judy Collins, Bob Dylan, Joni Mitchell, George Harrison, and a slew of other recording artists have all been clients of the Mandolin Brothers. This did not happen by supplication, the offering of endorsements, or direct mail campaigns. The Mandolin Brothers' clientele has grown out of their love for music and their support for musicians of all kinds. There has been such a rippling effect that the store remains on Staten Island, well off

the main thoroughfares of New York City, and receives a constant stream of
visitors. Instead of trying to achieve from a place of supposed isolation,
working from the heart creates an increasing opportunity for mutual recognition and collaboration because others no longer feel you coming from a
place of need, or from an ambition that must use manipulation as a modus
operandi. People therefore willingly extend their support to you. This point
is crucial: As long as you exude need, you will drive people away from you.
Consciously or unconsciously, they feel you sucking their energy. When you
exude generosity, an energy of giving from your heart, people naturally
want to support you—they want to be on your team. By supporting you
they sense that they are supporting something greater than an individual,
for you have begun to align yourself with the heart of humanity. It is no
accident that two of the greatest fund-raisers of modern times have been
Mohandas Gandhi and Mother Theresa.

The heart is the place where we begin to put our priorities in the service
of the community. We begin to think and act in terms of sharing our bounty
with the world. We begin to receive because we are able to share, and as this
process develops momentum through experience it begins to cascade until
the most important question becomes this: To what degree can I open to
receive and to share the bounty of existence? The sharing heart is the place
where other's fortunes become our fortunes. Instead of being envious of
another's achievements, we are able to support them, and we in turn are
supported in our achievements because we have taken our true place.

Support is a great mystery, and it takes many forms. On the outer level
there is backing, patronage, encouragement, votes of confidence, and the
rest. But there are also more subtle ways in which support comes to us. How
many times have you felt invisible help coming from somewhere? One
person I know had an experience at the age of five when he was roller
skating down a mountain road and suddenly heard the command: "*Stop.*"
He followed the directive, and just then a huge truck came whizzing by from
an unseen direction. On the average, two thirds of all anti-career workshop
participants have had such experiences. Often however these experiences go
unacknowledged, in part because they are not supported by our general
social environment. But it is the articulation and acknowledgment of such
experiences that will legitimize them in peoples' minds, inviting them to
occur more often. These invisible alliances, these threads of support, are all
around us, and they can be cultivated. If we consciously open to receive
them, we begin to acknowledge the miracle of creation and live in its
dimension.

WORKING WITH THE HEART

There are a number of methods you can use to facilitate the opening of your heart space. One of the strongest, particularly in group work, is the creation of a ritualized sacred space, a *temenos,* in which people can share from the heart. The advantage of this is that you acknowledge your human limitations and create a safe form to explore your edges. You do not try to dissolve into a sea of loving bliss with everything and everyone, and then kick yourself every time you fall out of it. Rather, with each person's agreement and support, you create a sacred circle. You might meet once a week, or perhaps on every full moon. The circle is the nonhierarchical form of sharing that allows hearts to open to each other. There are only two rules for communication and participation in the circle—love and trust. You may like or dislike someone, but within the circle you can love them. This allows the creation of deepened mutuality that enables the heart energies to be expressed beyond romantic or family bonding, which are about the only places where the general culture permits heartfelt expression.

In recent years, we have seen many people free themselves from drug and alcohol dependency through the powerful support of such groups. One may wonder what the ritualized sacred space in Alcoholics Anonymous is? There are no robes or strange chants, no formalized initiation procedures—and this is precisely the point. It is simply the continuity, the support, and the bonding of mutual energy that allows the heart to open, that creates a field free enough from judgment that people can speak their truth. And the moment you speak your truth and are heard, you are creating a heart space that is the pathway of alignment.

Perhaps in the near future, like-minded groups will develop where people can support one another's efforts to manifest the work they love. This is helpful, not as a crutch for emotional weakness, but as a sounding board and support system for those daring to venture forth into the marketplace with a new idea, and for reinforcing the reality of abundance as opposed to the fear of scarcity.

Another practice of unconditional support that can be done individually will open the flow of giving and receiving. Simply choose three people who you want to work with and internally send them a flow of loving support every day. No one else needs to know about this—this is work on the nonphysical plane. Quietly support their essences, their heartfelt desires, and their truths. In doing so you begin to experience the joy of blessing others as opposed to experiencing the "other" as a threat. As idealistic as this might sound, it actually works. Buddhist practitioners have done this for hundreds of years, calling it *maitri* or the offering of friendship.

The anti-career bases itself upon this presupposition: that your life is a gift to be received, and when you receive life as a gift you are inspired to give back with gratitude. This is not obligation, and it is a far cry from the prevalent idea of life as a struggle for survival and/or dominance. Why might it be that so many people struggle to "make it," to "get to the top," and then self-destruct when they get there? Could it be that they finally "arrive," only to find that no one is home? A colleague of mine who is well known in the field of psychology once confided to me that, in his experience, at the end of his profession there is nothing. After all the institutional games of standard setting and certification programs, only the human heart remains.

Another heart-opening technique is applicable to any emotional reaction we experience, especially the so-called negative ones. Instead of riding the roller coaster, we can actually bring our reactions into the heart and work with our experiences of them, as opposed to projecting them onto some one or some situation. At first the heart may remain closed, but by gently bringing our reactions into the heart we begin to acknowledge the possibility of a new kind of resolution, a resolution that is not dependent upon an us-against-them mentality. The Buddhist image for this idea is that of riding in a rowboat and being rammed by another rowboat. Just when you get ready to rant and rave, you see that the other boat is empty. There is no sense of fault to be projected outside, or inside, oneself.

P. D. Ouspensky reports that his Sufi-inspired spiritual teacher George Gurdjieff cultivated these kinds of blameful first reactions in people in order to encourage them to work through such reactions internally. He would invite a group to dinner and everyone at the table would begin to insult one unsuspecting guest, at first very subtly and then more overtly.[6] As the insults grew more intense and the guest reached the point of exploding, Gurdjieff would exclaim "Stop," and instruct the person to follow the path of their reactive anger within.

You do not have to find someone to do this to you. If you drive in New York or on the L. A. freeway, or deal with the errors made by your bank, phone company, credit card company, and the like, there will be plenty of opportunities to practice this inward-looking exercise. It is a good bet that, wherever you may live, your tolerance level toward anger will be challenged. You have the choice to use this energy to move into greater alignment or to remain in the chronic condition of reactive frustration. This does not mean that you should not fight to remedy a negative or unjust situation, but it does mean that you can wage your fight from the place of clarity of purpose as opposed to fighting from your reactions to something or someone else.

FORGIVENESS PROCEEDS FROM STRENGTH

Forgiveness is often regarded as a long, hard task, or else it is believed to be possible only in a flash of divine grace. While the latter may in some instances be true, forgiveness also unfolds as a natural consequence of alignment. When someone has said or done something that hurts you, you do need to acknowledge your woundedness, but you need *not* take on the posture of the victim. You feel the pain of your wounds so that you will respond, and although the intensity of your initial response will be in direct reaction to the way you were injured, the heart's hope is to grow through response, to discover the root of imbalance within yourself, to have the courage to find strength in adversity, and to work to keep the heart open out of this strength and not sentimentality. Courage is associated with the heart center just like openness is. From the place of heartfelt courage it is very difficult to be shaken by another. Someone who has hurt you in the past is no longer threatening. Just as you do not get upset if a five-year-old picks up a stone and throws it at you, you are no longer moved by the ignorance of others. Their actions proceeded from *their* problems, guiding them to act in an inappropriate way in the moment. Most often, hurtful behavior is but a stunted effort at loving. Forgiveness is therefore not necessarily an act of kindness or mercy on your part; it is rather the natural consequence of being filled with universal power, of taking your rooted place in the world. From the place of alignment we take appropriate action. When the other person realizes that they do not have anyone fighting back at them, the situation is open to change.

In meditation classes Hilda would ask us to put two hands in the air, then withdraw one and try to clap. "You see," she would say, "it takes two to create an argument." I remember sitting with Hilda in her living room one day when a call came in from out of state. A former student was on the line, saying: "Hilda, I just want to tell you how sorry I am for you. From my present enlightened condition, I look down and see your plight. Perhaps some day you will attain to my level and be able to see things as I do." Hilda did not wince. She simply said, with sincerity, "Well, that's wonderful, dear. I am so happy for you," and that was the end of it. Hilda was full and free in her power and did not need to create any emotional residue. So let us not misidentify the open heart with flowery softness. The heart is the place of great strength, the lion's strength that is exuded when we move from our authenticity.

The strong heart also allows us to receive valid criticisms and to grow from them, because with courage we are willing to expose ourselves, to listen, and to be vulnerable. When someone points to something that we could be doing better, we need not take it as an affront to our being. We can receive, consider the situation, and move to change ourselves if change is appropriate. A number of spiritual teachers with whom I have worked would save acute criticism for their most advanced students. These were the students who had developed enough strength and balance to receive without being wounded. When the heart center is open, we need not be intimidated by anyone. We are alert and open to share with all. There is a wonderful mantra to use if you ever feel intimidated in a job interview. You simply focus on the person you are meeting and say to yourself, "The God in me meets the God in you." No force, no flight—just honest meeting, heart to heart.

The point of the alignment process, then, is to strengthen the heart. The will becomes tempered in the heart—it develops lion-hearted courage to act from strength and compassion, to act for the greater good. We forgive because we have outgrown the need to react, not because we ought to or because we have learned to wear a sweet, brain-dead smile. We need not walk around with *love* written on our sleeves either, for the heart will transmit its energy in a way that is appropriate for any given situation. The I-Ching tells us that when King When was imprisoned by the tyrant Chou Hsin, he had to darken his light to meet the situation correctly. Otherwise he would have provoked a negative reaction.[7]

The ability to deal directly with situations as they are, as opposed to holding preconceived notions within, is an essential aspect of the heart's wisdom. When I first decided to return to college after seven years of travel, I walked into the Indian studies department at Columbia University and informed the chairperson that I was interested in graduate studies.

"Have you been to India?" he asked.

"Yes," I replied.

"Have you lived in ashrams?" he asked.

This, I knew, was the test, the sticky question. People who have lived in ashrams have a bad reputation and are generally not welcome in universities. I answered honestly, telling him I had lived in ashrams, and proceeded to tell him about all of my travels through India. It turned out that this conversation sealed the success of my admission. I was up front with my answer, and that straightforward approach was greatly appreciated. Had I *thought* more about it at the time, I probably would have answered differently. This was an early teaching for me, and it has been confirmed continually. The heart center is activated through a direct approach to situations, when the God in me meets the God in you.

SURRENDER IS THE ESSENCE OF THE HEART CENTER

Surrender is not an abdication of will or power, but a deepened intimacy with living. Relationship is the means of surrender, for in relationship—whether to people, places, or things—there are no ends that justify the means. However we interact with the moment, we are becoming—being shaped by the offices, typewriters, coffee machines, schedules, looks in the eyes of doormen or cab drivers, and we are shaping them in return.

The heart center is by nature inclusive, while the pursuit of one's private design excludes. Our work habits have become such that we no longer have much time for anyone or anything outside of our daily milieu. The stranger is suspect, and the constant shoring up of our walls has lead to mass exhaustion. The openness to shared pleasure and experience is intimacy, warmth, compassion, and love—it lets "the other" in.

Ultimately we have to decide if we are going to live for love or for our impoverished and fearfully conditioned concepts. Compassion does not mean martyrdom; it does not require us to be available for everyone else until you have nothing left. It does mean having an inclusive vision so that your work supports those around you. This does not exclude competition, for even competition can be supportive as the mutual inspiring of one another to do better, as shown in the film "Chariots of Fire."

As the youthful J. Krishnamurti said, "The first step is the last step." It is the living, the offering of our energies to the machinery of the world, that is the challenge, and this is why the heart center is a place of courage and action. Without the courageous actions to live what we know is true in our hearts, we remain on the outside. Taking time for another, widening the perspective of the job search to see how it can support existence, risking rejection or failure, and believing in our God-given abilities—these qualities will move us into work that will be effective, no matter where we are in space and time. And so we ask with every career move, "How does this support life?" Trust, Ask, Listen, and Live. The reward of the heart is community in its highest sense.

Green and Gold:
A Prosperity Meditation

Work meditatively within yourself to establish the strength of the base triangle—strongly rooted in the earth, at ease and flowing in water, and burning strongly in fire. Breathe in and out of the heart chakra, the spiritual center located behind the midpoint of the breast bone, in front of the spine. As you breathe in and out, feel the electromagnetic current of the breath warming you, relaxing you, softening you. As your heart center softens, it begins to glow in tones of soft green and burnished gold.

Green—the color of ever-renewing life and the flower-bearing spring, bringing with them unforeseen openings. Love, once off in the distance, now comes closer. Feel the rhythm of all life as you move deeply into the region of the heart. Gone are the fears of not being accepted. Gone are the worries of yesterday, tomorrow, and even today. Gone are past, present, and future.

Within the heart you approach presence. Feel this inner presence, and let the soft green energy wash over you and through you. If there is anyone against whom you have been holding a grudge, or anyone with whom you have been feeling annoyed, bring them into this soft green and feel a spark of renewal, a gentle letting go. Breathe freely now, soaring through the inner air, borne as on wings—the air messenger, eagle's wings, on to the Spirit most high. Allow the heart to open gently unto this sensation. There is no enemy for one who holds the sun in the heart. Let the experience of these words sink in deeply: There is no enemy, there is no fear for me who holds the sun in my heart.

The brilliant, blazing sun—let it shine within. In its rays visualize a temple with a gold, arching stairway and two lions on either side. This is the inner sanctum. Walk slowly and with dignity up the stairway and through the lions who guard the gates without fear, for they now protect you and reflect your courage to live for love in a love-starved world. Feel your entire being strengthened and radiant with the power of creation. For it is at the heart where the divine intersects with the human, and it is here that human life is forged into its offering to shine forth in the world.

Inside the temple is a great open space. There is a place for you to sit before a golden altar. You are guided to sit in this place, from which you may ask the questions: "How can I live from my heart? How can I love and be loved? How can I heal and be healed?" Ask, and feel inside for the answers, be they in words, colors, sensation, or song. See yourself moving and acting from this place in your life. See how everything you touch with your hand is consciously extended from your heart, how all your thoughts and ideas are touched by the grace of loving kindness.

When you are ready, when you feel filled, proceed to the altar and receive an object that will remind you of who you are, that will remind you that at heart thou art. Now slowly rise and exit the temple, leaving the door open so that you can return when it is appropriate to be renewed and to renew. As you breathe in and out, feel the depths of your heart touching the heart of God. Let gratitude come forth—gratitude for the miracle of life, gratitude for being who you are and where you are, gratitude that you can participate at this time in the renewal of the world. And as you feel this sense of appreciation, let three people come into your mind—whomever happens to appear first—and send them a loving flow of energy from your heart to theirs in support of their soul journeys, their growth, and their lives. Then visualize a rainbow of light that extends from the hearts of others to yourself—from your parents, ancestors, teachers, friends. Through the generations this extended rainbow of giving and receiving exists. We receive from others and open ourselves to transmit, thus receiving more and extending ourselves more. We are part of a never-ending rainbow of caring and sharing, a rainbow that extends from heart to heart, through space and time, since the beginning.

Stay in this energy for as long as you feel it moving. Breathe in and out. Be at peace.

8

The Fifth Chakra: Creative Vision

In dreams begin our possibilities.
William Shakespeare

What is popularly called *vision,* as in the vision of a person or an enterprise, is neither about visualization, planning, or mission statements, although a vision can include any of these. To be a visionary is to be able to sense what is still unknown, to be able to conceive of and imagine a possibility that does not yet exist in physical form. The traditional color associated with the creative visionary center—the fifth chakra—is blue, perhaps related to the spaciousness of the sky into which we can look up from the known and dream. The throat and voice are related to this center, indicating the creative power of the word—not only the specific, culturally bound word of signifier and signified, but the preconceptual vibratory energy of sound that words hold like a chalice when they are filled with soulful presence.

Sound strongly enters and effects the unconscious. The trumpets of Joshua sent the walls of Jericho tumbling down; the sound and rhythm of rock music brought down the Berlin wall. Music carries the vision of a culture, penetrating conscious barriers. The energy of a vision, then, is not necessarily found in statements and declarations. The lyrics and melodies of rock music would be ineffective without the underlying rhythms that communicate their essential energies. In a similar way, the vision of a society is encoded, often covertly, in its various forms of culture. Even if symbols of religion and statehood, the traditional carriers of vision, are seemingly done away with, the visionary domain reappears in our distractions. Advertising, sports, and situation comedies now transmit our collective visionary energy.[1] Its underside is carried in the classified ads of tabloids and by thousands of fringe groups passionately attached to their particular ideologies.

Creative vision is as natural as breathing, and it will emerge naturally and powerfully to the degree that one is aligned in body, mind, and heart. As our priorities are clarified and we become established in our self-worth and passion, our heart connections will generate enthusiasm like sunshine. The mind glows, reflecting this creative emergence, and begins to picture a world full of possibilities. This sort of imaging is a natural corollary of growth and has nothing to do with deliberate manipulation of the imaginative faculty used in certain techniques of visualization or self-programming. If our imaging is not genuine, if we have to go against our own grain to create a form, we are at cross-purposes with ourselves and are again setting ourselves up for sabotage. When our visionary faculties are aligned with our core energy, emotions, will, and heart, the visionary faculty extends our personal purview to the social and ultimately to the higher collective body.

Living with vision enables us to conceive of new roles for ourselves in the cosmic marketplace, and to transform the expectations we hold of others as well. When someone prefaces a statement by saying, "I know this sounds crazy, but . . . " it indicates that what they are saying is truly important, as it likely contains a kernel of vision. The apprehension around sounding "crazy" has to do with the fear of being exposed, of losing the protection of the habitual posture to which we have attached our self-worth. This posture often relates to a collective vision to which we are bound—as in believing, as people once did, that the earth is flat. In leaving a collective vision behind, we risk ridicule and rejection from those who are accustomed to our former patterns. To break through such consensus hypnosis takes great energy, the energy garnered through alignment. The more comfortable we become with the promptings of our own being, the safer we will feel about going out on a limb.

When we give up a collective construct, it is not other people who will reject us. Rather, we create opposition to the degree that we ourselves are still unsure of our visions. Consciously or unconsciously, we hold on to our ideas of how others will see us. We expect to be opposed or ridiculed, and such a response challenges us to reexamine our intuitions and motivations. Is the opposition due to the content of our idea, or the baggage from our own labyrinth that we are dragging along with it? A man I know who is passionately involved in the effort to reintroduce bicycles into our auto-gorged world complained that he felt like a black sheep whenever he spoke of his work in a social situation. Upon further examination he realized that the fact that most other people drove automobiles was not what was making him feel ostracized. There were personal factors involved, inner disharmonies that he was re-enacting in his current situation. Once again we return to the need to continually do our own inner work to successfully enact our visions.

As an emerging vision gathers momentum, it infiltrates our conscience. We can no longer live a lie, and the vision thus moves us to change our patterns and to share our insights with others. George Bernard Shaw, for example, was quite commercially successful as a young man, but he felt like he was wasting his life away in the business world and could no longer walk on a road that was not his own. The truth and power of the inner being overrides our self-possession, and we find that when what we want to do becomes okay with us, it is okay with everybody else. There may certainly still be opposition to the project, but we will not be stung personally by that opposition. We will be able to understand and work with it as part of the overall situation. As the I-Ching says, "On your own day, you are believed."

Through the visionary element, then, we are able to open doors and enter into new roles in the world. But these roles will be actualized only to the extent that others accept and work with them. Working with visionary energy has to do with much more than going out and finding one's vision. Yes, we must believe in ourselves or we will never be believed, but there is an interactive process to consider as well. In fact, in order to simply interact on a social level we have to accept the visions of our community as expressed in its language and customs.

Developing our visions, then, has to do with developing the correspondent quality of our interactions. Will our actions be determined by preconceived kinship roles or corporate standards of conduct? Will our professional lives be determined by the visions of others as we spend our days trying to fit into a strange suit of clothes? Will we get sucked into the vision of a profession, learning a jargon and believing that we are now knowledgeable? Will we learn to think like doctors, lawyers, or media people and lose our authentic selves in the bargain? Will the people we work with be the same people we would like to invite to our homes, or will we find ourselves socializing out of obligation? Will our visions be synchronized with our work, or will our lives be split into necessity and escape? Being conscious of one's integral vision will help answer these questions. The cultivation of that vision need not be an egocentric one. The passage of vision into form brings with it the potential for deep friendships and bonds resulting from sharing that which is meaningful and working toward its realization.

Developing our visionary abilities will not happen through adopting a cause, taking a course on psychic powers, or deciding to live a noble life. It will happen when we accept ourselves as we are, when we honor and act on our promptings and our fundamental concerns, whatever they may be. This will lead us to associate with people, places, and institutions that share our goals and values. Our enthusiasm shared with others will then generate sparks of life, and creativity will be at work. Even solo artists are mutually inspired by one another's works. Picasso and Braque frequently visited one another's studios at the height of the Cubist era.

Visionary capacity is a force of life, and it needs to be shared. It cannot be established in a vacuum.

VISION IS A COLLECTIVE PHENOMENON

There is no such thing as a singular visionary. Vision springs from the well of the collective. The time has to be right, the place has to be right, and there has to be enough cultural leverage to accommodate the shifting of paradigms.

How is this possible? Does one person suddenly and consciously conceive of an idea and other people then follow? This is highly doubtful, as the hundredth-monkey theory or Rupert Sheldrake's paradigm of the morphological field illustrate. The hundredth-monkey theory holds that when enough momentum builds in one place (that is, when one hundred monkeys on one island innovate a new activity) a similar paradigm shift will occur somewhere else (on another island). In Sheldrake's work, change is seen to occur with less effort as a new pattern begins to appear in several places at once. But such sketches only attempt to describe how mass change might occur; where innovation or mutation actually comes from remains a mystery. To be creative is to participate in this mystery, in its tribulations and challenges as well as in its inventive possibilities.

Vision wells up from the collective. It comes upon us. We can try to meet it but we cannot own it. Planning, when too tightly controlled and goal-oriented, does not allow space for the creative, and this holds as true in the job market as in any other milieu. If you have a preconceived notion of the outcome, of the job that you want, that is all you can achieve. Most goal-oriented people place a high value on outcomes because they still see themselves enmeshed in poverty. Therefore the best they can become is someone or something other than who or what they are. The practice of goal achievement, when not aligned with the creative center, is antivisionary and produces facsimiles at best.

Creative vision, on the other hand, constantly widens the field of possibility, putting people and situations together in new and unexpected ways. Where goal setting may actualize potential, creative vision synergizes potential: a person may thus attract employment possibilities that could not have been conceived of beforehand. When you love someone, you are always thinking about that person and ways in which you can be with them. Likewise, when your priority comes from the heart, you are always visualizing new potentials for its manifestation, and this ongoing process creates the etheric blueprint that brings its form into being.

After a good deal of self-reflection, Chris Townley realized that most of the work in his life had somehow been associated with the theme of housing. He had been a contractor, a construction worker, and a real estate agent. Chris realized that, although none of those jobs now felt nourishing to him, his overall vision and expertise was still focused on making a dwelling simultaneously more functional and more aesthetically pleasing.

Chris did not quit his job or immediately decide what his next move would be. Rather, seeing his life path as one of constant learning, he followed his vision, taking time to study the art of housing from different perspectives. He began to focus on the concept of inner environments, developing a deep sense of how a place feels and what its strengths and weaknesses are. This generative vision eventually led him to design school in New York where he was introduced to *feng shui,* the Chinese art of geomantic architecture and decoration in which one increases a person's or institution's potential by redecorating and arranging their residence or place of business. Chris's vision had led him to the place and to the person who would teach him this art. Within two years' time he began a successful real estate appraisal practice. He did not have to claim proficiency in *feng shui* on his business card, but he had greatly deepened his vision of what a residence was all about and could now employ that deepened vision in his work.

Growing organically, like a many-branched tree, Chris continues to allow new working possibilities to emerge from his matured sense of what a dwelling can be. He has developed a high-end finishing business, creating fine store and building fronts using decorative plaster techniques learned from Italian fresco paintings. His business has financed his study of fresco design in Italy, and he has pursued his interest in the "alchemy of dwelling" by learning to mix various elements such as cinnabar, marble dust, and various oxides and pigments into the plaster to balance out a dwelling and maximize its energetic potential.

WORKING WITH THE CREATIVE CENTER

The fifth chakra opens us to visions as opposed to fantasies. Fantasy is not necessarily negative, but it is *the energetic response to fantasy* that will bring positive results. If fantasy is not responded to, it becomes, in the words of Robert Johnson, an energy leak.[2] It is the creative faculty squandering itself into wishful thinking. Wishing for what one does not have is a symptom of unaligned energy. This energy can continue leaking, or it can be used as the raw material for creative action.

Traditionally the fifth chakra corresponds to the word and its creative power. And it does what word, as *logos*, implies: it creates and orders, it brings in the new as it crystallizes the full spectrum of our powers and aptitudes. The creative imagination operates more powerfully through pictures and feelings than through words or concepts. A strong priority becomes stronger through envisioning its possibility and cultivating the feeling that arises with it. To cultivate a vision we need to maintain a relationship with our emerging fantasies, dreams, and ideas, paying attention to their signs. The actual growth of a vision is organic. It moves to its own rhythm and cannot be jump started or pushed from behind.

The beginning of a new vision may be felt as restlessness or a vague uneasiness with the way things are. Such a feeling needs to be allowed to come in and be paid attention to, not disposed of or ignored.

It takes a certain maturity to translate such a feeling into effective action. As one participant in a workshop noted, "If I articulate my vision, I will then have to do something about it!" You may feel restless at work and begin to constantly fantasize about being somewhere else, or come home every night and sedate yourself with television just to relieve the unpleasant tension. The energy required to bring the restlessness into line is found in the will to ask, to inquire into this restlessness, to see where it is leading. You might bring it into the women's lodge on the medicine wheel and discover layers of feeling underneath it, explore how it appears in your dreams, and begin to connect with its power source. In this way, you move feelings and occurrences into insights about where you need to move forward. You begin to galvanize the energy into a vision and ultimately take action that will respond to your feeling. If it is boredom, for example, acknowledge it, notice its qualities in detail, ask for its message, listen to your dreams and to the reactions of other people, and notice exactly where and when this feeling comes upon you. In this way you make initial contact with the messenger of a possible future.

The messenger—be it a feeling, incident, or physical symptom—is the harbinger of the visionary process, and patient attentiveness is the key to its fruition, for the fifth chakra has as much to do with listening as with creative speech. When it is time to listen to the messenger, listen. You cannot force his hand. If you are dissatisfied with your job, you must move into the source of the dissatisfaction, dialogue with it, and allow it to bring you its message. Perhaps the answer is not to look for another job, but to begin developing a skill that you have always toyed with but never taken upon yourself to do. Stan Jay collected vintage guitars for years before he began selling them, and he was selling them on the side for a number of years before opening Mandolin Brothers. Perhaps dissatisfaction with the job is pointing toward a necessary attitude change or a need to rework a relationship with someone. Very often clients will say "I hate my job," when the truth is that they dislike their spouse.[3] Patience and attention will allow you to direct this initial energy rather than dissipating it.

As you listen to the message of the initial energy, you are gradually able to envision a new possibility. And because you have listened to the messenger, your new idea is more than a reflex reaction to your discomfort. It is able to carry the power of change. You begin not only to imagine another way but to take actions, even if they be symbolic ones like buying an article of clothing that relates to your evolving focus. [Such actions signal your subconscious that you are indeed ready for a change.]

As a vision develops, your dreams will provide guidance, as will the course of your original symptoms of dissatisfaction. And you can always open to this course by imaging the symptom. In a technique similar to the Jungian practice of active imagining, you feel into a symptom such as boredom and ask for its image, then allow the image to move, change, grow, and speak to you. Perhaps boredom will appear as a yawning spinster in a large white house in the 1800s. Following the image, go into the details and let them begin to uncover the issues that underlie the emotion or symptom. For example, perhaps the spinster suddenly develops a patch of gray around the throat area. You then move into the image of the throat, asking for its qualities. Going right to the gray, you might find a smoldering fire, squelched energy that has not been expressed. In this way you trust your inner being to guide you as you open to the feeling power of each new image. Such work will enable your visions to take form, for you are no longer covering up but are rather *uncovering* your life energy.

At one point in this process you will be challenged. An opportunity will be presented—a door will open or close. Sometimes an entire company relocates or goes under, or a friend may call with a new job prospect. Whatever the situation, the test is one of action. Are you willing to act on your feelings and intuitions? Are you willing to risk change?

The moment we opt for action, the door opens wide. It may not be the particular situation we expected, but we have crossed over the line of doubt and hesitation, and the natural release of energy will begin to activate and concretize the vision. We will begin to move with enthusiasm. New energy will create new ideas, new enthusiasm, and new resistances. This is all part of the process of trusting, asking, listening, and living.

Our visions becomes more firmly implanted in the ether as we begin creating inner foundations from which outer form will grow. The word *ether* in this case refers to the element of space, the element of the fifth chakra. Space, or *akasha* in Sanskrit, is the element that contains all others: earth, air, fire, and water float in and are interpenetrated by space. Having sufficient space around oneself is a necessary condition for the growth of a vision. If we are cluttered, the seeds of vision will not be nourished, for a new imprint needs to be made and to take hold in the psyche. As discussed earlier in regard to time management, when we allow enough space in and around ourselves, we will be able cultivate a new possibility. We will have room to begin acting a new part.

The person who holds an authentic vision of being a doctor and is pursuing medical training may begin to act like a physician or will model other doctors who are aligned with his vision. Modeling is very effective, as the practice of Neuro Linguistic Programming has shown. In traditional cultures, modeling was known as transmission. It was not a calculated modeling, however, but an organic evolution that resulted from working with a teacher. Such transmission occurs automatically as we gravitate toward people who embody our developing visions and learn from them. There is no need to consciously copy the master. Rather, when you stay in a teacher's energy field for a certain period of time, you automatically absorb the discipline in a way that is right for you.

During the time I worked with the shaman Orestes, a group of thiry people met every Monday night and participated in healings. During my five years with Orestes I do not remember him teaching us anything! Never did he say, "This is how to contact your guides," or "This is how to remove negative energy from someone's field," although this is what we were doing. We learned from Orestes because we were aligned in purpose. We all wanted to help others and to explore exciting and then unknown practices of healing. Orestes was the embodiment of our vision; he activated our energies by example. During those five years we unconsciously attuned to his way of working and by doing so learned to develop the same energies that he used in healing. I did not fully realize this until two years after his death. I was working with a client and noticed that I was tapping my pencil on the table, exactly like Orestes used to do. Suddenly various configurations of subtle energies around the person were visible to me, in much the same way that Orestes used to describe them. There had been a transference of wisdom, energy, and technique in working with him, but it had never been forced at any time. It was a natural outcome of alignment.

One of the chief ways that an initial vision develops and matures is through this kind of mentorship. By aligning yourself with the particular field and your own authenticity, you will be drawn to the mentor who is suited to your growth and who needs your kind of stimulation, for the mentor needs to teach as much as you need to learn.

Ron Young' story is a good case in point. Ron apprenticed with Orestes for a number of years. He did not find Orestes in the phone book or through a professional institution. In fact, before meeting Ron Young, Orestes had not taught Americans at all. When he met Orestes, Ron was already an accomplished healer. He had been initiated into a number of healing modalities and had a thriving practice. His passionate interest was the human energy field, as he sought to understand how various visible and non-visible influences worked on the body, mind, and spirit. Through the healing community in New York, Ron had heard about a man who would put your head next to a bowl of water, look into the bowl, and accurately diagnose illness as well as its cause; about a man who cured people by wiping their bodies down with flowers.

Before he met Orestes, Ron had a series of dreams indicating that he was about to encounter someone who embodied an entirely new understanding of the art of healing. A short while after these dreams, Ron was visiting a friend whose cancer had gone into remission after working with Orestes. The person casually mentioned that he was going out to see Orestes that day, and Ron went with him. After Orestes worked with his patient, he looked at Ron and invited him into the circle to be worked on. Ron Young was in the right place at the right time. He was deeply impressed by the initial experience with Orestes, and the resonance was apparently mutual, for Orestes invited Ron to bring to him people who were in genuine need. Young would repeatedly give up an entire day's work to bring one client to Orestes. He would arrive early and leave late, sweeping the floor and cleaning up after Orestes had left. Young describes his initial experience with Orestes as one of being in a "pressure cooker." He had to learn an entirely new way of perceiving, a totally unfamiliar language for understanding health and illness. It took months before Ron developed confidence in his ability to actively participate in this sort of shamanic healing, and he wondered at times if he was meant to be there. Then, just when Ron began to feel some assuredness with the work, as if on schedule Orestes said, "Okay, you can bring as many people as you want on Wednesdays." And this is how the teaching began. Within six months there were full-fledged classes and healing sessions happening two days a week.

Ron Young worked well with Orestes because there was an alignment of sensibility, a deep commitment to the path of healing, and a mutual modality of intuitive comprehension. Ron enjoyed learning by osmosis. He had already done much work in the inner realms and was quite gifted intuitively. But Orestes actually acknowledged him as a healer and taught Young how to "earth" energy for manifestation. It was through this acknowledgment, as much as through the teachings, that Ron's innate abilities blossomed, and extraordinary healings and transformations occurred through his work. In Orestes' tradition the teachings are meant to be passed on, usually to a family member. Orestes had traced his own lineage from his grandmother to his father; no one in Orestes' immediate family, however, was willing or able to receive these teachings. Orestes well understood the laws of giving and receiving. What was the value of a teaching that could not be passed on for future generations? Orestes found a vessel in Ron Young, someone who was ready and willing to accept the teachings. In Orestes, Ron Young found someone who could move him into his greater power as a healer. This is how mentorship is born.

After a number of years, however, their visions began to diverge. Young realized that he had to heal in his own way as opposed to working uniquely from the perspective of Orestes' traditional practice. Once again Ron had a number of dreams that indicated the need to change directions, and once again—as if on cue—Orestes responded. One day after a strenuous session, Orestes turned to Ron and said, "When I learned all I could learn from my spiritual teacher, I said 'Good-bye, I'm leaving,' and I never went back."

Leaving a mentor is never easy, and yet if you stay past your term you become a perpetual disciple. You never achieve your own integral power but instead remain a branch on someone else's tree. Traditional cultures had initiations that ritualized the process of departure and enabled one to go through it with minimal psychic damage. We may not have this option nowadays, but we have the gift of sensitivity to our inner beings. We know when we pass the moment that we are no longer in training. If you hold to your vision and pay attention, you will know when it is time to go. The vision itself will create the circumstances of its manifestation.

Your truth will create the right action and the right people to bring that about, so notice who you are drawn to. Athletes will be drawn to other athletes, musicians to other musicians, and so on. This is, in fact, a very good vocational barometer—not filling in the slots of someone else's vision disguised as an aptitude test, but noticing who you are repeatedly drawn to, who keeps coming into your path. This is the way a vision generates and perpetuates itself through the collective. One person is drawn to another, or you are drawn to a particular discipline or a vision of a way of doing something. You may carry a vision for a while; a vision may even move you or be seemingly forced upon you by circumstances for a while, but you do not own it, just as you do not own your career. Both vision and career are vehicles for your growth and for the growth of the world.

SUSTAINING VISION THROUGH RITUAL

The manner in which contemporary Japanese exchange business cards, the way Americans celebrate the Super Bowl, and the practice of graduation ceremonies are all ritualistic gestures that perpetuate a collective vision. These gestures convey the particular values that are being fostered in a way that mere words cannot, and they maintain the form of a collective vision to such a degree that to not have them present is to feel disoriented.

The fact that ritual can be deadening need not be detailed: most of us have first hand experience of that. What many people have not experienced is a ritual practice that stems from the living spirit. It is just this kind of practice, which can only take place at the grass roots, that keeps our visions alive on an individual as well as a community level. As the dominance of the national states and old-world religions continue to wane, rituals will arise that again reflect particular localities and the deep concerns of the beings who live there. As we allow ourselves to be drawn by our visions and to share them with others, the proper rituals will arise from the community itself.

In my own community of Cold Spring, New York, a winter solstice ceremony was begun through the vision of a pioneering woman named

Jane Marcy. Jane named her photography studio Inner Focus, and developed it into a space that also serves as a meditation and alternative education center. At first there was an idea for a single winter solstice celebration. Other people from the community got involved and offered the Manitoga Nature Center for the location. Another local resident, a professional storyteller, became involved, and on the night of the solstice, in the pouring rain, stories were told around a bonfire, candles were lit, drums and instruments were played, and prayers were offered. The rain did not put the fire out; instead they glistened and reflected off of one another. With no public announcements, more than thirty people came together in the freezing rain. Many present experienced a sense of timeless connectedness that could not have been planned. When the next winter approached, a few people came to Inner Focus to discuss the possibility of creating a similar ceremony, perhaps with a different theme or in a different location. But this was not to happen. It was impossible to change the format, the location, or anything else. It was as if it was written somewhere that things had to be done just as they had been the year before. Suddenly we realized that we had a ritual on our hands.

Ritual is more than a set of conventional or symbolic practices. The word itself stems from the Vedic *rta*, which refers to the inherent order of things—the time when the sun rises, when the frost appears, when the spring returns. This order also applies to the organization of the human psyche. When one is inspired (or one may even say impregnated) by a living vision, the psyche and hence daily life will organize itself around that vision, not around the contemporary nine-to-five expectation. And true magic can be effected by the way in which we order our daily lives. It is a magic borne of organization in its most organic sense. Instead of sacrificing our lives to the crippled vision of industrial productivity or to the whimsical apathy of nonengagement, we can allow our heart's vision to create its corresponding lifestyle.

There are many ways this might come about. Some people are inspired by visions, some are impregnated by visions, and others are burdened by visions. To be true to one's vision does not necessarily mean that you will sail through life with a healthy smile or retire to millionaire acres. There are those who take on visions through illness or depression. Marcel Proust unraveled the desperate life around him through a vision of a cookie taken from a jar. Stephen King has been inspired by and has expressed horrific visions that strike deep chords in the present generation. The morbid so-called negative and painful sides of our beings also need expression, and therefore being true to our visions of weakness or depression may lead to extremely creative states and gifts to be offered to the world. It is crucial to understand that holding to a vision and working with it is different from identifying with it. Whatever plot of ground you are given, that ground is yours to till, and from that plot will come your offering to the world.

Whatever the content, receptivity to your vision will bring an increased strength to organize and to create, for an inspired vision marshals higher forces around it and engages others who have a congruent purpose. When the purpose becomes clear, anchored, and conscious, the time, space, and personnel become available, because the forces that are bringing it into being surpass individual intention. One can literally feel the thrill of working with the forces of creation.

APPROACHING THE JOB MARKET AS A VISIONARY

Unless and until one is working with a conscious vision, the job market will be a threatening behemoth. Many try to avoid it or to eke out just enough subsistence from it to try and live their real life on the side. The concept of the market itself puts certain people off and causes others to again miss the mark by living in the market instead of in the world.

Like a body, a market is a living organism. It is a collective body and its form is determined by collective values. The market perfectly reflects the values of the collective. If a certain group is able to rig the market, it is because the collective allows this to happen. Dictators exist because enough people want them to; they may offer a convenient way of abdicating individual responsibility. The same is true for multinational corporations. They, and the quality of life they bring with them, are not the villains; they are our own creation. When there is sufficient alternative visionary activism and activity, their forms will change.

Many career counselors speak about the market in terms of forecasting. They might come out with an article on jobs that are hot in the nineties, for example, or where the "smart money" is going. This follow-the-market thinking may create brief stints of success, but it will not create an anti-career, for it is still based on the selling of one's integrity to the system. On the other hand, if you align with your authentic connection, allow your feelings to lead you, focus your priorities based on the truth of your inner being, and open your heart to the community, you will begin to create your vision and share it with others. Because this vision is your own, no one can steal it from you. It cannot be compromised for marketing purposes. And because the vision is authentic, it will resonate with others who have congruent visions. You will be led to be in your right place at your right time.

The true visionary does not cater to the market. Rather, a market grows around a powerful vision, for the vision is itself an expression of collective energy and desire. Therefore every authentic vision carries within itself its own market, but it may not be the market you currently imagine. If you are serious about your vision, you have to give it higher priority than the market. Otherwise the market becomes your vision, and you end up spending your life enmeshed in some popularity contest.

As your vision gains strength through action, its alignment will move you to where you need to be in order to accomplish each phase of its development. How, when, and where this might happen is not your real concern. All you must do is hold to your authenticity and be willing to pay attention and learn from life. No one is promising you a trip down a yellow brick road. If you do what you love, the money may not follow, but you will become yourself—you will ultimately understand the wisdom of your life process and you will die with integrity and in peace.

Edgar Cayce had the vision of founding an institute that would educate and heal people. He was led to a specific area and piece of land. The first building he erected burned down. At the second attempt he went bankrupt. Does this mean that he was on the wrong track? No. The Association for Research and Enlightenment in Virginia Beach, Virginia attests to the authenticity and power of Cayce's project and its purpose. But the vision manifested in its own time, and the lessons learned through the manifestation process were just as important as the developing form. Therefore, do not judge or measure how you are doing by how many clients are coming into your office. The measure of a successful vision is how you go to sleep at night and how you wake up in the morning. If you pass into sleep at peace with yourself, the world, and everyone in it, your vision is working for you. If you wake up filled with energy and enthusiasm to begin a new day, you are successfully engaging in an anti-career.

DEZANGER PARADIGM SHIFTS

At times in our lives we seem to arrive at a stalemate. Our visions are going nowhere, and we tend to get down on ourselves. If we fall prey to such judgments we may prematurely abandon our projects as we go looking for greener pastures. We have then forgotten the cardinal rule of the anti-career: Be where you are! Instead of damning your situation, you can re-envision it. You can begin to see that right in front of you is a clue pointing toward another way.

The paradigm-shift exercise stimulates your vision, encouraging you to open your perceptions to another way of seeing the very same situation that was apparently blocked. Andre Dezanger, the inventor of this visual exercise, co-authored the book *Tao of Creativity* with his partner, sculptor Judith Morgan. They have included the paradigm-shift exercise in creativity seminars for a number of years. The exercise is used as a method for breaking old patterns—visions that have fossilized into habitual ways of seeing the world and that no longer serve us—and for instigating new visionary possibilities. The exercise is as follows:

> Copy the figure below onto a piece of paper that you can put in front of you for meditation. You may want to copy the figure several times using different colors of paper, and work with the color that inspires you that day. At the same time every day, stare at the figure with your eyes unfocused until it shifts, that is, until a new way of seeing the figure reveals itself. Dezanger suggests that while you are doing this, you may also fold your arms or hands in the opposite way than you usually do. You will notice that when you fold your arms or hands, the dominant hand usually places itself on top of the other hand. Reverse this position. As you gaze at the figure you might also repeat the mantra, "There is another way."

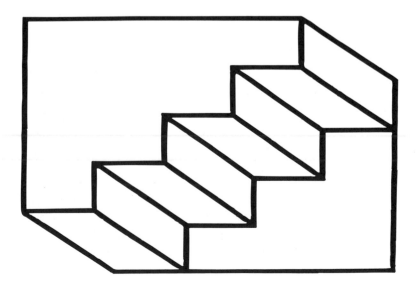

According to Andre Dezanger, only one minute per day of concentration on this figure is necessary, but the practice should be sustained for a minimum of twenty-one days, which is time enough for new neural pathways to begin to form. You are thus retraining your visionary faculty to perceive new possibilities. Once another way is acknowledged, it will manifest in tangible areas in your life, for a subtle change in perspective can have a powerful effect down the line.

From the perspective of the fifth chakra, the paradigm-shift exercise is a marvelous tool to energize originality and to help us move out of visionary standstills. This model supports the idea that we have much more energy and opportunity available to us than we habitually believe. There *is* another way, there is *always* another way to view a situation, one that will give us greater options and opportunities. If you feel blocked, this is a good place to start: Do not fight where you are, but try to see it in another way.

Vision is not made, it is born. But you are the midwife. If you do not assist in its birth, it will retreat back into fantasy or wishful thinking. You assist in its birth by working to align the vision itself, and then to align yourself with the vision. The visionary faculty is aligned with the heart center through the desire to love and to give. This process calls in the future. The future is then able to enter your present space and inspire the process of creation. This is not achieved by coercion or calculation but by trust, alignment, and the subsequent exercise of visionary action. Through such action you begin to play again, for visions are extremely energizing. Following them turns a mundane life into an adventure.

Fifth Chakra Meditation: Anchoring into the Future

Breathe in slowly. Breathe out fully. Allow yourself to center. When you have centered, work to establish the base triangle in your being— the precious alignment of trust, feeling, and focus. See this triangular alignment of the first three chakras rooting you, empowering you, and giving you the energy to move into the heart center, to open your heart to the world community, to share what you have to give, to become a force in the realignment of this world through love. Feel this possibility in your heart.

Place your attention in the heart center. Receive on the in-breath; offer on the out-breath. Take your time to move consciously into the circuit of giving and receiving, into a place that is free from the need to dominate or be dominated by anyone, able to exchange and share in an open flow. And as you become established in this circuit, receive again the energy from previous generations and offer your own life energy to the community of the future.

Imagine now that a path slowly emerges from your heart center to your throat. Work with the breath to open this channel, visualizing the energy of giving and receiving being expressed through your own voice. Open this channel from the heart center to the great, infinite, open space of creativity that is the throat center.

You are now able to express your desires. You are now able to articulate how you really feel without shame or fear of retribution. Instead of worrying about what to say or what to do, you can allow the creative flow to move through your heart and your throat out into the world as the Word itself.

If you feel any blockage in your throat chakra, breathe the color of a beautiful deep blue into the throat center, stimulating your ability to listen as well as to speak, generating the ability to shapeshift and to move through time and space. Feel your power to open to new possibilities, to new ways of seeing reality. Feel your ability to play with the energies of creation, to dance with the great wisdom, and to move into being something beyond anything that you have ever imagined because your imagination is now set free.

Envision an etheric stairway of seven steps emerging from your throat and imagine that this stairway, made of the element of space, allows you to move into other dimensions. See yourself walking very gracefully up the seven steps of this etheric stairway, at each step dropping more of your preconceptions of how things are. With each step, let go of any fixed ideas about your possibilities. Walk through the etheric clouds right through form, through time, and through the three-dimensional world.

At the top of this stairway you come to a doorway. Open the doorway and perceive into another dimension, into future time, not simply ten years from now but eons ahead, where the self that you are, the self that is unfolding like a seed within you, has achieved its full potential. See yourself in all your glory radiating energy and freedom, fully accomplished, working in a way that is perfect and excitingly creative for everything and everyone. Allow yourself to attune to this radiant being who is you in your future. Ask what it is that you need to learn, what you need to do, what you need to create in order to move into your optimum future. What qualities do you need to develop in order to become who you ultimately are? Allow yourself to receive the answers in a flow of radiance. Take them fully into your being, feeling subtle changes in your body, in your thought structure. Be open to the new, to the re-creation of your life's pattern. As you radiate gratitude toward this being, leave a doorway open, knowing that you can return to this place whenever it is appropriate for you to connect with the pull of the future.

Gradually descend the etheric stairway step by step, but do not simply put on the layers of the world. Only accept that which is truly aligned with your future. Take those colors, vibrations, and possibilities that have called you to the future as you move back to the throat chakra. Breathe in and out. Feel the connection between the throat and the heart, and between the heart and the base triangle. Feel the power of your passion and your purpose. Feel an alignment from the etheric plane right down to the earth, and know that you can walk forth and do things that you have never done before, because on some level you have already done them. There is no need to be limited by your thoughts. Feel your unlimited creative potential as you breathe in and breathe out of the fifth chakra, bathing in a blue ocean of etheric creation. Feel the part of you that is beyond time and space openly connecting with that part of you that is in time and space, that the different aspects and dimensions of your being can be integrated to make your life on earth a reflection of your living being that lives on and on and on.

Before you come back into your physical form, notice if there is any particular obstacle or frustration that has been around you recently. Instead of seeing it as a problem, bring it right into the creative center. Allow yourself to see this so-called obstacle in another way. Allow yourself to see how seeming blockages may be a gateway to growth. You might ask yourself, "Is there another way that I can grow without needing this obstacle to do it?" Follow the resonance to find the answer. Take this information into your consciousness, knowing that as you move down to the heart center and root yourself in your base triangle, your higher and lower worlds will begin to align. There is another way. There is a way in which all obstacles can become openings, and all openings can be channeled into effective action in the world. Breathe in. Breathe out. Contact your center. Bring the energy from the higher world into the lower world. Feel them aligned in your heart, your solar plexus, your sacrum, and your root. Walk forth from this meditation as a conscious and multidimensional being, ready to integrate past and future, possibility and probability, lofty vision and authentic action.

9

The Sixth Chakra: My Will and Thine

The movement of heaven is full of power.
I-Ching

As a university student I once asked one of my religion teachers, "How do you know when you are doing God's will?" The answer he gave was something to the effect of, "Oh, that's easy. Whenever you don't like what you're doing, you can be sure that you are doing God's will."

Our ideas around divine will and guidance may be the most charged subject we deal with in establishing a vital and authentic vocational path. On the one hand we do not want to fall prey to egotism, simply doing what we feel like doing in the moment and coming up empty in the end. On the other hand, we are expert at fooling ourselves, pretending that we are getting satisfaction out of something because it is "God's will," or because it is going to save the environment or the planet. We may well be doing what we are doing for reasons such as unworthiness, fear, or some need to justify ourselves and using an ideal as a glorious smoke screen.

The acid test of our work is not its effect upon the world, but its effect upon ourselves and our intimates. The world, after all, is what we see, and we see what we want to see. Those who live with us, however, see us. And they are wise to our ways.

We are habitually subjected to heroic models, people who seem to effect the world in a very progressive way but whose private life is in shambles. The unwritten rule is that it is noble to sacrifice one's intimate life in order to serve. If we can thoroughly understand that the ends never justify the means, we will see the fallacy of this attitude. The purpose of our work, like everything else in life, is to learn to love and to be loved. If our job is not helping us move in this direction, it is a problem. If the external payoff yields inner emptiness for ourselves or for those around us, we have fallen into the trap of externalities. And it is a serious trap. What is the good of tall buildings and fine cars if you cannot trust the person standing next to you?

Our work has value if it is nourishing the entire life process; the symptom of such nourishment is relaxation and radiance. The purpose of the medicine wheel and similar exercises is to help process our will instead of abdicating or inflating it. Thus, when we come to the sixth center, where vocation can take on divine proportions, we do not inflate ourselves out of proportion altogether.

The sixth chakra, situated between the eyebrows, is traditionally associated with the higher vision of clairvoyance. It is the place in the subtle body where we receive supernormal powers and experiences, the place from which we see, hear, and sense that which is ordinarily hidden. It is the place where we are no longer working under the illusion of our own powers, but are instead consciously aligned with a greater power for a greater good. After we have established our self-worth and worked with our emotional patterns, after we have conceived of our proper priorities and allowed them to be established in the heart, and after we have begun to cultivate our visions—in other words, after *we* have done all that *we* can do—we let it all go! We say, "Here God, this is yours." We allow the intelligence of the cosmos to guide us, to harmonize our visions and priorities with those of the world's evolution. We align ourselves with the forces that are working for the harmonization of the world. The fullness of our alignment draws in the universal power, and there is no task too large or too small. Thoreau expresses this understanding when he writes at the end of *Walden,* "Every nail driven should be as another rivet in the machine of the universe."[1]

This experience of alignment and divine relationship is one of exaltation. Thus it also carries danger and hence, responsibility. It is therefore most important to have thoroughly worked in the heart area and explored our motivations before giving it all up to God, for it is at this point that one becomes either a true visionary or a megalomaniac, and the difference between the two can be razor thin. When the sixth chakra opens, miraculous phenomena can and will occur, because as one works with and becomes more attentive to cosmic forces, there is a tremendous power that accumulates around one's energetic field. The danger is that one will become inflated around a personal myth and contract from sharing and interaction. To have a Christic experience is one thing; to think "I am the Christ" is another. The minute I believe the latter, in whatever veiled or overt form, others can only be followers or poor and unfortunate nonbelievers. There is no mutuality. The megalomaniac is afraid to share his or her vision, to take it into the open marketplace, because it will be challenged and exposed. The cosmic visionary, on the other hand, can live the miracle *and* share it. True visionaries know that alignment is one piece of a greater puzzle, that visionary action is necessarily cooperative, and that monopolies on the so-called truth are part of the warped use of power that has haunted our cultural history. It is just this type of misuse that has made many sensitive and intelligent people wary of higher visionary possibilities. But if *you* do not take on the challenge of working through this realm with humility and clarity, imagine who will!

GOD'S WILL AND THE LUST FOR TRUTH

In Umberto Eco's *The Name of the Rose*, the anti-Christ is identified as the lust for truth, and with good reason. If the ego is not supple and healthy, or if the emotional center has been bypassed in spiritual ascent, the overwhelming experience of a higher force so threatens the personality structure that it is either categorically denied or corralled into a dogmatic and oppressive ideology. The cardinal principle of inner work is trust. If trust is not present, there will be a quite strong pull to distort inner experience to conform to one agenda or another. The ideology then begins to encroach upon the creative vision. This occurs with groups as well as with individuals. Sects and cults of one form or another often create their own communal cosmologies, and the rich variety of inner experience is laid out on a procrustean bed of group expectancy. The result is a group of people who hold a congruent worldview, but who are unable to share that view in mutuality. Those people either have to convert you or shun you. So the quest, when dealing with the very real fact of universal guidance, is staying out of the childish belief that my god is better than your god.

The way out is to not get sucked in, to never—under any circumstances—give away your power, integrity, and the validity of your experience in the hope of an all-encompassing answer. To work with intuitive guidance is to take the responsibility of developing a long-term dialogue with your inner being, with Being itself. And choice is part of this process. You can challenge your information, you can turn off the faucet if it is running out of control, and you can determine the type of relationship you feel right with in terms of your intuitions. For too many, the parent/child relationship remains the prevailing model for human/divine interaction, but this does not have to be so. We can become psychological and spiritual adults, responsible for ourselves. Spiritual language does not have to be regressive, as in addressing God as Father, and the feeling that we are guided does not have to make us a favorite son or daughter.

Asking for guidance has much more to do with creating a mode of interaction than simply asking and waiting for an answer. In the same way, prayer does not have to be reduced to a child begging for some magical outcome. As the visionary mechanism matures, it begins to interact with other levels of being. We become aware that there are other players in the game, ones that we were not previously aware of, who have a definite interest in and power to influence the way things unfold. This is why we need not be afraid of continuing economic and social difficulties. They are a weeding of the garden, a preening of the cosmic marketplace.

Institutions that do not have planetary service as a high priority are going to find the going quite difficult, if not impossible. The visions that exalted productivity and profit as primary values are simply no longer viable on a global scale. And while there may be particular instances of regression into one authoritarian form or another, such periods grate strongly against the movement of the spheres. Fascism, authoritarian religious ideologies, octogenarian oligarchies, and cowboy drug-enforcers are futile attempts to recapture a paradigm that no longer serves evolution.

The ideology of absolute knowledge may be one of the most subtly destructive forms of the power-hungry worldview. The desert fathers characterized the sin of anger by the phrase "I am right." It is this defensiveness that must be left behind if we are to receive nourishing guidance from the higher forces. Much courage seems to be required to give up the ritual of transposing our legitimate human knowledge onto areas that we know nothing about. The sixth chakra asks us to relax the need for ultimates, and to share our insights without forcing them upon others.

Our visionary activism has become more significant than ever, for we now have something we have never had before: a cosmic marketplace with a full planetary exchange of information, ideas, hopes, and visions. In this wide open marketplace, visions can be shared. The more cultural interchange and recognition of mutuality there is, the less worry there will be about maintaining a particular standard of knowledge at all costs.

To be guided does not mean to make ourselves slaves to a new self-created authority. To create functional, prosperous working situations that honor the best in ourselves, we need to accept the challenge of our human freedom and align it with the corresponding realities of our human destiny. The deep acceptance of such a paradox is the essence of an unfettered mind. It is not simply tolerance, but the receptivity to paradox on increasingly deeper levels. Such receptivity is achieved through personal humility before a greater wisdom, and the willingness to share our received insights through our unique individuality.

SIGNPOSTS OF GUIDANCE

There are certain signposts that appear when one is in harmony with inner guidance, and they are worth noting. The first and foremost is an inward peace—not a self-enclosed peace that avoids relationship, but a deep and abiding sense of flow in the way of the cosmos. Being guided does not mean that you will not get the plague or that you will move to the country at the right moment to avoid a devastating earthquake. Guidance emerges as an evolving trust and experience in something deeper than self-preservation. It is an inner depth that allows you to work with any situation, because your self-worth is not dependent upon a particular set of conditions.

Another characteristic of allowing yourself to be guided is the occurrence of little miracles, the definite sense that you are being supported by the universe. The phenomenon of synchronicity is one of the most frequent of these manifestations. An example of synchronicity is when you just happen to run into the right person for your project, or meet the cousin of a friend who soon becomes your ally. In the beginning such occurrences are emotionally uplifting; after a while they are almost expected, for the world "out there" is no longer a stranger or an enemy.

Another earmark of guidance is mutual joy. It is not just recognizing that you are becoming successful, but everyone around you is becoming successful as well, for you are creating win/win situations wherever you go. Because you are not trapped in scarcity, you are not perceived as needy; you are therefore not an energy thief, and people enjoy your association. Because your authentic feelings are flowing, you create good heartedness, mutual bonding, and positivity. Because you are aimed in your true direction, you do not waste your time and the time of others. People you meet are uncannily attuned to your vision, therefore every situation is a potential to experience the miraculous, the higher forces in action.

This does not mean that there will be no obstacles—indeed, obstacles are a necessary part of this path. They make you aware of where you need to grow and change. If you keep running into a brick wall, it does not mean that you or your idea is invalid. It means that there is a blind spot somewhere, and the proper question to ask is "What must I learn from this situation?" Asking this question opens you to the way of inquiry, and inquiry generates its own momentum. By articulating the problem, you create its solution. And the solution may well be the unexpected, but it is just this that will widen your horizon and open you to new values and visions. To be guided does not mean that the cosmic deck is stacked in your favor. It does not mean that you will necessarily become rich, happy, or successful by anyone else's standards. But it does mean that the jewel, your jewel, will shine one day, and you will see it and know in your heart that your life has been worth living.

GUIDANCE TAKES MANY FORMS

Some people receive strong guidance from the Bible, others from an inner voice, and others from divinatory tools such as the I-Ching, the Tarot, or even from fortune cookies! There is no one way to ask or to receive. Napoleon Hill reports that Thomas Edison created his own inner "board of directors," peopled by the likes of Galileo and Copernicus, with whom he would consult about his work.[2] The sincerity of the inquiry is of great importance, as is the willingness to trust, ask, listen, and live, and then to put what you receive into practice. As you begin to live from your intuitive faculty instead of simply theorizing or wondering about it, you develop a working relationship with your source of guidance and begin to evolve your own way of receiving and responding.

Different kinds of people will receive legitimate guidance in different forms. A kinesthetically oriented person might be handed the perfect job offer, but feeling it accompanied by a tightening of the gut and other bodily discomforts, she will know that the job may, in reality, not be best for her. The visually oriented individual will see guidance, the auditory dominant person will hear it, and so on. Following your primary mode of perception, you may find the others will eventually open. It is common for people to see things that offer guidance in meditation. If you do not see, ask yourself what you feel or sense. What you feel as sensation or emotion is as legitimate a way of receiving guidance as what you see or hear. One Buddhist text speaks of a realm where the holy teaching is communicated by fragrance alone!

The way of inquiry is helpful in this regard. If you hold the question or concern strongly enough in your consciousness, you will begin to receive the necessary feedback. It may come through a television commercial or a conversation with friends about a completely different subject. The messenger is unknown, but if your antennae is out, it will pick up the necessary frequency. Therefore, you need not depend on professional channelers or others who might absolve you of personal responsibility. You alone are responsible for opening to guidance, but the content and manner in which you receive it may vary. Edgar Cayce went into a complete trance every time he gave a reading and would not remember a thing afterward.[3] No matter how you receive material, however, you are responsible for your response to it.

You can test, study, and work with your intuition, and you are not obliged to believe or disbelieve. When Stan Jay exchanged his first vintage instrument for a summer car, he did not need anyone to tell him what the message was. That one incident was his guidance: it was a lot more fun and lucrative than what he had been doing. We too can learn to trust ourselves and our promptings, and we can work with teachers, therapists, and others who will respect us and encourage our own self-empowerment.

THE POWER OF LINEAGE

Whatever guidance we receive is normally filtered through our conditioning. While we may strive to be as open as possible, there are different kinds of preparation that are helpful. We already discussed the sacred circle. Setting up a sacred place in one's home and putting aside a certain time everyday is another effective way of working to receive guidance. After all, our homes are manifestations of ourselves. If we do not have the time or place for spirit at home, where will we have it? The ritual organization of the psyche begins in the home, and the successful anti-career grows out of the balanced home, which is itself a reflection of the balanced soul. If we want to be moved by greater forces, we need to make a place for them in our lives—a quiet, receptive place that declares that the movement of life itself has become a priority for us, and that we are ready to listen to a plan that might be greater than what the mind alone can conjure.

Another way that guidance comes into being is through a thoroughly internalized body of knowledge or experience. This is the potency of lineage, and the lineage of a particular discipline empowers you to the degree that you can be an open and responsive vessel for a discipline that is entrusted to you. The power of lineage is more than the sustained influence of others. Influence occurs in the stage of mentorship, but in order to receive the lineage itself, you must have attained a certain mastery over your chosen field. You must be so permeated by that field's history and mythos that its various elements imbue you with an emergent wisdom.

The dedicated doctor, poet, engineer, builder, or artisan becomes more than a professional. Commitment and openness to their disciplines make them recipients of the insights that are not transmitted by textbooks, teachers, or repetitive experiences. Through mastery, they receive the genius of inspiration streaming from the very origins of their discipline. A dedicated poet will not only feel attuned to certain poets of the past or to a particular tradition of poetry, but will also feel the empowerment of the muse herself. The guardians of the poetic discipline take on and work with those who give themselves to her. This is the true reward of loving your work: Work itself becomes the way into connectedness and beauty; work becomes a vehicle for the soul's growth. It is no longer tolerated as a dreadful necessity. The elements of your work—tools, soil, oils, cloth, flowcharts, keyboards—respond to your touch. To work is to be blessed. You are animated, and the guiding energy of your work likewise becomes a blessing. Guidance becomes available because you are able to receive the full force of a tradition, assimilate it, and perpetuate it in your own unique way.

A person who gives him- or herself over to the muse may feel a strong affinity for the material of the work. There is a fascination with wood or words or animals or an early exposure to trauma, illness, and healing. This fascination evolves and can often be traced metaphorically. An early interest in planes and surfaces and fitting things together may evolve into the study of engineering and later into the study of the structure of the body. An early affinity with horses may be metaphorically connected with a desire for the freedom and beauty of the natural world and can lead to a career in the outdoors or to the designing of a new kind of motor vehicle. The possibilities are endless. The metaphor is continuous.

As you eventually commit to a particular form, you align with its discipline or with its lineage of teachers, be they educators, statesmen, athletes, actors, or astrologers. Through your desire—that is, through the power of eros—you become thirsty for the essence of your desired field. Study becomes an exploration, practice an affirmation. With time wisdom comes, the intuition transmitted through hands-on experience, through practice, and error and success. The relationship with the tradition itself matures. The student now is entrusted with its continuity through time. He or she cannot now rest on established conclusions, but must be willing to receive the mastery of a body of knowledge without being paralyzed by its form.

There is always the possibility that guidance may seduce and thus dull our responses. We can be seduced to abandon ourselves either to a tradition or to a spirit guide. We can be seduced into thinking that we *are* the tradition or the guide. And we can be lulled into a listless repetition of a once workable formula and thus lose the energy of the revealed present. This is why the base triangle is so important. If the root connection is strong and integral, if we have accepted our humanness, then the ego can negotiate a healthy relationship with the numinous world, a world in which personality, individuality, and fusion can coexist, for paradox no longer threatens but embraces the big heart and the open mind.

Sixth Chakra Meditation: The Open Door

Establish your base triangle so that your posture reflects the alignment of your purpose, your feeling, and the ever-present current of earth energy. As you breathe in and breathe out, feel the integration of earth, water, fire, and air within you as your purpose ascends to the realm of the heart and offers itself to the greater whole.

Working with your mental attention and breath energy, feel the throat center opening into a beautiful blue pool. As the throat center expands and loosens, feel your ability to speak your truth, to express your essence, as every breath further aligns your creative energy with the wholeness of your being. Imagine an entire day, from morning through night, in which every action and every detail expresses your inner depths, your joy, your passion, and your conviction. See yourself waking up, walking, working, and retiring from this space of beauty. Allow this vision to unfold in front of you and follow its exquisite details.

When you have finished, come back to the current of the breath, the rhythm that is synchronistic with all of creation. Invite the breath energy to move upward to the forehead.

Breathe in and out of the sixth chakra or the third eye, located between the eyebrows. Feel a delicate silver energy moving through this most sensitive membrane. As you breathe, let yourself relax so deeply and so completely that all of you becomes still, quiet, and open, like a delicate lake on a clear autumn day.

In this clear, open space imagine a funnel of energy above you, a funnel that is able to receive inspiration and guidance from the greater forces of existence. Open yourself to receive from this subtle level in whatever form is appropriate for you. As you breathe in, receive radiant streams of heavenly energy and feel yourself rising in light. As the rarified channels of your intuition open, bask in the glow of heavenly radiance. The upper radiance, the inner light, the glow of luminous existence flows freely through you. It lifts you and inspires you to know in a new way and to allow the greater forces to guide your movements in the world. Stay in this state for as long as you feel the flowing streams of energy.

When you are ready, come back to focus on your breathing. As you gently return to corporeal consciousness, leave a doorway open so that you can return to this place to be renewed and to align your own life with the energy of the cosmos. As you breathe in and breathe out, let the energies of earth and the energies of heaven meet in your heart. Walk forth from this place holding the beautiful balance of earth and sky within you, knowing that your way shall be guided and your path shall open.

10

The Seventh Chakra:
My End is My Beginning

I have heard what the talkers were talking,
the talk of the beginning and the end,
But I do not talk of the beginning or the end.
Walt Whitman, "Song of Myself"

The form of the human fetus curled in a full circle with the feet touching the head is symbolic of the entire life process.[1] Archetypally, the feet represent Pisces, the watery sign of dissolution, and the head signifies Aries, the fire sign of beginnings. The end and the beginning join, bringing us back to the wholeness of the sacred circle, now complete and awakened within our consciousness and yet no different than it was in the beginning.

In the arcane Puranic lore of India, the great and hoary sage Markandeya, after meditating for thousands of years, makes a pilgrimage to the source of creation. There to his surprise he finds a baby, who is Krishna, curled into a fetal position on a leaf, sucking his big toe.[2] In the end is the beginning: the sage meets the child, and all self-important effort and striving becomes humorously absurd. If our vocational paths are to reflect the reality of the whole, they must manifest both completions and beginnings.

The seventh chakra, the crown of creation situated near the top of the head, has been visualized as both the end of human experience and the gateway to higher worlds. It may also be seen, such as the Taoists see it, as the point of return, the point at which the cyclic current of being begins its descending course.[3] The current that begins at the root now returns to the root. The cycle is complete, but the cyclic flow has no ending. In the end is the beginning.

Fittingly, the symbolic color for this area differs from one tradition to another. Some traditions see it as violet, others as pure white light, while still others view the crown chakra colors as a rainbow. In all cases the color signifies completion. And while various cultural systems have different ideals as to what constitutes a complete human experience, the possibility of completion is offered as a noble end to human effort.

The current Western model of vocation sees completion as retirement, something that comes toward the end of one's life. Having supposedly reached the pinnacle of one's working capacity, the retiree can now spend the day playing golf or shuffleboard and taking pictures of his or her grandchildren.

Another myth of completion existent in our culture is the heroic one of finishing the "great work" before one dies. After fourteen years of analysis or the one hundred and thirtieth workshop you might hear someone say, "I am growing, developing, and improving," as if such perpetual movement holds the hope of change. The ideal of personal improvement through time can work as a double-edged sword. Certainly the human capacity for transformation is a real and vital one, but it is not something that can be contrived. If the desire to change is predicated on the idea that you are not all right exactly as you are right now, you again reconfigure the circle of scarcity. Markandeya, after a lifetime of hallowed work, finds a baby sucking his big toe—not quite what he expected! A conscious path of vocation, then, is different from self-improvement. It is a way of involvement in which completion occurs organically. Unlike the politicians and prize fighters, we know when it is time to withdraw from the arena because our self-esteem does not depend upon performance. Besides, there are other paths to walk on.

Certain cycles and progressions of life and work are evident, of course, and need to be acknowledged and understood. Fear of retirement and the frequent inability to let children be children by picking out their colleges at age five, for example, attests to our ignorance of these cycles. Most of us are locked into a pattern by age twenty-nine and spend the rest of our lives treading water. Old age is feared, its dignity and possibility unknown. Death is kept far from view.

In terms of the cycle of vocation and productive work, there is an important figure/ground relationship to consider. If you live and work like a forward-rushing train, never experiencing the stops along the way or the very real background of changeless presence, you will arrive at your destination feeling depleted, exhausted, and cheated—the end will mirror the beginning. However, if you begin with the mystery, you end facing it in awe. If you begin your job search by aligning with your integrity, fulfillment, and joy, your work will flower from this authenticity. On the other hand, if you see yourself as a college survivor walking around with a begging-bowl diploma, you will become the victim of every self-compromise ever made.

In the last step in working toward authentic action, we allow ourselves to be clear about our life's work in relation to the timeless present. The seventh chakra, known as the gateway to the other world, is really the gateway to *this* world seen beyond the veil of scarcity. If we remain attached to working in the scarcity model, we become unduly concerned with the legacy that we will leave to the world. We will place the heavy burden of the world on our shoulders instead of travelling light.

Nisargadatta Maharaja, a holy man from Bombay, was a cigarette maker before his enlightenment and remained a cigarette maker after his enlightenment. In *I Am That,* he tells the story of receiving a young westerner who wants to save the world.

"The only thing the world needs," replies Nisargadatta, "is to be saved from you."[4]

This story does not invalidate or devalue the very necessary work of social and economic development. It does, however, charge us with the responsibility of clarifying our perspectives around such endeavors. When Dr. Kevin Cahill, an eminent New York toxicologist, served in Africa, he stopped his work every evening in order to relax and dine with the local people, eating gazelle and other customary foods. Other doctors came into the disease-ravaged zone to serve and worked themselves to the bone, silently upbraiding Dr. Cahill for not working like them. No other doctor was able to last for more than six months in the area. Dr. Cahill remained there for six years.

Service to humanity and social responsibility and reform are constructive to the degree that they are aligned with the entirety of our being. There are some whose calling is to serve in such a particular capacity and the realization of that calling brings deep satisfaction. But such a calling is no better than any other. When we do what we genuinely love to do and deal fully with the circumstances we find ourselves in, we are already in a state of completeness. The rest is unfoldment, and our legacy is in the small acts of love and dedication that may never be visible in the world but will create a blueprint for the world to come.

Until we understand that the end is the beginning, our vocations will always bear the cursed stamp of work. They will never accede to play. Vocation, therefore, need not be found. It is within us as the tree is in the seed, and will unfold in time if we will just get out of the way.

COMING FROM A PERFECT SOURCE, BOUND FOR A PERFECT GOAL

This heading, the first part of a popular affirmation, expresses an incomprehensible truth about completion: *We come from a perfect source.* That is, perfection is a reality to be reckoned with. Imperfection is easy to see, and we are assaulted with the grossest examples of it every day. But to be able to first conceive of and then actually experience the simultaneous perfection of things without becoming inflated is extraordinary, or as Eileen Caddy of Findhorn says, it is "extraordinarily ordinary." Whitman saw this same perfection and exclaimed:

> One world is aware and by far the largest to
>   me, and that is myself.
> And whether I come to my own today or in
>   ten thousand or ten million years,
> I can cheerfully take it now, or with equal
>   cheerfullness I can wait.[5]

Perfection is our goal, not because we are striving for excellence, not because we are idealists, and not because we are mad. It is our goal because it is our source. At the seventh chakra we become comfortable with the realities of both acausality and causality. At the seventh chakra we move into completion before we begin. We move through the linear world while acknowledging the nonlinear. We give up the need for melodrama and accept the actuality of play.

The Indian concept of *lila* holds that all the world is God's play. Martin Buber objected when he heard this, saying that the world was not divine play but divine fate. But the validity of our life histories need not be threatened by lila. On the contrary, our histories, our world, and our work become transfigured when the awkward thorn of self-concern is removed from our side. The burden of heavy fate—be it tragic, comic, or just plain boring—vanishes when we see and feel the baby sucking its toe. We still chop wood and carry water, but instead of being empty we are full. When we are full we have no place to go, nothing to accomplish, no drama, cause, mission, or illness to sustain us. There is no reason to work, and no reason not to.

The energy of the seventh chakra can be met with despair or joy. The shadow side of the seventh chakra is nihilism. In nihilistic completion there is no more meaning, no more future. The love affair can only end in death, and the only alternative to rigid order is chaos. But the other side of this nihilistic conclusion is play. There is no meaning, no future, and no heavy melodrama because everything has its own meaning. Fulfillment is in the doing. We are no longer separate, striving entities. Rather, we are in the band, and everyone is playing together. We celebrate today in all of its wonder, and when tomorrow comes, we will celebrate it as well. For in our end is our beginning. We have trusted and we have been betrayed, and when the protesting and howling has ceased, we have followed that wound through the labyrinth, and it has taken us to the very bottom. And the bottom falls away, and the never-ending beginning lies in the palm of our hand.

11

Bringing Our Work into the World

The cultural icon of "the perfect job" is, of course, a come-on. But notice how most of us react to that pitch. We are seduced by the possibility of the quick-fix, all-worries-ended jargon. The intrigue we feel goes to show us the degree to which we need to continue to work with the first chakra issue of inadequacy versus abundance in order to refocus a scarcity-based mentality.

The fact is, you will never find the perfect job, just as you will never find the perfect lover. Both belong to the adolescent ascension ideal that dominates our culture to such a degree that it becomes difficult to conceive of alternatives to the linear, achievement-oriented model of living. We must reimage the job search and open to other ways of relating to work, money, and the marketplace. By doing so, the job begins to find us, for we are creating new space around ourselves and envisioning new possibilities that will ultimately lead to new opportunities.

The issues addressed within the chakra model have been presented in a format that can be easily incorporated into a personal meditation. If we work on a daily basis to align each of our energetic centers to support the others, we enter into the process of manifesting authenticity as opposed to staying at the discursive level of random action and unmet dreams.

In the next chapters I address the practice of creating a job out of priority and desire. In order to do this, the alignment process must be thoroughly internalized. The following meditation, which takes you progressively through the chakras and their specific issues, can be practiced as part of a daily routine, insuring you against falling back into the negative spiral of fear-based reactivity. In this way you begin each day by refocusing and reaffirming your alignment as you prepare to create the work you love. As your vision materializes in the inner world, you create pathways that will open into physical manifestation. These pathways may not literally correspond with your inner vision, for visionary energy is metaphorical, but the pathways *will* create possibilities for manifestation.

Begin by establishing a place and time where you can be undisturbed for at least twenty minutes. This time is dedicated to your inner being—it is not to be interrupted by phone calls or other distractions. Find a sitting position in which either your feet or your buttocks and knees can be in contact with the ground. Make sure that your spine is straight but not rigid. Begin to relax your body, first relaxing your physical form, then your feelings, and finally relaxing your thoughts.

As you breathe in and out, allow your body to receive the gift of the air and its electromagnetic energy. Notice the places in your body where you hold any tension. Gently and attentively breathe in and out, allowing the circulating flow of energy to loosen these places of tension. There is no need to banish discomfort from your field, nor is there any need to manufacture a specific type of experience. Trust, ask, listen, and allow each aspect of the meditation to unfold in its own way.

The Alignment Meditation

Direct your attention to your contact with the ground. Notice if you are fighting the earth, either pulling away from or trying to push yourself into it. Relax your efforting, allowing yourself to be fully supported by the earth. Let the earth's energies enter your body from below and fill you, just as a plant is filled with precious sap. Allow these energies to permeate you and stabilize you as you move your attention to the first chakra, the root chakra, element of earth, located in the area of the coccyx. Breathe in and out of the first chakra and feel your connection with this earth elemental. Allow the image of the earth to take a form that suits you and that will, by its nature, empower you. Then let that form inhabit you—you might feel like a piece of granite or a finely cut emerald. Notice the color of your earth energy and let it nourish you as it radiates through your being. Breathe in and out, feeling fully connected with the earth's energies. Gradually allow your breathing to descend lower and lower still, encouraging your center of gravity to fall until you let go and are completely supported by the earth.

Recognize the fulfillment that comes from being who you are, from being an organic part of the whole. Feel that fulfillment in your body. Feel the current of energy rising and falling with the breath, the breath connected to the universal energetic of expansion and contraction and the ebb and flow of the seas that rise and fall inside and outside of your body. Feel the one body of life—the boundless patience, tremendous capacity, and vast space that is the earth. Feel the capacity to be one—to connect, to receive, and to be fused with her life—to know that you belong here with earth, with her density, patience, and power, with her passion and with her silence. Know that you are a part of all this, and that your place is unique and special. This is the seed of your beginning—being at one with the universe, with her delicious darkness, fullness, and all-pervading flow.

Allow your attention to move up to the second chakra now, the area of the water element in front of the sacrum. Breathe in and out of this chakra, allowing a feeling of liquidity to permeate your being. It is here that you contact your emotional realm—the buried shame, hopes, and histories as well as the buried matriarchal history of the planet. And it is here that you contain within the rhythms and the cycles of life, the ebb and flow that is most suited to your biological being.

From the second chakra, look back on your lifetime and see the roads taken and not taken, the paths that you have walked upon, those that have brought you joy and those that have brought sorrow. Allow yourself to drift backward into your life history. If you find yourself blocked, ask for a guide to take you by the hand and show you the things you have truly loved doing, the places you truly loved being, the causes that touched you most deeply.

Allow yourself to return to the first moment in your life when the great wonder of being alive descended upon you, when you felt: Now I know what I am for. Remember in your body the impact of that vision—sense again what it felt like, smelled like, and looked like. Allow yourself time to savor that remembering, to be fully in your feeling world.

Think of one thing you can do every day that will be an expression of this passion. It could be anything from watering a plant to doing an hour of yoga to writing letters to your politicians. Whatever it is, allow that activity to manifest in your mind and, ultimately, in your

life. Let there be at least one act per day that announces to the world:
"I am here to manifest my joy. I am here to express my passion and
purpose."

   We now move from the watery domain of feeling to the element
of fire, the third chakra, located in the solar plexus. Allow yourself to
feel the very real power of fire in your being. Let it blaze and burn
away the dross, hesitations, and useless baggage around you. Let it
burn to ashes all the outworn accumulations—projects, people, and
places that are no longer part of your passion. Let your brilliance
shine forth as purified will, clear in its objectives because what you
want is supported by life itself.

   Observe what you have been thinking, doing, and feeling for the
last six months. Now slowly let your current priorities come to the
surface. How have you actually been spending your time? What has
continually appeared and reappeared in your dreams, visions, and
fantasies? What have you been resistant to or envious of in these past
six months? What do you need to work on, to manifest above all else
at this moment in your life? Do not force a response, but allow the
base triangle of your being to sort things out in its own way. If you
cannot articulate your first priority, do not coerce one into being.
Stay with the uncertainty in an attentive and open way. Feel the
force of the unknown just beyond your door, and know that it will
manifest in its own time. Come through the solar plexus, feeling your
razor-sharp, laserlike energy, imbuing you with the power to choose
a direction out of integrity rather than fear, and point yourself in
that direction.

   Once firmly established in strength of essence, feeling, and will,
you can allow the energy to move gently upward. The celestial realm
gently leads you into the center of the heart. Breathe in and out of the
heart center. While the physical air enters the nose and mouth, the
more subtle component of the breath follows one's attention. Just as
you allowed your breathing to relax your body, now let it flow
through and around your heart, warming and opening the chest
center. Feel your heart space gently unfolding like the petals of a
flower, radiating its energy outward. Just as you received energy from
the earth, as you breathe into the fourth chakra you receive energy
from the deep heart, the collective heart of all beings. Allow a feeling
of interconnectedness to penetrate you as your heart moves in the
rhythm of giving and receiving. With each in-breath, receive the

bounty of life. With each out-breath, share that bounty with the world. To fully participate in the universal flow of giving and receiving, bring three people into your field and send them your unconditional support. Do not try to heal or change them in any way. Simply share your essence from your heart to theirs, acknowledging the reality of unity and the love that is the source of all care.

Breathe in and out of the heart center, established in the flow of giving and receiving. Allow the heart to lighten, to soften, to encompass all. If you are having difficulty with a particular person in your life, or if you have feelings of envy toward a particular person, gently bring that person into your heart center, accepting them as they are and yourself as you are. Allow the energy of life to heal the wound. As you open the heart, you open yourself to your vulnerability and thus to grace. You no longer crave anything from anyone, and because you have made a space to support existence, you are supported in many unexpected ways. Allow a sense of gratitude for the wonder of life to come into your being, letting this gratitude become established inside you. It will deepen on its own. It will make a space for love, the love that comes from the source and is communicated throughout the deep heart.

Whatever your priority is, let it filter through the heart center. Ask: How might this project of mine express and support the heart of hearts? How may it serve all? Feel the subtle rhythms flowing within, nurturing the seeds of vision that will be the answer to this question.

Now allow this energy to move up into the throat center. Feel its spaciousness, the clear blue sky that opens further and further as your heart-centered vision pulls you with its own inherent potencies. Breathe in and out of the throat center, allowing your imagination to run free as your energy flows into the future and retrieves its message. In your mind's eye or in your heart's core, see how your vision may emerge, what forms it may take. If you are surprised, so much the better—you are allowing your visionary faculties to guide you. No judgment is necessary. Ask the future to come in and take you by the hand. Remember, what you are seeing is possibility, not fate. Your vision may also show you what roads need not be traveled, or it may show you the unproductive patterns you have lived out in the past. You may see or feel nothing at all. This, too, is perfect, for at times the imagination lies fallow. Wherever your vision takes you in thought or feeling, be faithful to it. Work backward to see how it is supported by your generosity of heart, by your clarity of purpose, by your real feelings, and by the energy of the world. Feel this alignment and open to that which is beyond the realm of your conscious mind.

Now bring your energy up to the sixth chakra, directly behind the eyebrows. As you breathe in and out, you may feel energy pulsating in the center of your head, or you may sense light filling this area. Do not be afraid to go into the experience, opening to receive guidance in whatever way is right for you. Open your mind and heart to be rightly guided by the highest forces of good. Ask that your vision be aligned with the universal vision, that you be inspired to be in the right place at the right time in order to serve and to love. Never feel that you are unworthy to be guided or that you need another to fulfill this function for you. You have your own rightful place in the world and that place will be given to you as you ask. The law of the inner plane is noninterference. Your guidance will only be mobilized if you request it to be.

Breathe in and out of this light-filled center and allow the feeling of higher energy to move through you. Know that it is your human birthright to be in contact with this level of universal communication. It is not a matter of religion, belief, or theory; it is simply a matter of honoring the yearning of your soul.

As you breathe in and breathe out, allow the energy circuit to complete itself at the crown chakra. The energy flows up to the crown and down through the entire system, drawing from earth and sky. This circuit is balanced in the heart. Feel the place that is beyond space; be in that moment which is not in passing time. Be at rest, at peace, at one with all that has been or may be: in the end is the beginning. In this present moment is fulfillment. Here, now, there is nowhere to go, no one to become. Here in this present moment is the beginning, the great play of being.

Continue to breathe in and out and allow the circuit to fill you with its power. When you sense your readiness to contract into your physical form, do so slowly and deliberately. Allow the energy to recede gradually, checking your alignment at each level. Let the descending flow harmonize your thoughts with your emotions and your physical body, all the way down to your very cells.

Allow the energy to reestablish itself in its own manner. Find your contact with the ground. Breathe in and out, experiencing the consolidation of your alignment into your physical form, ready to go out into the world and be your God-given self. Your vocation is in the making; the circumstances that reflect your inner disposition are unfolding. At any time during the day you can quickly reconnect with your priority, with your ideal, and with the forces that are quietly moving within and without, guiding you to consciously take your place in the great play of the world.

FOUR KEYS TO AN ANTI-CAREER

Practicing the manifestation meditation on a daily basis opens the way toward transforming our work in the world. Patience is necessary, as alignment generally arrives as a consequence of encountering and processing our various resistances. We may think that we have overcome the scarcity mentality, for example, when a new challenge suddenly raises its head. The more energy we are able to clear, the deeper and more complex issues we are able to face. And face them we will, as each encounter moves us into a closer alignment with our power. There is not necessarily an end to this process. But with each unveiling of mistrust one enters into a more profound level of conscious participation with universal energies, and that in itself is a constant source of renewal.

We are now ready to complement our meditations with practical applications of anti-career concepts as we enter the job market. The goal is to create a working situation that will allow us feel good about ourselves, with all aspects of our being pointing in the same direction, inner world supporting outer world and outer world nourishing inner world.

The concepts discussed in the following chapters represent four keys for turning a dream into a concrete reality. I associate these concepts with four goddesses of the Greek pantheon, reminding us that our work in the world is never divorced from the greater forces of the universe. The myths surrounding the four goddesses help us understand what ingredients, attitudes, and practices are necessary to actualize authentic work in our lives.

These asteroid goddesses, although part of the original Greek pantheon, have been neglected in our collective cultural thought until recently, and their arrival on the scene of psycho-mythology may also correspond to the rising of the power of the feminine in contemporary awareness.[1] As discussed earlier, it is the feminine side of our consciousness that needs to be cultivated and listened to in developing an anti-career. The asteroid goddesses, however, point beyond distinctions of masculine and feminine to the qualities that we need to develop, both personally and in our institutions, if we are to experience wholeness through our work. The four major asteroids are Vesta, goddess of the hearth; Pallas Athena, goddess of wisdom; Juno, goddess of relationship, family, and service; and Ceres, the earth-mother goddess of nurturing and nutrition. My purpose here is not to offer these goddesses as archetypal examples of human experience and behavior. I have simply asked them to lend their energies and influences to the sacred project of realigning work with soul.

12

Investing in Your Ideals

The most important personal quality to develop and utilize in establishing an anti-career is vibrant, dynamic energy. If you have gone through the chakra system and have come up with a working priority, you have the added advantage of focused energy. As you take your priority out into the world, you need to apply this focused energy in tangible, constructive ways. What empowers your work is the courage to choose to be what you really are and the commitment to follow through on your principles.

This combination of courage and commitment is investment. More than the mere funneling of money into a project with the hope of a good return, investment involves risk and thus embodies the courage of directing your energy toward what you believe in. What makes a job search successful is the movement from idealism to actually investing your life in your ideals. Therefore, the first step in creating a work situation that will nourish your soul is the willingness to take the risk of making an investment in yourself and in your truth.

Examples from world mythology serve to open the multidimensionality of a concept such as that of investment, which carries with it many financial-world connotations. This is, however, precisely the reason why I am using this word, for a successful anti-career must combine mythos and finance, psychological depth and pragmatic functionality. To promote one without the other places us in the middle of the problem that has been plaguing us all along. Whether it is money without soul or soul without money—in either circumstance we will suffer and pay dearly.

The mythic image I am using to approach the way we may re-envision investment is that of the Roman goddess Vesta, the goddess of the sacred fire and the hearth. Her energies of heat and light inspire us and illumine our way, for she is the sacred priestess who enables us to externalize the primal fire that lies within.

Before we set out on an alternative job search, we must answer Vesta's questions to see what, where, and how much of ourselves we are willing to invest—we must pass her examination. Do we have a sacred fire burning in our lives? For the fire must first burn inside ourselves before it can burn inside our homes, and ultimately inside our life's work. This fire is the cardinal motivating energy that will transform itself into conscious intention. It also translates into the principles of loyalty and trust, words that have been used in the past to describe the ideal bond between person and institution, be it the company or the nation, but that are here applied to a much more fundamental allegiance. For genuine constancy is actualized when we believe from the core in what we are doing.

Vesta, then, governs the principle of investment in her challenge to place our energies into that which is most vital to us. It is not only money that we invest. We also invest time, attention, and imagination. Where or in what are you willing to invest these energies? If you want to start a business, it takes a major capital investment. If you think that you want to create viable work that you love but are not willing to invest your sacred time and energy into it, (as opposed to your extra time and energy), you need to think again, for Vesta demands one's *primary* dedication and focus.

Primary focus is reflected in the ancient image of the vestal virgin. The defining quality of the classical virgin priestess was not sexual abstinence but rather dedication to the temple goddess. The classical virgin may have initiated men through her sexuality, but she never gave up her life path for a man. Her vow to the temple goddess was her singular focus. Similarly, if our ideas are to become realities, we must cultivate dedication that resembles such single mindedness. Now you can see why it is crucial to have done the work of alignment: If your focus is not aligned with the thrust of your being, you get mired in obsessions, detours, and workaholic syndromes that require you to amputate part of yourself as a condition for success. The vestal virgin is dedicated but not amputated. She reminds us that the goals we seek are our own.

Investment, then, can be defined as what is meaningful or precious to us. It is what we keep close to the vest, the secret that we share only with those who we deeply trust. The word *interest,* defined as the measurement of return on our investment, can be read as "in trust." The return we receive on our career investment will be proportional to the trust we place in ourselves and our commitment.[1]

What, then, is your ideal? What is most important to you in this life? Where is your sacred fire burning? This is the primary question: Is it God? country? family? music? nature? wealth? athletics? justice? awareness? power? healing? glory? poetry? creativity? high-speed excitement? sex? humor? high culture? Which "god" are you ready to devote yourself to? The list is endless, and you have to be clear with Vesta because, if you invest in a place where your sacred fire is not burning, you will spend the rest of your life playing charades and trying to make up for it on the side. Any worthwhile achievement requires the fire of Vesta. When you actually enter into her sacred precincts, when you make the commitment to walk through her gates, she takes your fire and begins to externalize its dedication, bringing it into concrete form.

Vesta is also the goddess of the hearth. Her sacred fire is a communal one, and the level of that communion depends upon how one enters into Vesta's fire. Vesta can bring people together around principles as opposed to bringing them together around bloodlines, personalities, or individual opportunities. Mutual dedication to an ideal can draw out the very best in people and can energize a community in ways that no self-interest ploy can. The principle of Vesta must be served first, whether the work is individual or institutional.

In current institutions such as the corporation, municipality, or university, you may find the flame of Vesta burning intermittently, but it does not shine. There is little genuine dedication shared by management and workers or students, faculty, and administrators. Productivity depends almost exclusively on some form of individualized compensation. There is nothing wrong with being compensated for one's time and work, but when people have to be coerced with benefits and vacation packages, it is difficult to develop loyalty or pride in a communal endeavor. The recent baseball and hockey strikes have shattered any remaining vestiges of the myth of the team. In a similar vein, when large chunks of a university are bought by corporations with their own agendas, when learning proceeds without a sense of centered purpose and when students are seen as mere consumers, the loyalty that a student might have had to a school cannot be evoked.

A strong investment principle need not indicate conformity to a singular vision. Rather, it can be realized by the honest, open, and full participation of all involved in an enterprise or institution. When purpose is articulated and some consensus is formed, Vesta burns brightly and many are willing to serve. Therefore, before entering into any contract, be it personal or professional, the sacred fire needs to be be acknowledged, the purpose fleshed out, and the degree of willing investment of all the participants made clear.

The following exercise works along the lines of a corporate mission statement. The mission statement is an ideal Vesta exercise for any group endeavor. The archetypal Vesta pact is traditionally signed in blood. If you are ready to sign it in blood, you are ready to invest yourself in your work.

An Exercise in Investment

Take an entire day off (no small accomplishment these days), and go to a place where you feel empowered. This could be your favorite room or the forest or the seashore, but it has to be a place that will resonate with the best that is inside of you. Bring writing materials such as colored pens and a large piece of paper. The place is important, for this is an exercise in creating the space that will facilitate your ideal investment. Remember: the first principle in time management is space. Likewise, when you take the time to focus on your deepest investment, you want to first create the right space.

Spend at least an hour "doing nothing," just allowing yourself to acclimate to your space. You might practice the alignment meditation given in the first part of this book. Once you have sufficiently settled in, focus on your six-month priority. You may want to move it around the medicine wheel once again to check its alignment. You may realize during this decompression period that what you thought was your priority is not your priority at all. When you are certain of your priority, draw three concentric circles and write the priority in the center circle.

Now rewrite the priority in terms of a tangible form of work. No matter what the priority is, you need to frame it in the language of a project, a product, or a service. This is an essential step in moving your dream out into the world. The language of a project, a product, or a service allows you to concretely invest in your point of focus. If your focus is creativity, for example, name the creative project you propose to devote yourself to for the next six months. If your focus is expanding your consulting practice, name it in the form of a service that can be exchanged in the marketplace. Whatever your priority is, by turning it into the form of a project, product, or service, you give it tremendous power. This moves you forward from introspection into manifestation.

Take all the time you need to polish the statement. Read it out loud. Get it sounding just right and resonant with who you are. When it is polished, write or draw it in the center of your three concentric circles, sharing that place with your stated priority. You now have your own mission statement. Writing symbolizes the incarnation of thought into form and thus facilitates the process of manifestation. This is the first step.

Now that you have put your focus into a new kind of language, you need to detail exactly what you are prepared to invest in it. Before you invest time and money, two necessary ingredients to move things on the three-dimensional plane, you want to clarify your investment of psychic energy. So in the middle circle, list all the mental and emotional qualities that you will need to move your project, product, or service out into the world. For example, if your focus is to write a series of articles, you will need concentration, enthusiasm, patience, and stamina. By listing these qualities in the circle and seeing their alignment with your centered purpose, you will begin to sense the powers available to you. When you have finished writing, meditate on each quality and feel it emerging within you. Feeling these energies, your psyche will spontaneously begin to generate images and ideas of what you can do to make your priority happen. This indicates that you are ready for the third and most important step.

In the outer circle begin to list the tangible things you need to do to manifest each quality and thus move your priority into form. Be as detailed as possible. For example, in regard to stamina, you might write, "Three hours a day of rewriting and editing." In regard to enthusiasm you could list "Making fifteen calls and writing ten letters a day to people I want to meet and interview." Notice the detail here. It is not enough to simply write "I will go out and interview people." You need to write how many people, where you will interview them, and when. The details that you list in the third circle represent the concrete investments that you are prepared to make. The more clearly detailed they are, the more you are able to invest in your developing career.

At the end of this exercise what you come away with is an action mandala that you can put on your wall to serve as your aligned plan of investment. But you are still not finished. Once you have named all of your investments and revised them so they feel clear, put the paper aside and begin to explore the physical space, whether you are in your home or somewhere out in nature. Survey the area for an object in the environment that represents the exercise you have been engaged in. Let your intuition guide you through your space. At some point your attention will, of its own accord, be drawn toward an object such as a rock, a leaf, or a picture, that speaks to you, linking your present awareness with the greater forces that are working alongside your conscious intention. This object becomes your totem, your power object. Whenever you see it or touch it, it will connect you with the work you did this day, charging your focus and amplifying your willingness to invest yourself in your dream. Do not sell yourself short on this last part of the exercise, for the object will tie your inner work to the outer world, constellating forces that are presently beyond your imagination. If you take it seriously, it will begin to grow inside you and make you aware of new powers and potentials.

A CHARGED FOCUS CREATES ITS OWN ORDER

Vesta also represents the principle of ritual and order that lends consistency to our endeavors. When the sacred fire does not shine within, it must be forced from without, and it is at that point that ritual becomes obsessive. But when the fire burns, it creates its own unique form. In the 1960s, places like Berkeley and Cambridge were mushrooming with creativity (no pun intended). The creative passion, born of the fire within, sought to forge new forms of living. But when it came time to actually invest in a creative life with a new sense of order, a great many people fell away. For there was no vessel to contain the fire, no compelling form that could receive the burning energy and manage it. Other factors would have to come into play before investments in alternative living would begin to bear fruit.

Investment, then, is not simply about commitment, which can be a guilt-ridden word used to straitjacket our creative energies. Nor is it about family or institutional values, unless such values issue from the burning inner fire. Without feeling and honoring the sacred fire, we find ourselves going through the motions of living without much passion. Ultimately it is through the active inner fire, the blazing of the creative process, that an organic and functional order crystallizes through every one of our actions.

We cannot consciously create a new symbology or ritualize our lives. Such efforts too often smack of the ego's manipulative heroics. Just as with the manifestation meditation, our work is to come in contact with and to remain in contact with the source of universal energy. This will be enough to render us more aware of the archetypal dimensions of our present activities. Washing, eating, cleaning, driving—all the details of life can become life enhancing when performed with the clarity that evokes the depths that are guiding us at every moment. Are our rituals of work congruent with the fires burning in our hearts? This is the question to apply to all aspects of daily life in order to keep our energies aligned with our priorities.

FANNING THE INNER FLAME

The sacred fire of Vesta is lit when we devote ourselves to our truth, to our loves, to our passions—known or unknown. It begins as a spark and is fanned through the fuel of time, energy, and emotion. As we follow the heat and light that burns inside, we become ever more certain about how to organize these factors to support our investments. If our fire is art, for example, we might spend our time observing the work of kindred spirit artists, visiting museums and galleries, associating with artists and their worlds. Our energies, fantasy worlds, dreams, and desires become associated with art and begin to take form. Perhaps we are drawn toward painting or sculpture. Perhaps we are drawn toward the intellection of aesthetics. Wherever the passion is, there the path is also. As energy and emotion fan the fire, we become willing and able to commit our resources to our investment. Instead of staying up all night drowning over a beer with friends and talking about the sorry state of the world, we begin to paint or draw. Instead of watching television to anesthetize ourselves, we find the right place and persons to learn from, and so we are underway.

Normally when we speak of investment we think of money; this too is Vesta's realm. How you invest your money is a major indicator of what gods you actually worship. If the consumer and the financier actually invested in what they believed in, the world we know would be a totally different place. Every penny you spend is a statement about what is important to you. What is your pattern? Are you always trying to get away with spending as little as possible? Are you willing to invest in what you believe in? If you want a clear indicator of what you believe in, of what altar your fire is actually on, take a clear and fearless inventory of how you spend your time and money. If you work just to make money but do not know what the money is for, there will be little motivation but money itself. On the other hand, if you are doing something that is not your ideal but your ideal is in mind—for example, driving a taxi to put yourself through school—the energy will be present because the ideal shines through the action. Vesta's message is direct: Walk your talk. Back up your ideal with time, money, and energy. Invest in what you believe in.

EXTERNALIZING THE PRINCIPLE

Each of the four keys to an anti-career can open doors to specific areas of employment that correspond to its energetic. In order for this to happen, however, you must be in full possession of that key, maintaining the practice of inner work that will allow your outer life to gradually align itself with your inner being. It is not enough to identify a developing trend and move your service or product to catch that wave. In doing so, you once again run the risk of having your face contort to fit the mask you have acquiesced to wearing.

Developing trends are certainly valuable to identify.[2] Once identified, we must still align them with our integrity, feelings, and purposes. As we master each key to an anti-career we find ourselves able to engage the developing marketplace in a new way. We begin to create our work from principle and therefore connect with jobs and entire fields that are resonating with the power of principle. Thus, while maintaining a job we also maintain soul. This is the goal of our work in the world.

Vesta exemplifies the principle of security and trust. The fire secures and protects our dwellings, and we trust in those with whom we share our hearth, those who belong to the same clan. If we develop a strong sense of personal security and trust that stem from our inner fires and the flow of our resolve, we will participate in practices that affirm that flow in ourselves and in others. The recent crises in the securities industry has been a massive violation of trust. Securities have been exchanged, businesses have been built and torn down, homes have been lost all because no flame burned for anything greater than a misaligned concept of personal advantage. In our society we are encouraged to go into debt from college onward, hooking into the system for life. Many of us are actually living out a highly polished version of the coal miner's life, owing our souls to the company store. The securities industry is obliged to participate in this practice of coercion and control because there is no trust present, especially where money is concerned. The lack of trust, which produces elaborate contracts, mortgages, and burglar alarms, accurately reflects the meager flames that currently burn in our interactions. When there is no inner commitment, there can be no morality, vision, or spiritual upliftment in the investment process. The handshake has as much value as fast food, for everyone knows what the bottom line is.

This is typified by government investments in underdeveloped countries. Under the guise of helping Third World economies, we have invested principally in crops and products that serve the interests of American industries, encouraging South Americans, for example, to grow coffee as a cash crop instead of the foods they need to survive.[3]

From this debacle, however, new securities institutions might arise to rework the principles of investment all the way down to the neighborhood bank. Security might be based on trust by reworking the trust of the bonds between people. If your light shines and my light shines, we can find the ground to work together because we witness one another's dedication to a principle. Now we are called to trust the inner integrity of the other person. Otherwise we shall continue down the road of everybody suing everyone else, seeing how much we can get because of the ever-present fear that there is not enough.

Trust is a grass roots community issue: day care, car pools, food co-ops, and the like can be set up by people who see the value of a community based on principle. In the same way, the home, street, and town can be made more secure not by having more uniformed police walking the streets, but by kindling the fire that will inspire order and devotion to a locality and its people, as values and priorities emerge from the communal spirit. The fire of Vesta creates the bond, the franchise, the psychic space in which people experience their bonds not as bondage but as power.

The anti-career, then, demands a transformation of the bond. One need not be beholden to the firm or organization after all, since statistically speaking, a life built around a company or even around a single career is no longer viable. Most people will change jobs many times in their lives, organizations will crumble and reconfigure, and new careers will emerge while others that were once thought to be secure will suddenly vanish. If we tie our camels to any post but our own, we will find ourselves scurrying around worrying about coming trends. If, on the other hand, we turn toward the fire, even if there is difficulty in the early phase of ignition, we will be focused on the place where we can truly make a contribution. We will be able to offer our dedication, and dedication—the existential principle of the aligned will—creates opportunity.

The power of investment can be used to enhance or diminish our career prospects. By acknowledging the inner flame we develop a connectedness to that which is essential, to that which we need to live by. When Vesta is not owned she is projected outward onto externalities, and we create loyalties that do not have the energy to endure. This is the challenge around investment. To create a life work that is a statement of authenticity, we need to be ready to invest our full selves, to give all of what we are. And the exhilaration that arises from this fire is so intense and exciting that our old security fears begin to fall away. Finally we are living. Finally our work has meaning. Finally we are participating in life as true shareholders.

There may be times when we feel no fire, when we have no sense of the sacred guiding us, when everything before us is confused or apathetic. Where does Vesta stand in this situation? In the Vedas of ancient India it is said that the holy fire has three abodes: the hearth, the sun, and the ocean. When we do not find the fire in our hearth, we can look to the sun; that is, we can ask to receive guidance, opening ourselves to receive in faith in whatever form the guidance might come. I never understood the image of the fire in the ocean until I witnessed a flaming sunset over the Atlantic. There it was—the deep fire in the ocean—a vision of the flame emerging through the watery element of our labyrinth.

If we do not have a direction, our integrity asks us not to contrive one, not to desperately seek someone or something new to believe in. If there is no flame to fan, no investment to make, let us have the courage to face it, to stand naked in the pit of absence and let our processes be born from it. If we allow ourselves to go deep enough into the water, we will eventually find the fire. At these times of not knowing, I often encourage people to take a moratorium before changing course, taking the time to process and let external things unfold in their own way. The willingness to lie fallow invites the spark that will ignite the flame.

13

Discipline: From Inspiration to Accomplishment

If the inner fire does not burn brightly, attempts at discipline and mastery become coercive and ultimately futile. The intelligence employed from such a partial perspective may appear to be formidable, even stunning—we may become quite proficient in particular fields or experience great marketing success, but the long-term result is self-defeating. This is because the whole person is not involved, and so there is upset and rebellion somewhere along the line. The anti-career is concerned with the soul of work, and the soul needs to be nourished through activity in the world. Such nourishment will bring with it all other requisites.

The health-care professional who has lived to serve others and has never honored his or her own creative inclinations may begin to feel weary after each day and become more resentful with each client. Starting a regimen to combat fatigue with diet and exercise will only mask the issue. A vacation may provide temporary relief or reduce stress, as will an illness, but the resolution lies in a return to listening. The fire needs to be felt again and motivations examined. Discipline will crystalize into its proper form when we are open enough to *let* it happen instead of trying to *make* it happen.

The discipline I am speaking of is a form of applied intelligence. It is neither absolutely pragmatic nor purely theoretical, but is able to solve problems by understanding the actual patterns of things and acting accordingly.

It is intelligence in action that leads to the standard of mastery. The willingness and ability to undergo a discipline, to move from enthusiasm to sustained action, is the next key to developing your career.

Many dream of starting their own businesses or becoming advanced meditators or professional musicians, but it is the quality of determined perseverance that leads to the cultivation of skills that will actually bring about results. Turning your project, product, or service into a viable reality requires the development of a practice that remains constant through emotional highs and lows. This is why an authentic investment is a necessary prerequisite—mastery cannot be achieved by a singular act of will. Of course, there are many people who have trained themselves to master a particular skill or body of knowledge, but if that training comes primarily from willfullness, inner resistance grates on the personality structure. Even if it is not overtly evident, the imbalance will appear as a symptom in another part of one's life. The strongly disciplined achiever, for example, attracts emotionally imbalanced partners and thus lives out his or her own rejected weakness and vulnerability. The willful mastery of a discipline or a body of knowledge does not necessarily lead to authentic action in which one's work expresses one's being. Neurotic achievement or the exhibition of unusual powers may be prized by society, but they exact a heavy price in return. Emerson called talent that was not aligned with one's source an "exaggerated faculty, some overgrown member," and likened such strength to a disease.[1]

True mastery in a particular field—mastery that is not a compensation for some form of perceived inadequacy—will extend its beneficence to other areas of our lives. Life itself will become the work of art, with a particular field of endeavor but one manifestation of that art. The cultivation of such mastery involves craftsmanship and patience resulting from the love of what we do. When we love something or someone, they become a source of endless fascination. Every detail is a new discovery, as with the guitar maker who is aware of every subtle nuance in the quality of the wood he uses. The genuine pursuit of knowledge is also a craft in this regard, one that springs from eros, the fascination and desire to know. It is this spirit of caring skillfulness that allows us to develop in our chosen fields, that awakens the heart center to attract support, and that calls in allies from many unknown regions.

Developing a discipline allows us to work through the plateau period of any undertaking. In his book *Mastery*, George Leonard, using his own study of aikido as an example, discusses how in the beginning of a new endeavor one is motivated by the rapid improvements that are characteristic of the neophyte stage. There soon comes a time, though, when improvement is no longer so visible, the emotion slackens, and the only apparent reward for dedication is the work itself. This is the plateau, and it may initially be accompanied by self-doubt or the strained feeling that nothing is happening. Often it is at this time that a person wants to quit and is filled with judgments of one sort or another, blaming the system, the teacher, the environment, or oneself. But this is also the point where mastery can be born.[2] If we want to move our work out into the world, we must construct a plan, an ongoing strategy for developing our project, product, or service, and *stick to it*. This kind of discipline will only work if there is a genuine alignment between feeling and will.

Often after working with a group in healing sessions with Orestes, I would leave in disgust. "Nothing is happening," I would think. "I've been working for six hours straight in some so-called spirit realm and haven't experienced anything that I can be sure of. Why keep torturing myself?" As if on cue, Orestes would appear and I would hear him say, "Mister Rick, you gotta do it. You're with the healin' peoples." Orestes' understanding of the healing profession was straightforward. According to Orestes, one does not acquire healing abilities. One is born with them, and has the choice to develop them or not. Moreover, if you are a healer and you do not honor your calling, some part of you will suffer. It works like a curse. Why? Because you are not swimming in your own river. This was Orestes' constant refrain: "Everybody has their own river. If you do not swim in your own river, you will drown." The anti-career concept is simply an extension of this teaching. If you do not swim in your own river, you go through life like a fish out of water, and a fish out of water is, to say the least, uncomfortable.

The Greek goddess Pallas Athena may be envisioned to symbolize the kind of discipline that evokes the energy to sustain original enthusiasm, overcome inevitable obstacles, and deal squarely with worldly situations. Exemplifying the best of air-element wisdom, her qualities are good judgment, industry, enterprise, skill, artistry (Athena was a weaver), plurality, and problem solving. Athena's wisdom calls us to reverse the deep-seated message that fulfillment is found primarily through commodities or status. She calls us to the heart of courage, to remain genuine in the chaotic world, for Athena is a warrior. Her emblems are the shield and spear. Lean and clear, she is able to sacrifice comfort in order to achieve her objective. And because she is swimming in her own river, her sacrifice is not an artificial one.

Athenian discipline is more than conventional heroic energy. We are not asked to do something way out of the ordinary like leap tall buildings, throw away our television sets, or be the best at anything. In our own river, discipline is the organic outcome of the constant love and care we put into our project, product, or service. If you love the land you live on, your discipline may entail developing a profound knowledge of its geography, natural history, and culture, and perhaps becoming a communicator of its lore. If you love your partner more than anything, your discipline may entail crafting your relationship to become so full that your love can be shared and offered to the world. In this situation, you arrange your work to best support the relationship.

THE NETWORK OF MENTORSHIP

In order to get your project, product, or service into the world, you want to do more than define and develop it. You want to perfect it. And as you move into the marketplace, you want to be well established in your discipline, for this is what will sustain you. The question of how to do this is bound to arise at this point. How do you become truly adept in your field? How do you maximize the effectiveness of your project?

This can be a thorny issue. On the one hand, you may have all the natural talent in the world, but without the proper preparation and training it may not manifest at all. On the other hand, institutional tyranny standardizes much so-called expertise and shuts out creative and innovative forces in many fields. In some areas, the standard routes may be necessary and helpful, but a person must be clear about the motivation for undergoing any type of training.

Rabbi Joseph Gelberman, founder of the New Seminary, an innovative and successful facility for the training of interfaith ministers and counselors in New York, states very clearly when granting ministerial degrees, "We are only confirming what you have already affirmed." This self-affirmation is crucial in terms of gaining mastery in any field. There has to be an inner sense of I am—I am a writer, a photographer, a builder, and my project is right for me and the world at this time. This inner affirmation will guide you to the proper channels for training and subsequent confirmation. The gaining of necessary experience and mastery of a craft or tradition comple-ments one's sense of inner direction, and it is inevitably linked to the issue of mentorship and apprenticeship. For how many of us are born with a singular sense of "I am" . . . "I am a writer," for instance. We may catch the glimmer of our dream, we may have a sense of it as a calling, we may even be able to affirm it, but if we are not acknowledged by someone else it will be difficult to turn that calling into a vocation. There is a great and often hidden power in the transmission of a way, whatever that way may be. Very rarely is vocation totally self-generated. For most people a vocation has to be received, earned, or even stolen! The Biblical Jacob and the Greek Prometheus are both examples of theft as the mercurial, cunning element in vocational transmission: the ability to do what has to be done to achieve what is necessary. Let us not forget that Hermes—the first thief—was also the first merchant! Our idealistic voices might object to the linking of theft with vocation, but when seen from a holistic perspective, we can allow these very real aspects of the psyche to support our emerging careers as well.

There are some who look upon the mentoring relationship as an inevitable struggle, a recreation of the Oedipal triangle in the way that the mentor/apprentice situation re-enacts the father/son dynamic of the family triangle.[3] Others see it as a smooth, orderly transmission of knowledge. In just about every case, however, the mentor/apprentice pattern seems to be built into our species. The complex of mythologies around Athena can be instructive here, beginning with her birth from the cleft skull of Zeus.

The birth of Athena is a struggle. Uncalled for, she issues forth out of Zeus's head and releases an earth shattering battle cry. A woman warrior and virgin goddess, Pallas Athena must create her own place in a man's world. In a similar manner, as we develop our priorities we must use the principle of intuitive intelligence to situate ourselves in the pantheon, the cosmic marketplace. The ability to break into a field of work often requires the battle cry that is not simply content to find a place in the job market but is willing to work to make a place.

Another of Athena's well-known struggles is her clash with Poseidon over which of them would be the patron deity of Athens. Poseidon displays his unfathomable strength, shaking the earth and sending his trident up from the sea as a gift to the Athenians. But Pallas offers the olive tree, multipurposeful and symbolic of a different kind of strength, and becomes the mentor of Athens. Similarly, the strength we seek is not one of overwhelming force nor a singular burst of enthusiasm. Discipline is a result of commitment, consistency, and versatility. Commitment is synonymous with the inner flame of Vesta. Consistency is the hallmark of discipline, and versatility allows our essential energies to adapt and take on various forms of expression. The olive tree was used for fuel and decoration as well as for food. When we are aware of our talents and abilities at their root levels, we are able to cross over into any number of fields, as opposed to being trapped in a limited definition of ourselves. Instead of defining oneself as a secretary, for example, the Pallas energy understands that my strength is organization. I can organize an office, a community project, a newsletter, and so forth.

You want to be committed but flexible. To add discipline to your project or service means that you recognize that your commitment is to the core value, the passion that keeps your flame ignited. Therefore, your discipline is not rigid. You can modify your project or reframe a service to meet existing needs while maintaining its core value. The discipline of air-element wisdom is a discipline that promotes versatility. This cannot be emphasized enough, for what is of increasing value in the postmodern marketplace is not one skill but the skillfulness that can be applied to any number of jobs. In developing an anti-career, you are responsible for developing a project, product, or service that reflects your inner nature, that you feel is worth working for. You are not responsible for how it will manifest in the marketplace. Once you enter the marketplace new forces come into operation, and the mentor or ally is one who will help guide the project to its appropriate place.

Athena is also mentor to Odysseus, guiding him home from his twenty-year odyssey. She does this via a circuitous route, leading Odysseus to make necessary stops along the way. If we hold on to a fixed idea about how our work should unfold in the world, we are severely limiting our possibilities. The development of discipline, therefore, includes patience and the willingness to improve gradually. Just as a show makes a number of local performances before opening on Broadway, we must be willing to make stops along the way, engaging with new people and institutions to develop our work. Athena gives Odysseus cunning intelligence to overcome seemingly greater powers; she represents a discipline that utilizes more than brute strength and is concerned with more than personal glory. Through working with mentors we develop the ability to read situations for the purpose of evolving appropriate tactics and strategies of manifestation.

There must be an inner resonance between teacher and student; they need to recognize one another. This is an important point to consider when embarking on a training program or similar career path: the teacher needs the student as much as the student needs the teacher. Both grow through their respective roles. You are not valueless in front of your mentor. Your place is as essential as the place of the teacher, institution, or training program.

A mentor need not be physically present or even embodied in physical form, but the mentor's presence will usually be an overwhelming one in the initial stages of a developmental process. The student may learn by unconsciously modeling the mentor, as well as learning in more traditional ways. At a certain point, however, this honeymoon phase ends and the teacher becomes a challenge to the student. Many students prefer not to acknowledge this phase, trying to recreate the perfect parent they never had. If the teacher allows this to occur, a wonderful discipleship may develop, but there will be little growth into the student's personal power. The student will remain attached to the mentor like a parasite feeding off a great tree.

Interactions with the teacher can also reveal the shadow side of the parent-child dynamic. Much unprocessed energy from the past can emerge, and the student will come to realize that the mentor, who they had placed on a pedestal, is actually flawed, and the flaw is magnified without end. The mentor may even become a demon who is blamed for everything, including betrayal. The student may well leave at this point, but will carry the same energy with him or her until someone else comes along onto whom they can hang their projections.

If the interpersonal struggles are successfully integrated, the second stage of mentorship is reached. In this stage the student will struggle with the teachings or the methods of the teacher. This struggle, which may take overt or covert forms, causes the student to discover his motivations, weaknesses, and previously unconscious expectations. The student or apprentice is forced to constantly re-evaluate his relationship to the discipline and to the teaching. Sometimes the struggle can move the apprentice on because another teaching is needed. Most of the time, however, this struggle is part of an inner dynamic of discovery. In many ways, the median stage of apprenticeship is akin to psychoanalysis regarding the transference, projection, and countertransference possibilities between the mentor and student. But this struggle brings strength and endurance, yielding insight and understanding that cannot be found in any book or journal, for it plunges us into the heart of the work and tests us on every level.

After the tests have been weathered (notice I do not say "passed," for tests need not so much be passed as experienced), there will be a third phase of initiation in which the apprentice's affirmation is confirmed. The apprentice can now go out and practice and contribute his or her own uniqueness to the field.

The purpose of mentoring, then, is not the gathering of information or power. The purpose of mentoring is transmission. Whether there is one mentor or a series of mentors, as you progress on your career path all teachers will respond to what is inside of you. The mentor is entrusted with the teaching, but the mentor is not the teaching itself, and a good teacher knows this. Ultimately, through the crucible of relationship and practice, the student grows into the teaching.

The mentor and apprentice need to be right for each other, and you must trust your gut instincts on this. One young man who wanted to be a writer enrolled in a class at a university taught by a well-known author, but from the very beginning the relationship did not feel right. The teacher asked the class what books inspired them and frowned when he saw this student's list. The student realized then that their essential visions were not congruent. Rather than be awestruck by a big name or remain in a situation where all he was likely to receive would be negative feedback, he simply picked himself up and left without blame or reaction. You are not required to buy anyone else's bill of goods. Before signing up it is wise to know if the class is for you. The student in question went and studied with another writer who was not so well known, and this writer was ultimately instrumental in helping the student publish his first book.

The mentoring process requires enormous investment on the part of both teacher and student. Therefore, Vesta—strength of intent—is essential. The burning inner fire will attract the suitable teacher and teachings. Oftentimes one is simply propelled by the fire, and the form of its expression remains undefined. Then at a certain juncture, the mentor appears, and this mentor may actually play a crucial role in determining one's calling. The psychoanalyst and author Eric Erikson, for example, was a wandering artist when a friend invited him to come to Vienna and teach in a school set up for children of Freud's patients. There he met Anna Freud and the circle of psychoanalysts that had developed around her father. He was soon drawn into the work and wound up studying with some of the leading proponents of analytic theory at the time.[4] The self-evident point here is that, if we enter into the sanctuary of our inner priesthood, the experiences necessary for our development will come of themselves. We need only be aware enough to recognize them.

FINDING THE MENTOR

There are many ways to meet the mentor, and even if the situation is symbolic, as in the case of Jesus and John the Baptist, it is a crucial developmental event. We may affirm who we are, but when our affirmation is confirmed, a greater energy is called into action. When Walt Whitman felt ready to set out on his vocational path, he mailed a volume of his poetry to Ralph Waldo Emerson. In this case, the apprentice—already having affirmed himself—sought the mentor to validate his path, a very enterprising Pallas phenomenon. Emerson, being a genuine mentor, did not feel threatened or put off by the differing sensibility of the younger poet. He recognized the flame and sent to Whitman approving notices along with the question, "Where have you been all these years?" Whitman, who was thirty-seven years old at the time, replied, "I've been simmering." The willingness to let oneself simmer may be the most difficult aspect of developing discipline. In many cases it may well be that leaving the starting blocks too early has negative reverberations. A highly acclaimed child actor may not be able to handle the pressures of stardom, a young and highly touted genius may find himself lost at forty years old because he never took the time to find his own river. Many spiritual traditions believe that a person should wait many years before engaging in the study of certain bodies of knowledge. It is considered better to simmer, to wait until a certain personal integration is realized before moving into the transpersonal realm, for mastery requires more than initial success or public acclamation. It requires crystallized intention (Vesta) and initiation by a holder of the tradition through which one works (Athena). The modernist masters of art and literature, such as Pablo Picasso and James Joyce, thoroughly worked through the styles of their predecessors before forging their own unique forms.

Initiation by a holder of the discipline through which one works is the crucial second key to establishing an alternative career. This initiation, a crucial phase in any manifestation process, can take any number of forms. Sometimes it just happens. You meet someone or hear of someone and you immediately know that you need to spend time with them and learn from them. In other instances you have to take the initiative to find someone, and you may have to spend trial time with that teacher to determine if he or she is for you.

Whatever the individual case may be, the key to a developing discipline must be received from someone in some way. The following exercise helps open the gates of receptivity. It prepares one for the all-important stage of working with an appropriate teacher or guide.

Invoking Your Mentor

Go once again to your special place. The right place can have enormous significance and can often, in and of itself, set a career in motion. In some very special cases, the place itself becomes the initiator, the career guide. In all cases, you want to be in harmony with your surroundings, not having to fight against the energy of your location. Relax into gravity, feeling yourself supported by the earth. Breathe deeply and begin to reconnect with your project. When you feel centered and aligned, draw a fourth circle on your paper.

In this circle you will list people from the past or the present who you feel drawn to in regard to your project. Think of people who you can ask for guidance, people who have already done something that you have done, albeit in a different form. Allow your thinking mind plenty of latitude. Do not try too hard; just let your inner being bring these faces or names into your consciousness. You might be surprised by an image of a person who you do not know or have never heard of, and so much the better. This means that you are working from a deeper place, and it can only be fruitful. One by one, bring these people into the foreground of your thoughts and just be with their images. Bathe your being in their presence. You may even want to imagine them sitting in front of you giving you advice. As the image strengthens for you, write the name of one of those people and his or her field of work in the fourth circle. Then begin to ask that person questions about your current vocational plans, and write the answers alongside his or her name. Follow the same steps with each person who has appeared in your consciousness. Take all the time you need to complete this exercise.

Keep these people around you by repeating this exercise every evening for the next two weeks. Keep their names by your bedside and notice the dreams that come to you. An important mentor will often reveal him- or herself in the dream state. By the end of the two weeks you will notice that a number of the people you have identified will be more strongly with you while others will have begun to recede. You are now ready to concretize this exercise by contacting these people in the flesh. Be gutsy! Put yourself on the line and see if a door opens. Remember, one mentoring situation is often the stepping stone to another, but *you* have to take the first step. So go out and make contact! When Kris Kristofferson resolved to enter the field of country music, he is said to have rented a helicopter and flown it onto Johnny Cash's lawn. Now that's gutsy! Remember, Athena is a warrior, and if you want to partake of her power and cunning, you have to step with certainty onto the battlefield. If you get no response you can let it go—that contact was not for you. And there need not be any regrets. Getting doors slammed in your face and receiving letters of rejection are all part of the initiatory process and will test your commitment. Discipline, the sustained pursuit of your project, creates a thick skin that can withstand rejection. Charles Handy writes that successful entrepreneurs have an average of nine failures for every success.[5] The air-element wisdom of Athena allows you to reflect on so-called setbacks so that they may become valuable learning experiences. Discipline enables you to persevere. Gradually you create a network of people who can assist you in developing your objective, people you can learn from and with whom you can expand into new dimensions.

The process of finding your mentors can also bring you to meeting people who are involved at various levels in the field you are interested in. Create a file on each person as you gather information. Find out who's who and learn the ropes about your area of interest. People are usually more than happy to talk to you, especially when you make it clear to them that you are not asking for a job but are gathering information. In this way, you create a resonant network that supports and informs you, opening the possibility to make unforseen connections. The career counseling department at Columbia University called this practice of information gathering the "indirect job search,"[6] and Richard Bolles describes it in detail in his book *What Color Is Your Parachute?* This is why I refer to Athena as air-element wisdom, for air is the element of sharing and communicating information, and if you want to develop your project, product, or service, you have got to get on the airwaves. Who knows? In the process you may well meet the person who will be able to mentor you, take you to the next level, or show you how to find a niche for your service.

When your focus is strong, this wisdom can operate on a level deeper than conscious networking. By sustaining your pursuit, new and unforseen connections appear that draw your project onward. The story of Peter Nicholson is a good example of this kind of guidance.

One afternoon over twenty years ago, Peter, an artist from Soho, had a vision. Vacationing on the beach with his wife Ana Maria, Peter watched a beautiful sunset. As he looked over the ocean, he had an intuition about holograms, and holographic images kept coming to his mind. He could have passed over the experience, attributing it to dreams and the salty air. Instead he took action. He began to systematically investigate holograms and all their possibilities, including the idea of creating holograms through laser technology.

Around that time, Peter and Ana Maria were moving to a new apartment in Manhattan. As Peter was trying to fit a couch into the doorway of his new place, a man approached him and offered his help. It turned out that this man was a scientist and his specialty was holography and lasers. They began to work and plan together. Within six months they received grants from the New York State Council on the Arts allowing them to continue their work. As a working artist also he received grants, one of which was to develop an exhibition on holography for the New York World's Fair. Peter had ongoing intuitions about developing pulse-laser holography involving a radically new type of laser technology, but as a nonscientist, the art community was the venue that was open to him at the time. Peter was soon devoting all his time and energy to this work, never quite knowing where the money to proceed would come from. But somehow it always materialized (often at the last minute).

Peter began meeting people within the scientific community at his exhibitions, and continued to develop his ideas on pulse-laser technology. In the 1970s he put on an exhibition entitled "Sculptural Explorations of Holographic Space," and there met a number of people from the National Academy of Sciences. This meeting generated an entirely new network for Peter, who suddenly found himself being regarded as a scientist. This is a central point to consider in the development of any career. By being true to one's passion, one meets the people who are attuned to that passion, and it is people who create career opportunities. Eventually, the J. M. Kaplan Fund, which had earlier funded some of his creative exhibitions, created a Center for Experimental Holography in Brookhaven, Long Island, and Peter was appointed director.

Soon Peter took off to travel around the country in search of more sophisticated equipment. During the 1960s a number of corporations that had been developing laser technology were downsizing and looking to sell off their stock. While Peter was interviewing someone in Colorado, a phone call came through to the person he was interviewing from a laser technician who worked for McDonell-Douglas in St. Louis. The caller was looking for a job, saying that his company was abandoning their entire laser division. Hearing this, Peter got on the next plane to St. Louis, and discovered that McDonnell-Douglas had some of the most advanced holographic equipment in the world. They had bought out an electronics company in Michigan that had been making components for X-15 fighter planes, and had developed corresponding holographic equipment. McDonnell-Douglas was interested in the electronic capabilities of the Michigan company, but not in holography. They were ready to auction off millions of dollars worth of laser equipment.

Peter called the Smithsonian and pleaded with them to save a national treasure by keeping this equipment intact and putting it to good use. The Assistant Secretary of Science at the Smithsonian had heard of Peter's work at Brookhaven and intervened. Ultimately, McDonnell-Douglas donated their equipment to the Smithsonian and received a tax deduction, and the Smithsonian had millions of dollars worth of holographic equipment and no place to put it. The logical place was Brookhaven!

Peter Nicholson, an artist with no degree or scientific training, eventually found himself installed at the Brookhaven National Laboratories with millions of dollars worth of laser equipment, all from following an inspiration that visited him one day on the beach. Twenty-some-odd years later, holography is an established art, and the pulse lasers Peter developed are being used in a variety of ways, from creating exact three-dimensional recordings of the retina of the human eye to detecting microscopic cracks in airplane bodies.

This story shows us that support can be found in many areas; you might meet your mentor when you are moving furniture or walking down the street. Mentorship is an organic process of growth and development that emerges as you move into the world with your aligned power of focus. As you sustain your discipline, you meet people from different walks of life who support your work. And these people can come from anywhere. The mentor may not even be a living person. General Patton had a mentorship connection with Alexander the Great. Patton was inspired by a military man who lived thousands of years before him, but that did not effect the power of transmission. The mentor offers transmission of the discipline they hold. When you prove yourself, the mentor passes the torch on to you.

IDENTIFYING YOUR LINEAGE

Another powerful technique for developing your genuine vocational path is to identify your predecessors, recognizing those people who have gone before you whose ideals and energy resonate with your own. The more you can personalize your lineage, the more you move into the process of self definition and mastery. You may start by identifying yourself as a singer, but what kind of singer are you? You begin at this point to work backward: perhaps you are a blues singer like Muddy Waters. Then ask yourself whose work stood behind Muddy Waters's?

The further back you can trace your lineage, the more you can absorb the richness of the discipline. This is true for stand-up comedians, plumbers, psychologists, healers, psychotherapists, entrepreneurs, communications executives, contractors, or hardware store owners. It is true for any vocation of any kind. The urge toward mastery of your craft automatically leads you to its lineage—its past or present masters. Connecting with them leads to validation, self-esteem, and the emergence of your own fullness.

A powerful variant of the exercise for invoking the mentor is to make a list of people, past or present, whom you admire. Underneath each name, describe what you admire about that person, what it is about the way he or she lives or works that inspires you. As you do this exercise you may find that one or two of these people begin to speak to you; they may appear in your dreams, for example, or their life stories may come to mind when you have a difficult decision to make. In this way they, too, become mentors. As you move through different situations, different mentors will appear. Thomas Edison, as mentioned, worked with an imaginary board of directors that he consulted regularly.[7] You are not manipulating the imaginative faculty here; you are instead following its lead and opening to the wealth of possibilities that exist within the psyche. If all life forms are interdependent, then anyone anywhere at anytime who is in resonance with your work can be present as a guide or ally. Anyone who has dedicated him- or herself to a discipline knows how important such alliances are.

ATHENA IN THE WORLD

In the external world, air-element wisdom manifests through the computer revolution, which has made home offices and home businesses a realistic option for so many people. The home computer is rapidly redefining individual and collective possibilities. Within the next decade the cottage industry will again rise to prominence as centralized forces lose their grip on the economy. The era of the centralized organization is over. We cannot depend on corporations, universities, or the government for jobs. Inspired by Athena, we must, as Odysseus did, learn to live by our wits if we want to escape the oppression of bureaucracies and the chaos of their dismantling.

Athenian discipline meshes well with the Aquarian urge toward decentralization, which promotes small business and the innovative entrepreneurship that has already provided eighty percent of the new jobs over the last decade.[8] This Aquarian urge manifests as the ingenuity that will help create new infrastructures to link communities with one another and to instigate a global/communal marketplace by encouraging individual (as opposed to institutional) mastery of technology, resource efficiency, and local ownership. Athena will inspire governments to build bicycle paths instead of highways, to promote solar panels instead of bureaucratic panels, to clean the air and water and to promote the paradigm of health and wholeness. People such as business innovator Paul Hawken, author of *The Ecology of Commerce,* have documented possibilities of humanizing the way we do business as well as the technology we use to do it. This is the best of what Athena represents in the global marketplace.

The more we move into our disciplines, the more effectively we are able to serve our communities. This is as true for public and private enterprise as it is for an individual, and leads us to the third key of the anti-career: expanding our capacity and desire to serve.

14

The Service Economy:
A New Paradigm for
a New Millennium

The person who wants to create an anti-career needs to appreciate the full ramifications of the market transformation to a service economy. Once there is a steady flame burning within and we are cultivating a working discipline, the next step in successfully developing our projects, products, or services is to ask the question, "How can this project serve?"

In the chapter on the heart center I pointed out that the transformation of a focused goal into a career possibility is achieved when we put the focus of our lives at the disposal of our communities. I now seek to expand our notion of service, for to do so will put us on the cutting edge of socioeconomic evolution.

Our guide through the realm of service is the goddess Juno. Juno has had some rather negative press for the last two thousand years or so; our patriarchal culture has cast Juno (the Latin name for the Greek goddess Hera) as a jealous and scheming wife of Zeus. If your husband was transforming himself into a bull or a swan and chasing after young girls, you might also think of ways to retaliate. Juno, in fact, is a multifaceted goddess. To the Romans she was the family deity, the goddess in charge of the household and all its accoutrements. As Eleanor Bach has noted, Juno also manifests as a principle of service, such as the selfless service of hospices and hospitals as well as the service principle in hotels, social gatherings, and cooperative ventures.[1] Juno further represents atmospheric service in the sense of the ambience and decor present in a particular environment. Our environmental atmosphere is becoming increasingly polluted as Juno is violated by computer terminals that emit radiation, by boxlike highrise offices in which people spend all day under fluorescent lights, and by the rumbling of trucks outside every urban window.

Thematically significant here is the recognition that service is atmospheric as much as it is moral. To think that one is good because one is serving the municipality, the state, humanity, or God has little to do with the serving mood, which is the real power that will extend our effectiveness and possibilities.

Many in the business community have lately been emphasizing the importance of service—as opposed to productivity—as the paradigm for success in the marketplace. But in order for this principle to take hold and begin reforming our economy, it is crucial to understand the concept of service in a new way. As it stands now, the word *service* carries many negative connotations, two of which are necessary to mention here.

The first of these connotations is the equation of service with the servant/master relationship, a relationship that has fueled much destructive religious dogma as well as slavery, sexism, and class hierarchy. Religious and social rhetoric around the glory of service can be directly traced to denial reactions around situations of political powerlessness. The ideal of service thus becomes the Marxist opiate that justifies the acceptance of oppression.

When there was no longer hope of a conquering God, as for the Jews during the Roman Empire, the Christians after the failure of the Crusades, or the Hindus in Muslim and British-dominated India, the religious traditions often distanced themselves from the failing power structures and took refuge in either millennial fantasies or the ideal of being the suffering servants of God.

While most contemporary societies avidly disclaim such notions as class and hierarchy, many service professions remain tinged with an aura of martyrdom. Social workers and health-care providers, for example, earn much lower salaries than airplane manufacturers and nuclear engineers, and the disparity is deemed to be a result of market value. It is furthermore believed by many that service itself should be the just reward of the service professional, while others are entitled to more tangible forms of compensation. Moreover, the concept of serving often remains clothed in the apologetic and guilt ridden liberal rhetoric of helping poor, unfortunate people, and thus reinforces the hierarchical mind set.

The other negative connotation around the ideal of service that I would like to discuss is the self-righteous pose of those who believe that service is the only legitimate occupation. This attitude is often adopted by various do-good groups that cite the likes of Gandhi and Mother Theresa as they exhort their followers to be less self-indulgent about personal growth and "bourgeois" individualism and to give all they have, materially and energetically, to "the cause." The failed socialist experiments held this outlook, as do modern-day zealots of any stripe.

What these attitudes share is the disempowerment of the individual and the distrust in the integrity of the person. If you are forced into service to rationalize defeat, adopt it as a strategy to cope with the world, or uphold it as a spiritual path in a materialistic society, you are not coming from your fullness. So while your service ideal supports some, it quietly alienates others, much like rich kids putting flowers in the barrels of working-class soldiers' guns.

The revisioning of the serving disposition requires the development of the base triangle of personal power, united with a compassionate heart. When one is full and living one's truth, there is a natural overflow that is expressed as the desire to serve. When one is naturally feeling gratitude for the gifts of the world as well as for one's personal gifts, the instinctive reaction will be the desire to share that feeling. The redefinition of *service* shall be sharing from the heart, and such sharing will promote interactive models that move beyond profit and loss. The salespeople, then, will not sell in order to take from their clients. They will sell because they have something that they are excited about and believe in. Their natural enthusiasm for the product will attract others, and exchanges will be made in such a way that everyone feels they are receiving value.

Similarly, the research and development of products can participate in the service ideal when such activity emerges from overflow: invention proceeds from celebration as well as from necessity. The new questions that will be asked are, "How can this product serve?" and "What is the highest good for this product?" Andre Dezanger and Judy Morgan, authors of the *Tao of Creativity,* worked with companies in India that were developing ceiling fans. The question they put to the developers was "What is the highest good of a ceiling fan?" Some said "comfort"; others answered "relief." Finally someone said "health." "Now that is something we can support," Andre and Judy said. "How can we make a healthy fan?" Eventually an idea emerged to make ceiling fans out of neem wood, which is a natural insect repellent. Insects are a major problem in the heat of the Indian summer, and a neem wood fan would be potent medicine.

The entire enterprise of marketing shifts through the serving disposition. It is not simply a matter of creating a product or fulfilling a need. Marketing becomes a proactive endeavor that emerges from a vision of abundance, not simply promoting comfort but promoting well-being. As Andre and Judy said, "This we can support." The new service economy will lend itself to such collaboration and celebration.

The following exercise will help bring your developing focus in line with the greater energy of service. Tapping into the emerging awareness of the centrality of service is the third key to establishing an anti-career. To do this exercise you will return once again to your special place. Each time you return to this place to do soul work you are empowering both the place and yourself, for the energy of the work you do remains in the place where the work is done. This might be how certain places come to be designated as holy: rivers such as the Ganges that have received prayers for thousands of years contain the cumulative energy of those prayers, and you attune to this energy when you pray there. In the same manner, your special place will become a source of inspiration and creativity as you continue to return to it whenever there is major introspective work to be accomplished.

Always begin at the beginning. Return to your central focus—the project, product, or service that you are dedicated to developing. By cultivating a discipline, you create an energy of continuity that builds momentum. By going out and seeking people, places, and institutions that can facilitate your project, you begin to create the all-important network through which your work will find its right place in the world. You must keep at these two practices, your focus being continually affirmed through action. Establish your network by staying in regular contact with your mentors and colleagues. Networks are not static objects—they are ongoing, evolving streams of interconnectedness that need to be nourished and utilized on a regular basis. The path is only open if it is walked upon. Now you are ready to take the process to another level.

Creating for the Highest Good

Move into a meditative mind. Allow yourself to feel the energy of abundance, connecting once again to the natural rhythms of your body and the universe. Feel the power of your passions and convictions, and how that power has focused into the priority you are now working on. Allow the sensation to move up into the heart center, and feel there your desire to share your work with the world. Now bring your energy up to the throat center, and feel there the surge of creative possibility within. Finally open up at the crown chakra, feeling an inverted funnel of energy streaming down into you. From this centered and alive place, ask yourself "What is the highest good of my priority? How is my project, product, or service contributing to the larger picture of planetary evolution?" Open the screen of your mind's eye to receive whatever impressions come to you. What are you sensing within? Be patient. Allow your interiority to work at its own pace. Let the energy develop, and, when you feel it is complete, write down what you received. Then go back into meditation and ask "How can I realize the highest good of my priority?" Allow yourself to visualize the responses in detail; see your project unfolding through time. Write down what you received, adding a fifth ring to your concentric circle model.

When you finish this exercise, you should feel energized, vibrant, and enthusiastic, for you are aligning the best in you with the best for others. You are entering the great wheel of exchange from a totally new perspective, not out of dreadful need but out of the great flow of being that created and sustains you.

THE AQUARIAN JAZZ BAND AND THE NEW ECONOMY

Service is the expression of the overflow created through alignment. From this perspective, one can understand the famous verse from the Indian scripture, the Bhagavadgita:

> Better to do one's own dharma, even if imperfectly,
> than the dharma of another. For to do another's
> work is dangerous.[2]

To do one's true work, one's *dharma,* leads to the fulfillment that permits one to serve with no strings attached. In traditional Indian and European culture, however, one's dharma was determined by the elders of the family and community: you were told what you should do. Many people long for such certainty, and so we have ashrams and the armed forces. The fact that the principle underlying the American constitution is freedom from the stranglehold of European class culture and its concomitant traditions, however, offers each of us the chance and the challenge to find our own dharma. This is the purpose of anti-career work—to create the space and do the inner preparation to allow your dharma to find you. The native American cultural tradition of the vision quest serves as one possible model for the re-envisioning of work. In this practice, time is taken to cultivate the inner being and to allow the inner and outer forces to coincide into the revelation of an individual's calling. The culture creates the time, space, and social support for individuals to process their inner lives and so contribute to the community from their essence.

Each of us is a unique expression of the creative force, and each of us therefore has our own unique gift with which to serve the world. The development of the serving disposition asks us to create cooperative social models that will enable our project, which is our form of service, to come into being. One model that I have been working with in this regard is the Aquarian jazz band. Instead of a conformist orchestra ruled by an inflated conductor who plays no instrument himself—the hierarchical model in which power is projected onto the male elder—the Aquarian jazz band offers a manageable decentralized group of individuals, each with their own specific mastery and each respectful of one another's place. From this position the musicians improvise, the improvisation creating a flowing form that allows individuals to enter and leave as desired. There is a cohesive unity, but not at the expense of the individual and his or her service.

Part of our emerging anti-career work, then, is to create an atmosphere that will allow each person's service to be received and shared, an atmosphere of trust that validates the activity of exchange. This includes families, extended families, communities, and support centers on all levels. Such forms can only be created when there is a conscious understanding of the laws of giving and receiving, for service is about sharing—it is not about giving until there is nothing left to give.

On a deeper level, a service disposition points the way toward the model for a new economy. The new economy, as the poet Gary Snyder has suggested, is itself a branch of ecology. In the new economy, the self-evident truth of interdependence is acknowledged and respected as much as the truth of individual freedom. When one begins to realize that any act performed anywhere has repercussions everywhere, the whole idea of service transforms. The economy is not to be expanded or maintained at the expense of a particular group or region. Rather, economy is the sacred sharing of what we value, for all of life is serving life itself, and any form of exchange is truly sacramental. Service, therefore, is a deep recognition of the nature of things. The honorable exchange of value is a central part of this delicate fabric. As we recognize the truth of interdependence, we are not only able to share across the boundaries of race, religion, and state, but across the boundaries of past and future as well. We begin to receive support from our ancestors and predecessors in other times and places. We are able to offer our services to heal the past and reconcile differences as we move toward the creation of a collective future.

This reconfiguration of the individual and the collective is happening at an amazing pace. Nations and states are splitting apart and reforming; the concept of family has changed dramatically over the past ten years, and businesses go under and resurface in one week's time. From an anti-career perspective, this is not necessarily a deplorable situation. Rather, it points to the need to establish new ways of relating, ways that honor but do not isolate the individual, and ways that affirm the interdependence and individuality of everything and everyone.

The emerging service paradigm facilitates cooperative endeavors and the goal of developing work possibilities for all. It seeks to reunite hands and heart, to acknowledge the value of the craftperson—the potter, carpenter, designer, chef, naturalist, herbalist, and so on. When Juno's influence is present, the so-called menial tasks and the ordinary busy work of life take on new meaning. I may not want to push a broom for the rest of my life, but if I believe in the project I am working on and feel supported by the others who are involved, the work I do participates in a greater dimension of sharing. I sweep the floor and feel good about it because my work puts me in contact with another kind of joy.

Juno also represents the need to balance our personal lives with our work lives. An anti-career does not hold work as a substitute for intimacy, self-esteem, or spirituality. Its purpose is to align our work with our full life energies. When people say, "I am working to support my family," the declaration often carries undertones of resentment, as if this is seen as an obligatory burden. If your family is truly where your heart is, however, you will organize your working life around family priorities in terms of time, space, and energy. This is why alignment is essential: When we are clear about our priorities, not just for our work but for our lives as well, we can align our work around our authentic concerns.

One of the greatest challenges to establishing an anti-career is creating a situation in which your primary relationships and your work support one another. This is why it is essential that, from the very beginning, you know, define, and articulate where your flame is located, and make that knowing clear to everyone around you. A relationship or a job worth keeping is one that you are willing to build up step-by-step as well as fight for when necessary. The closer you move toward your authenticity, the deeper you will care, for what you care *about* will be what you are.

Caring is the characteristic energy of the serving mood. As postmodern industrialized nations consciously move into a service economy, who and what we care for, and how we embody our caring will be essential issues. In this regard, the re-envisioning and re-exalting of service will be one of our highest priorities, and as these priorities come into alignment, we can consciously put our caring into action. This is the project of Ceres, the goddess of interactive management who governs the distribution and arrangement of energy and structure in our lives, the final key in establishing our anti-career.

15

Interactive Management

There was once a time when the United States was glowingly visualized as a melting pot, an idealistic vision that was touted throughout the world as a new and humane solution to the clash of variant interests, races, and creeds arriving on the shores of the New World. It was also a vision that strongly supported the centralization of work into the corporate firm or government agency. Everyone could melt together and work for the same company—black and white, woman and man would be indistinguishable working on the assembly line or fitting snugly in parking spaces, with somber suits on and agendas in hand. These days the melting-pot model is no longer in vogue. Instead we now speak of a glorious tapestry emphasizing the creative possibilities of our cultural diversity. Why should our working situations not follow suit?

Instead of melting into a job, a career, or a firm for one's entire life, the anti-career person of the future will be a living tapestry, someone who is able to perform a number of services and expand his or her interests into complementary and simultaneous directions. The one-job-for-life ideal is as dead as the transcontinental railroad. Some people may still travel this way for leisure, but it is essentially a relic from another age. Even retirement is no longer a sought-after option. Most of us would rather retire at age twenty-nine and spend the rest of our lives working productively at what we truly love to do.

As the electronic information network continues to dissolve the increasingly irrelevant walls of class, greater numbers of people will have extensive and varied work portfolios. One and the same person will be a farmer, electrician, dowser, all-purpose handyman, and an opera singer who travels to Austria to perform every summer! I know someone who does this. This is not a utopian dream; rather, it is a necessity if we want to create the work that we love. What we love, after all, grows and changes. To limit ourselves to the concept of a particular job or the idea that certain types of employment are reserved for certain types of people, so that a laborer cannot be an artist, for example, is to draw artificial walls around ourselves and limit our opportunities.

This does not mean that one person can do everything; it is important to remember the pivotal management principle of going with your strength. But as we develop our projects, products, or services, we will see our vocations emerge thematically as opposed to linearly, and we must be prepared to branch out. Jan Nigro, for example, has allowed his passion for music to branch out in three or four directions. He gives guitar lessons locally, performs singing telegrams for birthdays and other occasions, and co-manages a production company that has so far produced two award-winning albums for children. His own group, Vitamin L, performs regularly on the East coast, and he is able to adjust his work schedule to accomodate these engagements.

In *The Age of Unreason,* Charles Handy defines the shamrock organization as an increasingly decentralized structure that branches out like a shamrock clover, preferring to contract work to smaller outfits than to maintain a top-heavy centralized organization.[1] This model of decentralization now holds true for individuals as well as businesses, for it no longer makes sense to keep your proverbial eggs in one basket, since the basket may not be there in the morning. A good friend of mine who worked for an elevator company for twenty-one years was recently called into the boss's office one day bright and early. "How would you like to take a long vacation?" he was asked.

"Does this mean I am being laid off?" my friend replied.

"No, it means you're being fired. We want you out of here by one o'clock," said the middle-management henchman.

The only striking aspect of this scenario is its common occurrence. Such experiences are shared by millions of people across the country and the world. The hope that the government will provide safety nets, retraining programs, and even jobs is an ultimate absurdity, one that, when taken to its logical conclusion, leads to the government becoming the big corporation and employing the entire nation. Thus the failed melting-pot schematic is repeated as we continue to hope and pray that someone else will take care of us.

The only way to step off this treadmill is to begin to take responsibility for ourselves and our careers. There is an appropriate native American proverb that states that the best medicine is always right under your feet. This is where we must start to create our careers, with the "taming power of the small."[2] A strategy is needed that will allow us not to simply create a career, but to create *a way* in the literal sense of *a path*, a network portfolio of genuine contacts that expands into a fully blossomed tree of possibilities. We can no longer afford to be dependent upon employers, governments, or entitlements. Just as the Samurai warrior cultivated alertness and our hunting and gathering ancestors knew the trails, seasons, and sounds of the forest, we must attune ourselves to the currents in the cosmic marketplace. We must develop our network of interconnections based on abundance, passion, and priority, not as a grid to fall back on but as a living resource to create from.

The final key to an anti-career is management, and it is the most interesting and difficult practice to master, because the concept of management is generally seen in a very one-sided way. When management is only understood in terms of organizational efficiency, we miss the point of Gary Snyder's comment that economics is a sub-branch of ecology. Management, as I refer to it, is interactive as opposed to hierarchical. It involves nurturing our projects, assimilating the elements and energies needed to manifest them fully, and distributing them to the places where they are needed. Ceres, the goddess of the earth who holds a stalk of wheat in her hand, is an appropriate representative of this principle, emphasizing its organic, whole-life aspect. As the mother of all forms of creation and productivity, Ceres represents the principle of proportion, of creatively balancing our lives as nature balances herself. If Mother Nature put all of her eggs in one basket, there would only be one species of life on the entire planet! But that is not her way. She has created a myriad of life forms that are constantly experimenting and interacting with one another. If Mother Nature loses one job, she does not have to worry because she has millions of other jobs on the side!

Even devastating events like forest fires are necessary for the ultimate growth of the forest and the emergence of new and stronger species. This is because Ceres views her work as her way. She does not work for a firm in trust that the parental corporation will see her into old age. Rather, her work represents her being in all its marvelous complexity: she may work for a firm, but she also works for her own creative pleasure. Moreover, because she values interconnectedness, her security is established through her reciprocal network of relationships. Because she does not need the firm, she exudes grace and dignity in every season. This grace is crucial for developing a successful anti-career: it is not enough to know what you can do; you must also know when and where you can do it and with whom you can do it.

To develop such creative balance in one's life is to cultivate grace and dignity, to transform the mayhem of day-to-day disjunction through the interaction of nurturing, assimilation, and distribution. Just as a distributor cap in an automobile allows the energy to circulate to its proper sources in measured amounts, so it is that we need to nourish the different aspects of our lives—home, family, community, work place, and inner being—in ways that are synergistic, as opposed to one side of life outweighing all the others. Interactive management encourages us to manage our available resources so that we can become working tapestries, rather than melting into the overburdened centralized economy.

Interactive management is an organic principle that indicates that the reciprocal balance we seek cannot be manufactured. It must grow. It must literally emerge out of our authenticity. The most evident application of this principle is seen in the rise of the home office, which along with the international telecommunications network is allowing us to create a new working culture. Without a strong ideal, however, we will become victims of this technology. We will all carry cellular telephones and portable fax-pads and allow ourselves to be tracked down by anyone, wherever we may be, at any time of night or day.

Sometime ago I had to have my car towed to an ultramodern garage for servicing. When I walked into the garage no one greeted me or said anything. Finally an attendant behind the desk asked me eight questions: when? where? make? model? year? automobile service card number? insurance? and method of payment?, without once looking up at me. All the while his eyes were glued to a computer terminal, and he had to wait about thirty seconds for each of my answers to be registered by the computer. This surrealistic scene, including my ungreeted arrival, the very manner of questioning, the time it took to type in my answers, and the wait for a computerized bill to come up on the printer, took over ten minutes. Standing there, I had the nightmarish thought that we human beings may just be a step in the evolution from nature to machine.

Technology may offer efficiency and power, but if it is not integrated into a wider vision it will destroy friendliness, intimacy, and the human contact that we live for. The home office can offer one kind of independence and versatility, but do you want your home to become an office? Do you want to surrender the last frontier of your inner world, or might there be other solutions? Perhaps the office could be reconstructed in a more humane way. In traditional Middle Eastern cultures, for example, the home is clearly partitioned into its public and private domains. These are the important issues that we must come to terms with as we continue to develop our projects, products, or services—not only how much, but how do we want to work? How do we want to relate to the people we work with, to the materials we use, and to the locality in which we work? Ceres exemplifies a nurturing as well as a productive principle, and she encourages us to balance our humaneness with our working needs.

These same issues are as relevant for organizations as they are for individuals. Tom's of Maine, for example, has been cited for its effort to create a corporate extended family. People who work for Tom's have an interest in the integrity of the product—healthy and additive-free toiletries—and workers share in company profits. Employees are encouraged to work for the community as well as for the corporation, and are given hours, benefits, and child-care facilities that enable them to balance community and family lives with their work. Similar corporate visions are being cultivated by emerging organizations like the Social Ventures Network, which among other activities monitors salary relationships between managers and employees, seeking to transform the paradigm that business simply exists to make a profit for its owners, to one that promotes humane reciprocity and respect for the natural world.[3]

In the past, such ideas would have been seen as counterproductive. But with the ongoing humanization of values fostered by interactive management, people will seek out employment that is geared toward fostering sustainable community as opposed to blind productivity, and people will be willing to give more of their energies to such an organization.

A chilling testimony about the prevailing noninteractive management paradigm was given by Konosuke Matsushita, executive advisor to Matsushita Electric Company, when he addressed a group of Western industrialists:

> We (Japanese) are going to win, and the industrial West is going to lose out. There is nothing much you can do about it because the reasons for your failure are within yourselves. Your firms are built on the Taylor model, where your bosses do the thinking while your workers wield the screwdrivers. You're convinced, deep down, that this is the right way to run a business.[4]

Interactive management offers an alternative to this paradigm. It supports systems that promote the alignment of love and work. Such systems can be created by individual communities to support their local industries, crafts, and particular uniqueness. The town of Sugarloaf, New York, for example, features a Main Street of shops run by local craftspeople. Instead of going to malls, people from all over the state drive to Sugarloaf for its uplifting atmosphere and artistry. The individual craftsperson can no longer compete with the mass production ethic supported by the mall and its faceless culture, but a community guild of craftspeople was able to create a self-sustaining town that has now gained a statewide reputation.

The interactive management that Ceres represents is neither planetary awareness, environmentalism, voluntary simplicity, community commitment, systems management, or self-reliance, but may include all of these to certain degrees. Proportion and balance vary with each individual, and cannot be measured or enforced by external standards. The anti-career person needs to create a nourishing balance that is at once independent and interdependent, a balance that promotes one's own interests and talents and serves those of others. In the spirit of biodiversity, there are many ways to do this.

The rock band Earth deliberately chose to bypass the commercialized music industry, refusing to charge more than five dollars for a concert, even after they made it big. Sometimes they would have to sell hot dogs on the street before a show in order to pay for their rental equipment for a concert. Their focus remained on the music they loved and the art-as-process culture that their music supported; thus they promoted not only their own band but other artists with similar perspectives, and they eventually built a following around the country. They did this by playing repeatedly in certain welcoming cities, eventually creating a community network in a circuit that traversed the country from Portland to Washington, D.C. to San Antonio. In this community, one person would rent a house and, when other bands toured the area, the band would simply rent sleeping accommodations from that person, rather than going through the trouble and expense of looking for and booking a hotel. A string of houses was thus set up that supported their particular art form, and in this way a mobile lifeline was created that sustained hundreds of artists all focused in a similar direction.

A member of this community told me how Jack Kerouac served as a model for many of the band members, not only because of his achievements, but because of his mistakes as well. The model of the open road and spontaneous expression sustains many of these experimental artists. Kerouac's self-destruction is seen to be a result of three errors that the community consciously avoids: substance abuse, sexism, and becoming a victim of the media.

Interactive management is not only a principle for the underground. It also suggests new strategies for employers, rewarding care and quality rather than hours spent on the job, creating a working environment that supports friendship and self-esteem, and envisioning business in service to the global community.

Alisa Gravitz, director of Coop America, wrote about the impact of attending a workshop on sustainable community design in which the concerns of the Ceres principle were demonstrated.[5] In the workshop, architects Peter Calthorpe and Andres Donnay discussed the long history of community design, from the church-centered towns of old to the modern suburb. I will quote the passage on the suburb:

> The suburb was developed at a time when people wanted to escape from the troubles of the city and was designed for two-parent families where the husbands were employed outside of the home and the wife worked within it. However suburbs no longer work well for the diversity of families that now live there. With so many single-parent families and families where all the adults work, having the home so far away from work, child care, stores, and recreation creates an enormous pressure on families and the environment.[6]

Gravitz cites the fact that Americans generally envy the European's typical five week annual vacation, but the average American spends an hour more per day than the average European commuting to and from work, which comes out to approximately five weeks' time in the course of a year.[7] Interactive management offers us the possibility of physically restructuring our lives so that we can live and work in such a way as to have the time and space that is necessary to fulfill our potentials as human beings.

DESIGNING YOUR PORTFOLIO

As you continue to develop your project, product, or service, you need a checklist to help you see to what degree your work is becoming akin to a work of art. Are you receiving the correct nutrition from your work, as well as from your food? Is your work leaving you energized or depleted? Are you living in a location that is suitable for what you wish to manifest? Interactive management is concerned with the sights, smells, and sounds that relate a place to a person. What is the value of being in New York for one business meeting and Paris for another if all you have done is move from one telephone-laden office to another?

Do you have the correct materials, tools, education, information, and helpers? All this is part of your nutrition. A Ceres-minded worker knows and loves his or her tools. Whether they be books, gardening tools, tractors, or musical instruments, they become a part of oneself. This is a good way to measure your relationship to your work. Look around your work space. Look at your tools, at all the materials that are part of what you do. Are they well cared for? Do they reflect your rapture at being fully alive? Are they part of an order that would make your life a work of art? Equally important here is the principle of assimilation. Are you able to digest and distribute the various elements in your life so that they function together optimally?

In order to become successful at interactive management, we have to be clear about our values and what it is that we actually need. For most of us the management issue is not one of not having enough, it is one of having too much. We feel overwhelmed by bills, meetings, deadlines, and all the things that must be done in a day, and this is a matter of poor distribution of time and energy. Well-managed work gives us the innate satisfaction of working in full presence. We may need to apply interactive management principles to our priorities, defining our work in such a way that it can branch out without splaying out and leaving us with no center.

As we trim and contour our work, we develop a portfolio—a series of skills and ways these skills can be utilized—by diagraming the different branches of our work, along with the who, what, where, or when these particular avenues might be appropriate. We develop this portfolio by cultivating a lifestyle that serves our purpose rather than impedes it.

In order to accomplish this, we must courageously eliminate what is unnecessary in our lives. The key here is to hold onto only those things that help you move in your direction. A fleet of first-class automobiles may be necessary for one person, while for another a bicycle will do. Interactive management is not simply about cutting costs or eliminating waste; the Ceres principle is even a deeper principle than voluntary simplicity. It is about redirecting resources and consumption to serve our deeply felt visions.

The interactive management principle builds upon the service paradigm and its recognition of the reality of interconnectedness. The Ceres community is bound by something more than a social contract. In a Ceres community the earth and water, the contours of the land, the history of an area, the caring for its people—all this is taken into account. When the principle is operating strongly, synchronistic events become the rule rather than the exception, as one becomes strongly aware that how one operates in the microcosm—washing the dishes, listening to the radio, and folding laundry—corresponds in a precise manner to one's work and circumstances. When we are in our own flow, we attract the people and circumstances who will nurture our energies. Thus, from the Ceres point of view, where one lives is as important as what one does.

I have stated something previously that I want to mention specifically here. A person can become empowered by a place. For many people, the matter of creating artful life work may not be so much a question of finding the right job as it is of finding the right place. If you feel connected to a place and many people report moving into the area on the intuitive strength of knowing that this is where they belong, honor that place. Find a way to develop a relationship with it. The place itself will then produce the work that is needed to keep you there. I cannot emphasize this strongly enough. It is quite mysterious how a place calls a person, and there are stories upon stories of peoples' fortunes changing when they change location. This does not mean that you must pick up and move somewhere because things are not going well; that would be giving into the scarcity principle in another form. On the other hand, honoring the energies and feelings that a place communicates to us factors into our personal management work.

Architecture and urban environments likewise need to offer something more than functionality and cost-effectiveness. As James Hillman notes, in urban and suburban areas you can walk for miles without seeing a public meeting place where people can gather together and share with one another.[8] Our project, product, or service, then, cannot be separated from community building, and the careers of the future will be found through shared concerns at a grass-roots level.

How can one begin to create community? One can learn from the story of David Hagstrom, the former principal of a junior high school in a rather seedy section of Fairbanks, Alaska. Hagstrom sent out invitations to parents and members of the community inviting people to a breakfast meeting that would focus on one question: What kind of future do we want to create for our children? Five people attended the first meeting. Within a few months attendance had risen to five hundred, and a number of fundamental changes were instituted in the curriculum and structure of the school. This was accomplished by a group of people who were all committed to the same area, who all felt a bond with the place where they lived.

The question that must be asked along with "What do I want to do?" is "Where should I do it? Where can I integrate into a community of likeminded people who are likely to support the creative expression of my work?"

Any sane-minded business will recognize the need for creating ties with the community. When the Missouri river flooded a few years ago and fresh water could not be pumped into most homes, the Anheuser Busch brewing company offered beer bottles filled with fresh water to the community. If our work consciously considers the community, we are creating the reciprocity that will sustain our work over time.

Along with the question of where comes the question of how, for the principle we are cultivating is creative balance. When we overprepare for a meeting, overstudy for an exam, overspend, or oversave, we are not circulating the energy in its optimal way. We will create swellings in some areas of life and shrinkages in others. The American work culture has evolved a nine-to-five workday that entirely ignores natural and human rhythms such as the passage of the seasons, the phases of the moon, childbirth and care, and so forth. The prevailing idea underlying the paradigm of productivity is that people should become like efficient machines. The result, of course, has been that people at work become akin to machines, and like machines they break down and are carted away. There is no purpose in producing a thousand cars a day if we do not know why we are producing cars in the first place. If such production is an unrecognized way to feel validated and needed by others, we would do better to focus our energies on learning new ways to be at ease with one another, exploring possibilities of human communication and interaction. The Ceres principle creates community by responding to authentic needs, not by creating artificial needs that do not ultimately serve anyone.

Interactive management, the directing and distributing of energy, is also necessary on the personal level. It entails, among other things, balancing our nutritional intake, sexual energies, needs for exercise, sleep, comfort, and recreation, and all else that is necessary for our beings to remain aligned. In our social and work lives, this principle also has to do with recognizing and respecting cycles. Visions, projects, societies, and individuals move through specific cycles of development. There may be different conceptual approaches to cycles of markets and nations as opposed to the cycles of any one person's life, but Ceres has to do not with the concept, but with being sensitive to the cycles themselves. If everything is falling apart, it may be a waste of energy to stick a finger into the dike and try to keep things together. Sometimes it is necessary, and even advantageous, to let things completely fall apart, for when we reach the bottom we will be able to reconfigure with much less resistance.

One exercise that may be of value in recognizing cycles and responding appropriately is looking at our career in light of the four directions. For a career, like the world market, proceeds not in a straight line but through the varied seasons of upswings and downturns. Many cultures have utilized the model of the four directions to recognize how one is going and where one is headed. The following model can be used by an individual or by any business. It is simply a way of seeing what is needed in the present moment.

We begin in the North, the direction that represents the winter, a time when things are quiet and in waiting. Waiting has its advantages. A colleague of mine who does business with the Chinese says that in many negotiations between the Chinese and Americans, the Americans lose because the Chinese know how to wait. Ultimately the Americans become impatient and accept the other party's terms. There are times when we need to simply wait, to be patient and allow life to unfold. The North represents this time of the tree in winter, shorn of its leaves, turned inward in its stillness.[9] The North often represents a down time, a period of scant resources and opportunities. It is necessary to recognize such times and honor them. By doing so, we are building humility as well as unseen resources that will be available to us in the future.

The East represents the onset of the flower-bearing spring. Spring often comes slowly—first the ice begins to thaw, and eventually bird calls can be heard again. But if we jump up and run outside without a coat on, we find that it is still too cold to play, and we might even slip on the remnants of ice. In the East we learn to respect the first stirrings of spring, the subtle rising of new ideas or projects that are like the early buds on the trees. If a cold frost comes blowing in, the buds will be destroyed; often we destroy new possibilities by trampling them to death with overbearing expectations. Buds are delicate and need nurturing and protection to allow them to mature. When we are ready to begin something, we are advised to be delicate, to proceed deliberately, to test the waters and see how the buds are developing. More than fifteen years passed between the time Stan Jay sold his first vintage guitar and the incorporation of Mandolin Brothers. The incorporation occurred at the right time, and the buds grew into great fruits and flowers. It is often unwise to advertise or publicize a new project or idea. Our budding ideas need to first be planted in our own gardens and watered regularly. When they take hold, we can then transplant them into the world. The direction of the East is filled with hope and the intimation of new life. It is this hope, one that stems from an inner sense of self, that can direct and sustain a new career.

The South represents the sun at high noon, the deep summertime when trees are full of fruit and can extend their shade to others. This is our time of fruition, a time when we can run full steam ahead. We can take risks and move into new areas because we recognize our fullness and power. This is the time when others will flock to our banner, a time when we are ready to make an impact upon the world. How fulfilling it is to be at one's zenith, to do all that one is capable of doing, to fully expand like the summer tree filled with sap and flavor. In the South there is no holding back. We can commit all of our time, energy, and resources. Here is where our self-worth, passion, and focus can join forces and build structures that will represent the legacy of our truth and caring. Here is where we can seize the time and expand without looking back.

Finally we come to the West, the time of autumn, the place of the setting sun. In autumn we acknowledge the need to die, the need to let go of a venture or a well-worn idea just as the tree lets go of its leaves in autumn. How often do artists keep with an act or signature style simply to maintain an audience, even though they themselves are no longer energized by it? It is painful to continue in a certain way when we know it is time to let go. If the tree did not let go of its leaves in autumn, it would die; its branches could not support the ice and snow of winter. When done with dignity, the time of letting go can be as awesome as the setting sun or the changing colors of the leaves, for letting go is also a time of flowering, enabling us to change and ready ourselves for that which is to come.

Before moving headlong into your project, product, or service, it may be helpful to ask what season you are in. Are you in a place of rest, emergence, manifestation, or dissolution? This information alone can save years of labor and misalignment. Interactive management is, above all, about knowing time. Ceres knows the cycles and respects them. Nothing is as important in the manifestation of an authentic career as timing.

INTERACTIVE MANAGEMENT IN THE WORLD

Ceres represents the true economic principle in a society, not economics as a bloodless and bodiless abstraction but as the flowing lifeblood of interaction. How do we arrange our homes and the energy we consume to support both nature and ourselves; transportation and its consequences; food grown on farms and its distribution; our relationship with the mineral, plant, and animal kingdoms; the total production, distribution, and circulation of goods and services?

The word *interaction* implies relationship. If there is no relationship with the food we eat, assimilation can only occur on a gross physical level. The food industry is removed from the process of interaction to the extent that animals are shipped, killed, and packaged with no ritual or regard for either the animal or the human. People buy packaged flesh in stores where they do not know the people who sell it to them, where the meat came from, how it got there, or what has been added to it. Animals themselves increasingly disappear from our lives except as domesticated pets or totems on football helmets. The majesty of the lion, the power of the cougar, the cunning of the fox, and the soaring flight of the eagle are all but lost to us. When plants and animals become objects of human consumption without any reciprocity, we violate the laws of nature. We may objectify the world, creating unlimited flavors, tastes, shapes, and forms, but we still feel undernourished. For objects cannot share life, and we find ourselves needing more objects to fill the lifeless void that we have created. Just as an anti-career is based on a revised service principle, an anti-career also needs to revise the management principle. Rather than imaging the manager who is removed from the system and controls it from above, the anti-career cultivates the interactive model—the Aquarian jazz band—in which there is shared responsibility and participation from a sense of interconnectedness.

The goddess Ceres helps us to revise management by encouraging us to understand that management is a nutritive principle. As such, interactive management has everything to do with health and healing. The United States is the only industrialized nation that does not consider health to be a human right. With no national health insurance or medical guarantees, health becomes tied to employment as the only way that most people can afford health insurance. The health-care business works alongside the education, automotive, and home-owning industries to keep people in debt. If health was insured by the collective, millions of people would immediately leave their meaningless jobs. The fear, of course, is that such an action would implode the system. On the other hand, if work is creative and challenging, if people feel that their work is making a meaningful contribution to the communities in which they have direct investment, there will be less illness and more individual productivity.

Presently it can cost over nine hundred dollars a day simply to stay in a hospital bed. The hospital is as much afraid of lawsuits as it is dedicated to healing. In the hospital one can receive treatments from highly trained physicians with their space-age machines, and later that day be subjected to lifeless, industrial-age foods. This disparity is another example of mismanagement growing out of the lack of the Ceres principle of nutritive awareness.

One way to implement Ceres energy in our communities is to promote local farms. The Genesis farm in New Jersey recruits members who buy shares which entitle them to fresh, locally grown produce for the entire year. The shares sustain a community farming project that employs local people and creates organic products that enrich both the members' health and the locality itself. Such actions help redirect the agricultural system in a sustainable direction; thankfully this kind of Ceres activity is already well underway in many areas. As reported by Coop America, for example, citizens in Santa Barbara started a local safe foods project, learning how to promote the sale and distribution of healthy, nutritious, local food on the community level.[10] The personalization of human services, the promotion of local responsibility for and control of nurturing one another, the recognition of the importance of healthy food and clean air and water, and community-oriented housing all point to vocational areas that will greatly expand in the next fifty years.

If you are serious about creating a career that serves your soul, start with your lifestyle, examining and reshaping your habits of production, consumption, and distribution. Take an inventory of everything in your possession and see what your possessions say about you, what your car says about you, what your clothes say about you. Operating on the principle of interconnectedness, a seemingly small change anywhere on the chain will influence the rest of the chain. How you treat what you have already received will determine your ability to receive appropriately in the future. A traditional Hebrew tale tells us that when God saw that Moses, the shepherd, cared enough to go after one stray sheep and would not stop until the sheep was found, He decided that Moses was the one fit to receive the Ten Commandments.

The interactive management paradigm also promotes alternative energy as the most caring means of productivity. Solar energy, wind energy, organic farming, and alternative health care are all fields that will dramatically expand in the next fifty years because they serve the most pressing needs of our time. The eco-job field is burgeoning already, and with enough Ceres energy in operation, corporations that produce armaments like Lockheed and McDonell-Douglas may be influenced to diversify and put their prowess to work for protecting and restoring environmental balance.[11] Ceres energy spawns new concepts of community and cooperative living, including cooperative banks that invest in people's visions, food coops, and new methods of public transportation.

On the social level, the interactive management paradigm is about the need to combine self-reliance and collectivity. If health care in the United States was instituted as a natural right, it would cover a collective need; but leaving the responsibility and choice of care to the individual is the self-reliant necessity. The collective response can only be effective when the individual takes personal responsibility for being healthy. This includes not only gathering information and seeking quality health care, but creating a lifestyle that promotes health. The stress of unfullfilling work promotes illness, which in turn serves the medical and insurance industries, and so the vicious circle is set in perpetual motion. Without a healthy relationship between collectivity and self-reliance, our fledgling efforts at authentic manifestation will be swallowed up by the cancer of overproduction and institutionalized selfishness.

The interactive management paradigm governs the principle of exchange on many levels, and how we handle exchange may well determine our future, be it the exchange of knowledge, commodities, or the visions of how things should be. In order to successfully manifest an alternative career, it is important to be very clear about what you need and how you can best utilize the energies that you currently have.

These are the four keys to the successful creation of an anti-career: If we are willing to kindle the inner fires of dedication, pursue discipline and mastery of our fields, serve in the spirit of sharing, and creatively balance the various forces in and around us, the external world will respond in kind, and step by step we will find our project, product, or service developing in ways we could not have previously imagined. These energies complement our inner alignment and allow us to effectively be who we are in the world of exchange, turning the work world into the cosmic marketplace.

The four keys are deceptively simple; their effectiveness is quite substantial when they are employed in aligned succession. Many people try to focus on management without a sacred fire burning within, and the result is simply boredom. Others may have a deep sense of self-investment, but little discipline to sustain the energy or build a network. Still others may recognize the importance of service but neglect the managerial skills that will allow a particular service to interface with the community. All four keys are necessary to unlocking successive doors—as investment creates the necessary energy for sustained action, discipline creates something of genuine value which can then be offered as service, and service sets in motion the interactive energies that are necessary to making life into a work of art.

16

The Alchemy of Transformation

The White Rabbit put on his spectacles. "Where shall I begin please, your Majesty?" he asked.

"Begin at the beginning," the King said, very gravely.[1]

The beginning is where you find yourself here and now. You do not have to eat brown rice, leave home, or quit your job to begin creating a new career. The beginning is accepting where you are now and gently allowing yourself to move into alignment with the greater forces of the universe.

There is a plethora of information available on career change and employment opportunities, and a bibliography is provided at the end of this book for the inquisitive researcher. We hear about micro- and macrotrends, about great shifts in the earth, about the effects of a global economy. With the rapid development of computer technology, no human brain can hold the smallest fraction of material available in any field. If we continually reach for ever more information, we fall headlong into the pitfall of consumption. What is important is not trying to gorge on this or any other book about career change, but to pick the weeds out of our own gardens and tend to the beautiful flowers that are already there, hidden though they may be. If we work our own terrains, the necessary information will be made available. Any more information is a burden.

Rather than information, what an anti-career requires is transformation, and transformation is different than what is presented in heroic scripts of self-improvement. Hucksters on television selling real estate or telling you that you can live in a castle are selling improvement, but the concept of improvement is built upon the blueprint of scarcity. To transform our way of life requires that we start at the very bottom: We must begin at the beginning. And the beginning is the breath. To breathe easily, to walk fully, to hasten slowly, to honor the power of the small—these are the initial acts that will open up our way to us.

The ideas discussed in this book will remain shelved on the conceptual level if they are not taken to heart and put into action. As we are willing to risk transformative action, we find ourselves less preoccupied by the ills of the world or by our own apparent shortcomings, for we are becoming part of the solution. To trust, ask, listen, and live is to create a way of life the concrete details of which reflect our aspirations. What greater gift could be given to our world and our children?

To forge our lives into works of art, to master the craft of living, to work patiently with the forces of life, and to become ourselves in action requires courage and genuine commitment. It is both an inner commitment—to accept who we are and what we stand for—and outer one—to take that into the marketplace. In short, we are challenged to make our lives into statements of that which we believe in. This sounds like a tall order, and it is. To touch our authenticity we will have to walk through the fires of ordeal not once but many times. But gold is borne of this fire. Our work in this world is the way in which the base elements are transformed. So start with an hour. Move to a day. Go for a lifetime.

Endnotes

Introduction

1. Henry David Thoreau, *The Journal of Henry D. Thoreau,* vol. II, ed. Bradford Torrey and Francis H. Allen (1906; reprint, New York: Dover, 1962), 317.

Chapter One

1. "The intellect of man is forced to choose
   Perfection of the life, or of the work . . ."
   From W. B. Yeats, "The Choice" in *Selected Poems and Three Plays,* ed. Macha L. Rosenthal (New York: Macmillan, 1962).
2. Ralph Waldo Emerson, "Nature" in *Selected Writing of Ralph Waldo Emerson,* ed. William H. Gilman (New York: New American Library, 1965), 36.
3. Genesis 3:19.
4. See Max Weber, *The Protestant Ethic and the Spirit of Capitalism,* trans. Talcott Parsons (New York: Scribner's, 1980).
5. See Carlo Antoni, *From History to Sociology: The Transition in German Historical Thinking,* trans. Hayden V. White (Detroit, Mich.: Wayne State University Press, 1959; reprint, Westport, Conn.: Greenwood Press, 1977), 156–57.

Chapter Two

1. Steven R. Covey, *The Seven Habits of Highly Effective People* (New York: Simon and Schuster, 1989).
2. I am indebted to my friend and colleague Ron Young, who first articulated this way of perceiving the dynamics of career making.
3. T. S. Eliot, "Burnt Norton" in *Four Quartets* (New York: Harcourt, Brace, and World, 1943).

4. Erik H. Erikson, *Childhood and Society* (New York: W. W. Norton, 1963).

5. Robert Johnson, *Inner Work* (San Francisco: HarperSanFrancisco, 1989). This particular statement was made during a lecture given at Wainwright House in Rye, New York, in October, 1990.

Chapter Three

1. Edgar Cayce, *Revelation: A Commentary on the Book, Based on the Study of Twenty Four Psychic Discourses of Edgar Cayce,* Twenty-Six Interpretive Readings Series (Virginia Beach, Va.: A. R. E. Press, 1969).

2. Emerson, "Self-Reliance" in *Ralph Waldo Emerson,* ed. Richard Poirier, The Oxford Authors Series (New York: Oxford University Press, 1990).

3. Walt Whitman, *Leaves of Grass and Selected Prose,* ed. Sculley Bradley (Fort Worth, Tex.: Harcourt Brace, 1949).

4. Isadora Duncan, *Isadora Speaks* (San Francisco: City Lights, 1981), 46.

5. Tapes of the meditations are also available through the Anti-Career Workshop. Write to: The Anti-Career Workshop/Soul Basket Recordings, RR 11, Box 20–214, South Kortright, NY, 13842.

Chapter Four

1. The correlation of the Minotaur myth with the second chakra was first shared with me by my colleague Ron Young, who has used this myth in his workshops for many years.

2. See Juliet Sharman-Burke and Liz Greene's *The Mythic Tarot* (New York: Simon and Schuster, 1986) for a poetic rendering of this myth. I have paraphrased their sentence, "she entered the bull and the bull entered her," as I can find none better.

3. Ralph Waldo Emerson, "Thoreau," in *Ralph Waldo Emerson,* 475–90.

4. Ibid.

5. Alice Miller, *The Drama of the Gifted Child* (New York: Basic Books, 1983), *Thou Shalt Not Be Aware: Society's Betrayal of the Child* (New York: New American Library/Dutton, 1988), *Banished Knowledge: Facing Childhood Injury* (New York: Doubleday, 1991).

6. Allan Bloom, *The Closing of the American Mind: Education and the Crisis of Reason* (New York: Simon and Schuster, 1988).

7. Ibid.

Chapter Five

1. Richard Bolles, *What Color Is Your Parachute? 1995: A Practical Manual for Job Hunters and Career Changers* (Berkeley: Ten Speed Press, 1994).

2. See James Hillman, "Oedipus Revisited" in Karl Kerenyi and James Hillman, *Oedipus Variations* (Dallas, Tex.: Spring Publications, 1979).

3. A case can be made for Horatio being Hamlet's one true friend and confidante, but Hamlet keeps Horatio at a careful distance. Hamlet demands allegiance but hardly confides in Horatio.

4. Carl G. Jung, *Nietzsche's Zarathustra: Notes of the Seminar Given in 1934–1939*, 2 vols., ed. James L. Jarrett, Bollingen Series 99 (Princeton, N. J.: Princeton University Press, 1988).

5. Emerson, "Nature," in *Selected Writings of Ralph Waldo Emerson*, 223.

Chapter Six

1. Murray, W. H. *The Scottish Himalayan Expedition* (London: J. M. Dent & Sons, 1951).

2. See Denis de Rougemont, *Love in the Western World*, trans. M. Belgion (New York: Pantheon, 1956).

3. For more on this topic, see Robert Thurman's introduction to *Holy Teaching of Vimalakirti: Mahayana Scripture*, trans. Robert A. Thurman, Institute for Advanced Study of World Religion Series (University Park, Penn.: Pennsylvania State University Press, 1976). Also see the epic poem and Hindu gospel, the Bhagavadgita, for the classic model of positive action in ancient India.

4. Erich Neumann, *Origins and History of Consciousness*, trans. R. F. Hull, Bollingen Series 42 (Princeton, N. J.: Princeton University Press, 1954). This book discusses the archetype of the wheel in great depth.

5. See Jack D. Schwager, *The New Market Wizards: Conversations with America's Top Traders* (New York: HarperBusiness, 1994).

6. Robert Moore and Douglas Gillette, *King, Warrior, Magician, Lover: Rediscovering the Archetypes of the Mature Masculine* (San Francisco: HarperSanFrancisco, 1991).

7. There is much literature available on time management, and most of it is more a waste of time than not. One of the few products that is actually helpful is Charles Hobb's Time Management Seminar, distributed through Day Timers, Inc. of Allentown, Pennsylvania.

Chapter Seven

1. Joe Dominguez and Vicki Robin, *Your Money or Your Life: Transforming Your Relationship with Money and Achieving Financial Independence* (New York: Viking Penguin, 1992).

2. Henry David Thoreau, *Walden* (New York: Collier Books, 1962), 81.

3. Thich Nhat Hanh, *The Miracle of Mindfulness: A Manual on Meditation*, trans. Mobi Ho (Boston: Beacon Press, 1992).

4. See Stephen Levine, *Who Dies?* (New York: Doubleday, 1989) and *Healing into Life and Death* (New York: Doubleday, 1989). In his books, Levine effectively explores the powerful concept of living in such consciousness.

5. See *Deliverance from Error,* vol.1 of *The Faith and Practice of al-Ghazali,* trans. M. Watt (Chicago: Kazi, 1982).
6. P. D. Ouspensky, *In Search of the Miraculous: Fragments of an Unknown Teaching* (San Diego, Calif.: Harcourt Brace and Co., 1965).
7. *I-Ching or Book of Changes,* trans. C. F. Baynes and Richard Wilhelm, Bollingen Series 19 (Princeton, N. J.: Princeton University Press, 1967).

Chapter Eight

1. See Mircea Eliade, *Myths, Dreams, and Mysteries: The Encounter between Contemporary Faiths and Archaic Realities* (New York: Harper, 1943) on the perpetuation of mythology in contemporary cultures.
2. Johnson, *Inner Work.*
3. This dynamic was presented by Robert Mulligan at the New York Astrology Center Conference, June, 1992.

Chapter Nine

1. Henry David Thoreau, *Walden,* 233.
2. Napoleon Hill, *Think and Grow Rich* (New York: Fawcett, 1987).
3. Interestingly enough, Cayce considered this phenomena of going deep into trance for every reading to be a form of penance. In a reading for himself, Cayce attributed his need to go into an unconscious trance to the misuse of power in a previous incarnation, necessitating that he abandon his ego every time he wished to serve another.

Chapter Ten

1. Randolph Stone, *Polarity Therapy: The Complete Collected Works,* vol. 1 (Sebastopol, Calif.: CRCS Publications, 1986).
2. *Bhagavata Purana* , skandha 12 (Gorakhpur, India: Gita, 1962).
3. See Hua-Ching Ni, *Tao: The Subtle Universal Law* (Santa Monica, Calif.: SevenStar Publications, 1995) and *The Taoist Inner View of the Universe and the Immortal Realm* (Santa Monica, Calif.: SevenStar Publications, 1979).
4. Sudhakar S. Dikshit, ed., *I Am That: Talks with Sri Nisargadatta Maharaja* (Bombay: Chetana Press, 1973).
5. Walt Whitman, "Song of Myself" in *Leaves of Grass and Selected Prose,* 40.

Chapter Eleven

1. I am indebted to the late Eleanor Bach, the "asteroid lady" and one of my mentors in the astrological arts, for introducing me to the asteroids and sharing with me her original research on their correspondences.

Chapter Twelve

1. This new way of understanding the meaning of the word *interest* was recently brought to my attention by a participant in the anti-career workshop at the Kirkridge Spiritual Retreat Center, Bangor, Pennsylvania.
2. See John Naisbitt, *Megatrends* (New York: Warner, 1988) and Faith Popcorn, *The Popcorn Report: Faith Popcorn on the Future of Your Company, Your World, and Your Life* (New York: HarperBusiness, 1992) in this regard.
3. See Noam Chomsky, "The M.I.T. Interviews," interviews with David Barsamian (Boulder: Sounds True Recordings, 1990).

Chapter Thirteen

1. Ralph Waldo Emerson, "The Over-Soul," in *Selected Writings of Ralph Waldo Emerson,* 291.
2. See George Leonard, *Mastery: The Keys to Long-Term Success and Fulfillment* (New York: New American Library, 1991).
3. See Harold Bloom's *Anxiety of Influence: A Theory of Poetry* (Oxford: Oxford University Press, 1973) for an example of how this dynamic relates to poetry and poets.
4. David M. Wulff, *The Psychology of Religion: Classic and Contemporary Views* (New York: John Wiley & Sons, 1991).
5. Charles Handy, *The Age of Unreason* (Boston: Harvard Business School Press, 1991), 69.
6. I am indebted to the indefatigable Richard "Buzz" Gummere, former director of Career Services at Columbia University, for introducing me to this process.
7. Hill, *Think and Grow Rich.*
8. *Coop America Quarterly,* vol. 4, no. 2 (Summer 1992).

Chapter Fourteen

1. Eleanor Bach, *A Graphic Ephemeris of Sensitive Degrees* (New York: Planet Watch Publications, 1987).
2. *Bhagavadgita,* 3.35.

Chapter Fifteen

1. Handy, *The Age of Unreason,* 89–102.
2. *I-Ching,* hexagram #9.
3. *Business Today,* citations from Jeffrey Green, Chairman and CEO of Hutchison Technology, vol. 30, no. 3 (Fall 1993): 28.
4. Cited by Richard J. Lambert, "Rethinking Productivity: The Perspective of the Earth as the Primary Corporation," in *Population and Environment: A Journal*

of Interdisciplinary Studies, Human Sciences Press, vol. 13, no. 3 (Spring 1992).

5. Alisa Gravitz, personal communication, March 30, 1993.

6. Ibid.

7. Ibid.

8. James Hillman, *City and Soul* (Irving, Tex.: University of Dallas Press, 1978).

9. The tree meditation was introduced to me in 1993 by Andre Dezanger at an anti-career workshop at the New York Open Center.

10. A book by the Santa Barbara safe-foods project, entitled *Increasing Organic at the Local Level: A Manual for Consumers, Grocers, Farmers, and Policy Makers,* is available through the Community Environmental Council, 930 Miramonte Dr., Santa Barbara, CA, 93109.

11. Some valuable publications about jobs in the field of ecology are *The Job Seeker,* which lists national environmental jobs (Rt. 2, Box 16, Warrens, WI, 54666) and the *Complete Guide to Environmental Careers* (286 Congress Street, Boston, MA, 02210).

Chapter 16

1. Lewis Carroll, *Alice's Adventures in Wonderland and Through the Looking Glass* (New York: New American Library, 1960).

Bibliography

Career Development

Bolles, Richard. *What Color Is Your Parachute? 1995: A Practical Manual for Job Hunters and Career Changers.* Berkeley, Calif.: Ten Speed Press, 1994.

CEIP Fund. *The Complete Guide to Environmental Careers.* Washington, DC: Island Press, 1989.

Covey, Steven R. *The Seven Habits of Highly Effective People.* New York: Simon and Schuster, 1989.

Cowan, Jessica, ed. *Good Works: A Guide to Careers in Social Change.* New York: Barricade Books, 1991.

Everett, Melissa. *Making a Living While Making a Difference: A Guide to Creating Careers with a Conscience.* New York: Bantam, 1995.

Fox, Mathew. *The Reinvention of Work: A New Vision of Livelihood for Our Time.* San Francisco: HarperSanFrancisco, 1994.

Gross, Ronald. *The Independent Scholar's Handbook: How to Turn Your Interest in any Subject into Expertise.* Berkeley, Calif.: Ten Speed Press, 1993.

Kaplan, Robbie Miller. *The Whole Career Sourcebook.* New York: AMACOM, 1991.

Leonard, George. *Mastery: The Keys to Long-Term Success and Fulfillment.* New York: New American Library/Dutton, 1991.

Sacharov, Al. *Offbeat Careers.* Berkeley, Calif.: Ten Speed Press, 1988.

Simpkinson, Charles II., Douglas A. Wengell, and Mary Jane A. Casavant. *The Common Boundary Graduate Education Guide: Holistic Programs and Resources Integrating Spirituality and Psychology.* Bethesda, Md.: Common Boundary, 1994.

Sinetar, Marsha. *Do What You Love, the Money Will Follow: Discovering Your Right Livelihood*. New York: Dell, 1989.

Finances

Clason, George. *The Richest Man in Babylon*. New York: New American Library/ Dutton, 1989.

Dominguez, Joe, and Vicki Robin. *Your Money or Your Life: Transforming Your Relationship with Money and Achieving Financial Independence*. New York: Viking Penguin, 1992.

Fisher, Mark. *The Instant Millionaire: A Tale of Wisdom and Wealth*. New York: New World Library, 1991.

Harrington, John C. *Investing with Your Conscience: How to Achieve High Returns Using Socially Responsible Investing*. New York: John Wiley and Sons, 1992.

Hill, Napoleon. *Think and Grow Rich*. New York: Fawcett, 1987.

Phillips, Michael. *The Seven Laws of Money*. Boston: Shambhala, 1993.

Ponder, Catherine. *The Dynamic Laws of Prosperity*. Marina del Rey, Calif.: DeVorss, 1985.

Business and Social Transformation

Berle, Gustav. *The Green Entrepreneur: Business Opportunities That Can Save the Earth and Make You Money*. Blue Ridge Summit, Penn.: Liberty Hall, 1991.

Daly, Herman E., and John B. Cobb, Jr. *For the Common Good: Redirecting the Economy Toward Community, the Environment, and a Sustainable Future*. Boston: Beacon Press, 1991.

Handy, Charles. *The Age of Unreason*. Boston: Harvard Business School, 1991.

Harman, Willis, and John Hormann. *Creative Work: The Constructive Role of Business in a Transforming Society*. Indianapolis, Ind.: Knowledge Systems, 1990.

Hawken, Paul. *Growing a Business*. New York: Simon and Schuster, 1988.

———. *The Ecology of Commerce: A Declaration of Sustainability*. New York: HarperBusiness, 1994.

Henderson, Hazel. *Paradigms in Progress: Life Beyond Economics*. Indianapolis, Ind.: Knowledge Systems, 1992.

Naisbitt, John, and Patricia Aburdene. *Reinventing the Corporation: Transforming Your Job and Your Company for the New Information Society*. New York: Warner, 1985.

Ottman, Jacquelyn. *Green Marketing: Challenges and Opportunities for the New Marketing Age*. Lincolnwood, Ill.: NTC Publishing, 1994.

Popcorn, Faith. *The Popcorn Report: Faith Popcorn on the Future of Your Company, Your World, Your Life*. New York: HarperBusiness, 1992.

Senge, Peter M. *The Fifth Discipline: Mastering the Five Practices of the Learning Organization*. New York: Doubleday, 1990.

Chakras and Spirituality

Bruyere, Rosalyn L. *Wheels of Light: Chakras, Auras, and the Healing Energy of the Body.* New York: Fireside, 1994.

Cayce, Edgar. *Revelation: A Commentary on the Book, Based on the Study of Twenty Four Psychic Discourses of Edgar Cayce.* Virginia Beach, Va.: A.R.E. Press, 1969.

Holy Bible: King James Version. New York: New American Library/Dutton, 1974.

I-Ching or Book of Changes. Translated by C. F. Baynes and Richard Wilhelm. Bollingen Series 19. Princeton, N. J.: Princeton University Press, 1967.

Lao Tzu. *Tao-te-Ching.* Translated by D. C. Lau. New York: Penguin, 1992.

Miller, Barbara S. *Bhagavadgita: Krishna's Counsel in Time of War.* New York: Bantam, 1991.

Sharman-Burke, Juliet, and Liz Greene. *The Mythic Tarot.* New York: Simon and Schuster, 1986.

Thich Nhat Hanh. *Miracle of Mindfulness: A Manual on Meditation.* Translated by Mobi Ho. Boston: Beacon Press, 1992.

Perspective

Antoni, Carlo. *From History to Sociology: The Transition in German Historical Thinking.* Translated by Hayden V. White. Westport, Conn.: Greenwood, 1977.

Bellah, Robert. *Habits of the Heart: Individualism and Commitment in American Life.* New York: HarperCollins, 1986.

Berry, Thomas. *The Dream of the Earth.* San Francisco: Sierra Club, 1990.

Erikson, Erik. *Childhood and Society,* 2d ed. New York: W. W. Norton, 1963.

Hillman, James. "Oedipus Revisited." In Karl Kerenyi and James Hillman. *Oedipus Variations.* Dallas, Tex.: Spring Publications, 1991.

Hillman, James and Laura Pozzo. *Inter Views: Conversations with Laura Pozzo on Psychotherapy, Biography, Love, Soul, Dreams, Work, Imagination, and the State of the Culture.* Dallas, Tex.: Spring Publications, 1983.

Miller, Alice. *The Drama of the Gifted Child.* New York: Basic Books, 1982.

———. *Thou Shalt Not Be Aware: Society's Betrayal of the Child.* New York: New American Library/Dutton, 1984.

Neumann, Erich. *The Origins and History of Consciousness.* Translated by R. F. Hull. Bollingen Series 42. Princeton, N. J.: Princeton University Press, 1954.

Weber, Max. *The Protestant Ethic and the Spirit of Capitalism.* New York: Scribner's, 1980.

Inspiration

Duncan, Isadora. *Isadora Speaks.* San Francisco: City Lights, 1981.

Emerson, Ralph Waldo. *Ralph Waldo Emerson.* Edited by Richard Poirier. The Oxford Authors Series. New York: Oxford University Press, 1990.

Thoreau, Henry David. *The Journal of Henry D. Thoreau.* Edited by Bradford Torrey and Francis H. Allen. 1906. Reprint, New York: Dover Publications, 1966.

———. *Walden.* New York: Collier Books, 1962.

Whitman, Walt. *Leaves of Grass and Selected Prose.* Edited by Sculley Bradley. Fort Worth, Tex.: Harcourt Brace, 1949.

Index

BOOKS OF RELATED INTEREST

THE BALANCING ACT
Mastering the Five Elements of Success in Life,
Relationships, and Work
by Sharon Seivert

CENTERING
A Guide to Inner Growth
by Sanders Laurie and Melvin Tucker

FINANCIAL SUCCESS
Harnessing the Power of Creative Thought
by Wallace D. Wattles

ENLIGHTENED MANAGEMENT
Bringing Buddhist Principles to Work
by Dona Witten with Akong Tulku Rinpoche

SHAPESHIFTING
Shamanic Techniques for Global and Personal Transformation
by John Perkins

CREATIVE VISUALIZATION
Using Imagery and Imagination for Self-Transformation
by Ronald Shone

LESS IS MORE
An Anthology Edited by Goldian VandenBroeck

LEADING FROM WITHIN
Martial Arts Skills for Dynamic Business and Management
by Robert Pater

Inner Traditions • Bear & Company
P.O. Box 388
Rochester, VT 05767
1-800-246-8648
www.InnerTraditions.com

Or contact your local bookseller